Frederick Denison Maurice

The Conscience

Lectures on Casuistry

Frederick Denison Maurice

The Conscience
Lectures on Casuistry

ISBN/EAN: 9783337033828

Printed in Europe, USA, Canada, Australia, Japan

Cover: Foto ©Thomas Meinert / pixelio.de

More available books at **www.hansebooks.com**

THE CONSCIENCE.

LECTURES ON CASUISTRY,

DELIVERED IN

The University of Cambridge.

BY

FREDERICK DENISON MAURICE,

PROFESSOR OF CASUISTRY AND MORAL PHILOSOPHY.

SECOND EDITION.

London:

MACMILLAN AND CO.

1872.

EDMUND LUSHINGTON, Esq.

PROFESSOR OF GREEK IN THE UNIVERSITY OF GLASGOW.

My Dear Lushington,

You kindly sent me a copy of those most interesting Remains of Professor Ferrier, which owe so much to the affectionate diligence and critical judgment of Sir Alexander Grant and yourself. It is not to prove my gratitude for this valuable gift that I take the liberty of dedicating these Lectures to you. Even the pleasure and honour of associating my name with yours might not have tempted me to that vanity. But a writer about the Conscience ought not to let any burthen rest upon his own. After I had delivered these Lectures, I turned to Ferrier's 'Philosophy of Consciousness,' and found that he had anticipated several of the remarks which I had made on the word I, and on the mischief of smothering it under general phrases such as '*Mind*' or '*Reason*.' I cannot be sure that sentences of his essays which struck me many years ago when I read them in *Blackwood's Magazine* may not have fixed themselves in my memory, and that I may not unawares have mingled his thoughts with my own. If so, I cannot do better than direct your attention to the plagiarism, and beg my readers to trace it to its source. They will find their recompense in the knowledge they will acquire of Professor Ferrier's teaching if it destroys their interest in mine.

You will perceive that in other respects there is very little in common between these rough Lectures and the books, so conspicuous for rich and various culture, which you have edited. I have had no notion of producing a 'Philosophy of Consciousness.'

My aim has been to associate the Conscience with the acts and thoughts of our ordinary existence. I have abstained, some will think even pedantically, from the use of philosophical terms: I have only touched on philosophical systems when I fancied they were interfering with the rights and duties of every wayfarer. If I can lead a few young men in what I must still call your University, to think more earnestly, to live more bravely, I trust that the many obvious deficiencies of my book will not hinder you from owning me as a fellow-worker. .

Believe me,

My dear Lushington,

Very sincerely yours,

F. D. MAURICE.

PREFACE TO SECOND EDITION.

Since these Lectures were published there has appeared an exceedingly interesting volume entitled "Colloquia Peripatetica, by the late John Duncan, D.D., Professor of Hebrew in the New College of Edinburgh." These Colloquies are reported by the Rev. William Knight, who seems to be admirably qualified for the task which he has undertaken. His friend must have been a man of rare originality, varied culture, great vigour in expressing thoughts which were worthy to be expressed and remembered. Mr Knight has listened to Dr Duncan's utterances with reverence and sympathy, and has the high merit of not distorting or colouring them by opinions of his own.

The reader who shall give himself the benefit and gratification of studying this short

volume (it will suggest more to him than many
of ten times its size) will find that I have not
been bribed to speak well of it by any praise
which Dr Duncan has bestowed on me. My
only excuse for alluding to it is that it contains the severest censure on my writings which
they have ever incurred; though they have not
been so unfortunate as to escape censure. If Dr
Duncan's complaint of them were established,
I should own at once that I was absolutely
disqualified for speaking on Casuistry or Moral
Philosophy; that the less young men have to
do with me, the better it will be for them.
He says that 'my system is pure illegality*;'
that Law is by me banished from Ethics or is
swallowed up in Ethics. What my system is
or does, I really am not able to say. I have
always professed with great earnestness that
I had never constructed a system; that if I
did it would exclude most of the truth which
I feel to be the support of my life, would
include most of the falsehoods against which

* *Colloquia Peripatetica*, p. 40.   Edmondston and Douglas,
Edinburgh.

I protest. But that I hold any Morality which banishes Law to be inhuman Morality—to be inconsistent with the Order of God's Universe, I think every reader of these Lectures and of those on Social Morality will be constrained to admit, whatever may be his judgment in other respects of them or of me.

It is, unfortunately, impossible to ascertain what passages in my writings conveyed this impression of my 'illegality' to Dr Duncan. If I ever meet with them and find the sense which he perceived in them to be their natural sense I shall be more anxious to blot them out than any one else can be. Against any ordinary criticism even a writer who is naturally thin-skinned becomes by degrees tolerably hardened. One proceeding from a man of such learning and worth as Dr Duncan I have thought it a duty to notice, less for my own sake than for the honour of the University which has permitted me to be one of its teachers.

CAMBRIDGE,
Jan. 1872.

CONTENTS.

LECTURE VII.

LECTURE VIII.

LECTURE IX.

LECTURE I.

ON THE WORD 'I'.

YOU may wonder at the title which I have chosen for my first lecture. I have taken it because I can find none which explains so well what will be the subject of all my lectures; what kind of facts will be considered in them, what claim they have to be practical.

Charges against the Moral Teacher.

There are grave doubts among men of the world whether the student of morals has any real subject to treat of. He can talk much about the blessings of virtue and the mischiefs of vice. But Lord Macaulay, who spent a great part of his life in dealing with virtues and vices as a legislator, or in recording the effects of them as a historian, said, you may remember, that the most brilliant writer upon them did not deserve half the gratitude from mankind which is due to the maker of a substantial pair of shoes. Again, the moralist may dwell upon different opinions which have descended upon us from other times, or have been produced in our own. He may speak of Sensualists and Utilitarians and Transcendentalists. Grand names assuredly; but how do they or the doctrines which they represent concern the business of life? Who that is occupied with facts can care about them? Who that is seeking for

(1) He is a vague declaimer.

(2) He is busy with idle disputes.

✗

amusement will not find elsewhere what is much more lively and stimulating?

(3) He prefers the possible to the actual.

Or if the moral teacher adopts the distinction which is sanctioned by one of the ablest and most accomplished of his class—if he says that his business is with what ought to be, that of other students with what is— can there be a clearer or fuller confession that he means to leave the actual world for some other world which he has imagined?

Such remarks as these you will hear in ordinary society, from dull men and clever men, from those who most profess the sober wisdom of age, or from those who most affect youthful fashions. Nor am I safe even in a place specially devoted to learning. Unpleasant comparisons may be made between my work and that

(4) He cannot point, like the physical teacher, to facts.

which goes on in other lecture-rooms. The Geometrician, the Geologist, the Astronomer, the teacher of any branch of natural history, can point to things with which he has to do; if he discovers secret laws they are laws which have reference to these things, without a knowledge of which they cannot be safely or effectively used. Of what things can I speak which answer to these? Shall I not be leading you away from objects which can be handled or seen, or reached by indisputable demonstrations when they cannot be handled or seen, into a region of shadows, where distinct apprehension, where secure proof is impossible? If the shadows ever become realities, must they not have undergone the change because I have travelled into a province which is not mine, because I have usurped duties which are much better performed by others?

The Word I—its claims to

These are formidable difficulties; if I cannot remove them, I can scarcely hope that you will listen to me

with patience. Beginning then with that objector who
especially boasts the title of the practical man, I ven- *be real and*
ture to ask, 'Does the word *I* seem to you an unpracti- *practical*
cal word, one which only concerns shadows? You do *generally*
not act as if this were so. You do not speak as if this *confessed.*
were so. You are rather angry if reverence is withdrawn from this word, if there is a hint that any can
be equally dear to him who utters it. In making your
calculations about the doings of other men or your own,
is it not your maxim that this I is entitled to a primary
consideration? Well! it is this which the Moralist
claims for his investigation. He agrees with you in
your estimate of its importance. He thinks as you
seem to think, that whatever may be the value or interest of the things which are seen and handled or tasted
or smelt, I who see and handle and taste and smell am
at least as interesting to myself as they can be.'

Then I should turn to you who frequent class-rooms *Not treated*
in which mathematical or physical or philological or *of by the*
mathema-
historical enquiries are pursued. I should remind you *tical or*
that in each of these rooms there is a teacher who calls *physical*
himself I, that there are pupils every one of whom calls *lecturer.*
himself I. But the I is to be kept as far as possible
from the lines and angles and parallelograms with
which the geometrician is occupied. The student who
is thinking of himself will not attend to the propositions of Euclid. One great duty of the teacher in any
branch of physics will be to warn you against the danger of confusing the objects which you contemplate
with notions and prepossessions of your own. The I
is not the subject there, but a dangerous intruder.
Wherever any language is cultivated, the I cannot be *Its import-*
ance to the
thus forgotten. If you take up Homer you will find *Philologer.*

that when he wants to express the distinction not between Trojans and Greeks but between both and the horses which they tame, the dogs which look up to them as masters, he calls them μέροπες. Articulate speech is the characteristic of *men.* How does the speech become articulate and human? What is the difference between the cries of beasts or the songs of birds which Homer must have known intimately, and the winged words which went forth from the mouths of his heroes? Each of them called himself I. There is the difference, there is the articulation. Ascribe that word to a cat or an elephant, and you are sure that you are in the region of fable, that the man is imputing to a lower race that which is the necessary condition of his own.

*He recog-
nises its
human
worth; but
cannot in-
vestigate
it.*

The philologer is much exercised by the different appearances which the I makes in different dialects; how it hides itself in some amidst the acts or passions in which it is concerned, how it comes forth obtrusively in others, as for instance in our own. He almost suspects that he could detect various forms of civilisation in this diversity; he is sure that the scarcely articulate, almost brutal, utterances of the savage are severed from the organic discourse of educated nations by this fact, that the one chiefly represents the impressions which are made on the beholder by the sights, on the hearer by the sounds, of the outward world; that the others have learnt to rise above these sights and sounds and to express themselves. But though he may perceive how this word has penetrated into the heart of human speech, though he recognises it as at once the most universal and the most exclusive of all words, he cannot look further into the marvel. He notes it and passes on.

The student and critic of national or of general history—or of any historical epoch—finds himself amidst a world of I's. They perplex him almost equally by their varieties and by the curious uniformity which he discovers in a number of their acts and movements. Sometimes he is tempted to resolve all events into the strange irregularities, eccentricities, contradictions of human beings, sometimes he flies to phrases about the species or the laws of Nature or Destiny. He is not satisfied with one solution or the other. He knows that they are both awkward expedients to escape from a difficulty, attempts to explain the *ignotum per ignotius*. He cannot rid himself of the I; what it means he leaves some other to interpret.

It is to this question, which is left with such testimonies to its significance, as a waif or estray by all those who are not afraid to face other questions, that I believe the student of Morals must address himself. He ought to explain why this I is so troublesome to the physical student, why it casts its shadow over all his enquiries into the order of the outward world. He ought to show why it has struck its roots so deeply into language. He ought to assist the historian in casting off some of those vague generalities which obscure the facts that he is describing, and yet offer themselves to him as such convenient modes of accounting for them. I do not think that the moralist can advance a step, can make out any reason for his existence, unless he girds himself to this task. And yet no one has more opportunities for evading it, more hints from illustrious practitioners of his art how he may evade it. Instead of using the word I, which men use in their common speech, he may talk about Individuality or

LECT. I.

Its place in History.

The Historian leaves it to the Moralist.

How the Moralist seeks to

escape from the consideration of it. His consequent failure.

Personality. And though, if he is rudely asked 'what is your personality, what is your individuality?' he may be obliged rather ignominiously to reply that it is a more philosophical way of saying 'I myself;' he will find so much comfort in this phraseology—such a graceful plea for it as being a refuge from egotism—such an apparent justification for it in the necessity of alluding to the mass of human creatures and not to a single unit of the mass—that the word 'I' will vanish out of his school dialect, whilst he is resorting to it every hour, almost every minute, if he is speaking not as a school-man but as a man. So the link between the two characters is broken; his talk is of men, but that which characterises a man is gone; you have killed him that you may dissect him.

At whatever risk of appearing egotistical—even of being so,—at whatever risk of exchanging grand technical words for common words, such as men speak in the market-place—we must make an effort to show that morality means the life and practice of each person who walks this earth and calls himself I, that it is not wrapped up in theories and speculations about some general human nature which is no man's particular

Professor Grote's plea for Egotism.

nature. I alluded in my inaugural lecture to a testimony of my excellent predecessor upon this subject. I will now quote his words in full, they exhibit so strikingly the method which I should wish to follow in these Lectures. "I send out these pages," says Professor Grote in the preface to his *Exploratio Philosophica*, "with much misgiving, not as to the substance of them —all that I can say about that is that they represent real thought—and of what value the thought is can only be seen when it is compared with the thought of others,—but as to the way in which the manner or method (if it is to be called method) of them may be taken. They are full of *Egotism.* I can only say that in reading what others have written, it is a matter continually occurring to me how much better it would have been if they had been more egotistic; how much better we should understand what they meant if they had described how the thing had come to present itself to their minds, and let us see their thoughts a little in the forming; and also how many pages of literary history ending at last in an unsatisfactory result would have been saved if this had been the case."

Every one who reads this passage, even if he knows nothing more of the writer, will say that he could not have been an egotist in the English sense, nor an egoiste in the French, that he must have been a man of singular modesty, with an unusual disposition to be fair and tolerant towards others, with a zeal for truth which overshadowed the desire to be himself the discoverer or promulgator of it. The egotistical method—he was too diffident even to give it that name—was attractive to him precisely because the thought of one person, if it is really his, calls forth the thought of another, to resist it, to conspire with it, or to complete it. Surely it is so with the most illustrious men and the least illustrious. No great man really does his work by imposing his maxims on his disciples; he evokes their life. Correggio cries after gazing intently on a picture of Raffaelle, 'I too am a painter,' not one who will imitate the great Master, but who will work a way for himself. The teacher who is ever so poor in talent or information, but who is determined to speak out the convictions he has won, who is willing now and then to give some hint of the struggles through which he has won them,—leads one or another to say 'I too am an I.' The pupil may become much wiser than his instructor, he may not accept his conclusions, but he will own, 'You awakened me to be myself, for that I thank you.'

The Anti-Egotists of the last Century.

Mr Grote applied his maxim to what is called Intellectual Philosophy. How important it is for the student of Ethics or Morals I have become convinced, whilst I have thought over some of the great writers who devoted themselves to this study in the last century, and have compared their influence with that of a philosopher who preceded them by 2000 years, and whom they greatly admired. The writers to whom I allude—they are those whom Sir James Mackintosh and Dr Whewell have described to us with so much ability—were men of serious purpose, with a desire not merely to talk of goodness, but to produce actual goodness according to their standard of it. They busied themselves with composing treatises on Human Nature or on Man. They were emphatically *not* Egotists. They were not generally as much interested in the Greek teachers of Ethics as men of a former generation had been. They dreaded the return of the influence which Aristotle had once exercised over Christendom; they looked upon Plato as a high-flown mystic. But they reverenced Socrates. They believed they could see through the reports of his imaginative disciple that he aimed at being real and practical, that he had, according to the old saying, brought Philosophy down to the earth. I do not think that their praises of him were exaggerated, or that they put these praises on a wrong ground. But when I ask for the secret of that

Their admiration of Socrates,

specially real and practical character which all ages have concurred in attributing to Socrates, I find it in his Egotism. I might give you instances of what I mean from either of his disciples, but Xenophon's testimony in this case at least might be more suspected. *who was emphati- cally an Egotist.* He was a soldier and a man of business; when he speaks of Socrates as practical, we might fancy he gave his master credit for the quality which he preferred to all others, and which he had acquired in the world. If Plato was the dreamer that some suppose (all will admit that he was a man of lofty imagination, a born poet), he might be glad to represent Socrates as a dweller in the clouds, not as a citizen of the earth. The passage which I shall choose from him, is taken from one of his most poetical dialogues; it occurs at the beginning of the Phædrus. Socrates and Phædrus are sitting near the spot from which Boreas was reported to have carried off the nymph Oreithyia. Phædrus wishes to know whether his friend accepts that legend as it stands, or adopts one of the physical explanations that had been given of it. Socrates has heard such explanations; they are ingenious; he admires the cleverness of those who invented them. But *Specimen of his Egotism.* if he resorts to this kind of interpretation for the story of Boreas, he must treat Gorgons, Centaurs, Chimæras, after the same fashion. Such a task would be tedious, interminable. 'And, my friend,' he says, 'I cannot find leisure for it. I have not yet complied with the precept of the oracle; I am not yet able to know myself. It seems to me ridiculous whilst I am in this ignorance to busy myself with subjects which lie at a distance from me. Allowing then those mythological questions to settle themselves as they may, accepting the ordinary traditions about them, I devote myself to the question what sort of creature I myself am, whether I am some wild beast more composite in its structure, and more fierce than Typhon, or a gentler animal with a nature partaking of the noble and the divine.'

It is the secret of his practical wisdom,

Here is the Egotist. And here is the practical man we have all heard of. He who could dismiss all questions about Boreas and Oreithyia that he might settle accounts with himself, that he might ascertain what he was, might indeed be said to bring philosophy out of the cloud-land to the *terra firma*. That, in the effort to do so, he should be accused of liking the region into which he was obliged to travel, cannot surprise us.

and of the love and hatred which he inspired.

Nor can we wonder either at the power which he had of attracting men, especially young men, to him, or at the bitter hostility which he provoked. There is no attraction in general formulas and propositions; there is an immense charm in one, however uncouth in his appearance, who can enter into desires and perplexities which he has first realized in his own life, and through which he has fought his way. There is no terror in mere propositions and formulas; there is great terror in one who arouses us to remember that which we had rather forget; he would take from us the Lethe cup; we may be willing that he should drain the cup of hemlock.

The geniality of Socrates, his hearty humour, his appreciation of all the forms of common life, his habit (indicated so well in the passage I quoted from Mr.

Influence of Egotism in the century of Butler and Paley.

Grote) of showing his thought, not formed, but in the process of formation,—were nearly wanting in his accomplished panegyrists of the 18th century. And, therefore, all their talent and all their desire to be useful could never obtain for them the influence which was exerted by men whom they could often despise for want of taste, by men whom they could often condemn for more grievous faults than any against taste, but who had the courage or the audacity to reveal that which had passed in the inmost sanctuary of their being. Amongst us the disciples of Wesley announced, often in grotesque phrases, often with a mixture of wild and morbid fancies, facts of which they had become aware, not in the world without, the world which they saw, but in their own very selves. The grotesque phrases might be ridiculed, the morbid fancies might be detected and exposed by those who were acquainted with diseases of the body or the mind. But the facts were recognised by men whose circumstances and education had been altogether different from those of the persons who disclosed them; chords which had been silent in the hearts of refined men and women responded to the touch sometimes of very coarse fingers; general moralities were rejected as feeble; he who used the Ego was hailed, for there was an Ego in the hearer.

There was a man who spoke in altogether different accents from those of the Methodists to the people of France. Amidst the voices of philosophers who were listened to with wonder and delight in the salons of Paris, because they struck at hypocrisies which were becoming intolerable, and did *not* strike at vices which were fashionable, there echoed from the hills of Switzerland the Confessions of Jean Jacques Rousseau. They were the utterances of a disturbed, even of a deranged mind; were outrageous in their display of the writer's evil acts and thoughts; did not spare the polite

The Methodist in England.

Jean Jacques Rousseau.

Power of the Egotism in France.

society of the day, or the notions which were popular in it. But in spite of their strangeness and madness, in spite of the disgust which they often excited, they had, for Rousseau's countrymen and strangers, a fascination which was found in no dogmas however destructive, in no jests however keen and brilliant. In the most superficial of all societies there was still a craving to look below the surface; where men were most crushed by conventions, there was still a welcome for any one who could prove that he maintained an existence, though it might be a very incoherent existence, under the pressure of them.

Limitation of these remarks.

I quite admit that there is in the English character something which shrinks from both these forms of egotism, even whilst it gives them entertainment. The silent self-contained man who avoids such exhibitions commands our respect; we have a certain dislike, even contempt, for the man who relieves himself by whispering his confessions into the ear of the public, though we are not unwilling to use our privilege of listening.

The Worth of Reserve.

The reserve of such writers as Butler often tells us more of their characters than any discoveries which they could make respecting their history. They hide, under language which concerns the world, many a struggle which they have gone through in themselves; slowly we become as much convinced that a man is speaking to us in these books as if he admitted us into his closest privacy. If such reticence were lost from our literature we should lose much that is most precious in it, much that has been ultimately very power-

Reserve and Egotism not incompatible.

ful. If we banished it from our own characters they would suffer a more serious injury; the most sacred treasures would be profaned. That danger should always be remembered when we commend Egotism. There must be some way of escaping these perils while we satisfy Mr Grote's demand, some way of uttering ourselves without talking about ourselves, some way of carrying on living communications with each other, even when we dwell least on our idiosyncrasies—when our dialect is even less moulded by our own habits and prepossessions than that of the philosophers in the last century was.

Such a method I have wished to indicate by taking for the title of my Lecture 'The *word* I.' 'If you must have that I for your subject,' some one may say, 'why not tell us of the *thing*, why give us the mere name of the thing?' I answer, I cannot call this I a thing; you would all be scandalized by such language. If the I were a thing I should have nothing to do with it; you would get your knowledge of it in the rooms where things are treated of. But, if not a thing, what shall I say of it? Am I to allow that it is a mere abstraction, that it points to no substance? Every man who is most busy in the affairs of the world would raise his voice against me if I did that. 'What! you put this slight upon number one! You say that I am a nonentity. What then, pray, is not a nonentity?' A question which I should find much trouble in answering. If in this perplexity I resort to the phrases Personality or Individuality, I have told you already what consequences I foresee must follow from that proceeding; how, after all, I should be driven to the shame of giving I in exchange for those splendid polysyllables. In despair then of getting a substitute for this word, I content myself with drawing your attention to the fact that you do use it, that you must use it whenever you

The Word points not to a Thing,

nor to an Abstraction.

speak the speech of men. And so I would lead you to reflect a little on the grandeur and power of words; of those words which we repeat most frequently, which we trifle with most. Not the words which are appropriated to the service of Art and Philosophy, which are withdrawn from daily usage, but those which are passing from hand to hand, those which are the current coin of every realm, those which are continually liable to lose their image and superscription from the friction of society, are the truly sacred words; in them lies a wealth of meaning which each age has helped to extract, but which will contain something for every fresh digger. The word *I*, with its property of being demanded by a whole community, and yet being only capable of denoting a single unit, is a key to that mystery in words which makes them interpreters of the life of individuals, of nations, of ages; the discoverers of that which we have in common, the witnesses of that in each man which he cannot impart, which his fellows may guess at, but which they will never know.

This use of common speech was understood by Socrates; it enabled him to detect a number of tricks which the young men of Athens, in their zeal to make words serve the purposes of persuasion, were practising upon themselves; it enabled him to bring to light a multitude of thoughts and convictions that were lying in them crushed under the weight of customary and traditional notions, or of the vanity which aspired to catch at the newest and most paradoxical notions. If he could persuade them to account to themselves for the force which they were giving to words, if he could shew them what force lay in words which they did not recognise, he would teach them to reverence an

inheritance which had come to them from their fathers,
and at the same time to feel that unless they reduced it into possession it might be their burthen and
their curse. In no way had he so much learnt to
fulfil the oracle 'Know thyself,' as by reflecting on the
words which were continually passing from his lips;
in no way could he so effectually stir his pupils to obey
the same oracle as by leading them to cultivate the
like habit. Often, no doubt, he was betrayed into extravagances and puerilities by his passion for etymology. If we would observe carefully how men of the
old world fell into that temptation, if we would faithfully use any lights which philology or experience have
supplied to preserve us from it, modern students might
have a great advantage over the ancient. But they
often, it seems to me, turn their dread of what they
describe as verbal quibbles to a mischievous purpose.
They refuse to recognise any life in words; they quote
Horace as an authority that it is only usage which con-
fers any value upon them. I wish they would consider
that passage in the Ars Poetica which they claim in
support of their doctrine. Horace illustrates by a beautiful analogy from Nature the changes which words
may undergo in different periods:

> Ut silvæ foliis pronos mutantur in annos
> Prima cadunt; ita verborum vetus interit ætas
> Et juvenum ritu florent modo nata vigentque.

He recognised a winter and a spring, a decay and a
renewal for words. The usage therefore

> Quem penes arbitrium est et jus et norma loquendi

can never mean the fashion which makes a word bear
a certain impress without reference to its origin or

*His me-
thod open
to correc-
tion but
not obso-
lete.*

*The opin-
ion that we
may put
what sense
we please
on words*

history. He says that Virgil and Vari
vate and adapt to their own time words
Cato which had become rusty, that

Licuit semperqu̅
Signatum *præsente* nota producere nome

Take the other course, and we may pro
phical slang, or a slang of any other kin■
debase the language of our fathers, and
for the education of our sons.

There is one class of words which e
against arbitrary definition, and which
cially profitable for the end that Socra
himself. I mean such words as 'Con
'Conscience.' There are a multitude r
discover by degrees to be of the sam
point in the same direction as these;
centres from which light falls upon the 1
inseparably connected with that prono
have been speaking in this lecture. Tẽ
from language, and they must disappear
no demand for them in any of the things
taste or handle. They come into exis
cause there is an I who sees, tastes, 1
there no such words, the Delphic oracle
tried to obey would seem the most
uttered. How can I know myself?
creatures then, I and myself? It do
strous. But, monstrous or not, these
that duplicity, they associate it with a
thoughts, they remind me that I am ᳝
condition of a brute, not asserting my r
if I disavow it. For they are not word■
to the inarticulate nomenclature of th■

are like the I, characteristic portions of organic civilized language; they appear in the discourses which have exercised most influence over bodies of men, as well as in those which discover the fears, conflicts, hopes that belong to the secret chamber.

They are full of difficulty, full of apparent contra-diction. Yet I must grapple with them at once if I pursue the course which I have marked out for myself. I have proposed to treat of Casuistry. Now *the* subject of Casuistry is the Conscience. The illustrious man who thirty years ago restored this chair to dignity and efficiency, and began to endow it with some of his vast intellectual treasures, abandoned that title for his lec-tures, deeming Moral Philosophy a more suitable one in this age. The Conscience therefore was only *one* of the subjects which he had to examine; he could deli-berate where he should introduce it into his system. But whilst I yield the greatest weight to his arguments as well as to his authority—whilst I entirely accede to his doctrine that the intentions of founders may often best be fulfilled by a departure from the letter of their instructions, whilst I have no doubt that the main duty of a teacher is to consider how he may meet the re-quirements of his own generation—I am led by these very maxims to accept the term which Dr Knightbridge chose for his professorship, as denoting the first divi-sion of Moral Science. I have told you in this lecture that I dread the temptation to lay down a general scheme of morals or of human nature. The examples of eminent men in former days who have adopted that course—the craving for facts, the impatience of mere opinion, which I welcome as some of the most hopeful signs of our time,—alike lead me to desire, as my im-

Casuistry is occupied with them.

Casuistry why useful for this age.

M. C.   2

mediate predecessor did, a more egotistical kind of study. Casuistry, it seems to me, is such a study. It brings us face to face with the internal life of each one of us. The world without, it leaves to the examination of other enquirers. The Casuist's business is with him who looks into that world, who receives impressions from it, and compels it to receive impressions from him.

Fichte the Egotist among modern philosophers.

There is a writer of the eighteenth century—he lived into the nineteenth—who was singularly unlike those anti-egotists of whom I spoke, one who more than any philosopher since Socrates took the question, ' What am I ? ' as the subject of his thoughts. I should not introduce him here if some of his books had not been set down in the list of those in which students for the Moral Sciences Tripos are to be examined. That being the case I wish that you should know the man better than his books; for he deserves to be known better; his books are valuable chiefly as they help us to know him. I may not have occasion to refer again in any part of this course to *Johann Gottlieb Fichte;* but to this present lecture he specially belongs. He will shew you that an Egotist, in Mr Grote's sense of the word, may be a very brave and noble man, one of the sternest antagonists of that egotism which we ought all to hate.

Fichte's education.

Fichte was a poor man, one however who contrived to obtain a higher culture than rich men generally enjoy; he went to Switzerland and became a teacher of boys. In that occupation he discovered what seemed to him the secret of all philosophy.

Some admirable lines of our own poet, very appropriate to my present subject, will tell you how that secret was brought home to him.

LECT. I.

*Tenny-
son's* In
Memo-
riam
XLIV.

The Baby new to earth and sky,
    What time his tender palm is prest
    Against the circle of the breast,
Has never thought that this is I:

But as he grows he gathers much,
    And learns the use of 'I' and 'me,'
    And finds I am not what I see,
And other than the things I touch.

So rounds he to a separate mind,
    From whence clear memory may begin,
    As through the frame that bounds him in,
His isolation grows defined.

Well, Fichte's lot was cast among those who were thus learning the use of the I and the Me. He did not adopt a theory about the Ego in himself, and the Ego in his pupil; he found that one responded to the other. There was no learning if there was no such communication; the name signified nothing. A vast amount of what was called learning existed in Germany, philosophical speculation without end, heaps of information that could not be measured. But the speculator, what was he? who was informed by all that information? Fichte believed that the vocation of the scholar must be something different from that which the German schoolmen were dreaming of; he believed it must be connected with the vocation of a man.

And now there rose a cry beginning in France, spreading through Europe, about the Rights of Men. The ears of the schoolmaster opened to that cry; it met cries which had been in his own heart long before. He liked it better because it rose from hovels, not palaces or colleges. But *was* each of these men claiming his rights? Had they not been reduced into a dead mass of animals; were they not now feeling their animal

2—2

power and trying to put that forth for the destruction of those who had not recognised them as men ? Must not the scholar's vocation be to give as many as he could the sense of their right to be men; their right not to be lost in a crowd.; their right to be each verily and indeed an I ? For this end and in this spirit Fichte worked in Germany. But against what enemies! The issue of the cry for right had

The Napoleonic I.

been the domination of an emperor. The great Bourbon had said, The State, it is I. Napoleon trampling on the Bourbons said, The Republic, it is I. He said that not only in his own land. Austria and Prussia bowed before him; the country which Rome could not conquer crawled at his feet. In Jena, Fichte had proclaimed that no tyrant can bind him who does not bind himself. In Jena, it was shewn that Prussia had bound herself, and therefore that no army such as

The prophet of Freedom.

Frederic had bequeathed to her could save her from being the bondsman of the foreigner. There were none so hateful to Napoleon as the scholars of any land which he subdued; that is to say if they cared for men; he was willing to patronise them if they would only speak of things. It was specially perilous for any one to maintain the ground which Fichte had taken up. But he never flinched. The hymn of freedom and of its future victory,

Unawed he sung amidst a slavish band,

till the slaves began to shake their fetters and to believe that there might be a deliverance from them. The men of Fichte's own class awoke first. In the lowest depression of Prussia they established the University of Berlin, as the Dutch had established the University of Leyden during their struggle with Philip II. Then

came an army born of the new craving for liberty. The
military arrangements of Frederic were gone; a
Spirit came to take their place. Fichte would have
gone forth to the battle ; his monarch commanded him
to stay in the city and do his country's work there. He
lifted his voice to denounce the compromises which
Austria tempted Prussia to make. He heard that the *His oppor-*
last Frenchman had crossed the Rhine. He was saved *tune death.*
from seeing the disappointment of his hopes from Germany, the degradation which it had to undergo from
those who now claimed to be its emancipators. His
wife, whom he had loved from his youth up, nursing
the wounded in the hospitals, took a fever. He caught
it from her lips and died.

I have told you nothing of Fichte's system. I *Difference*
mean to tell you nothing. When he spoke of that *between*
the Man
which had become a part of his life, of his very self, he *and his*
seems to me a grand teacher; when he tried to speak *System.*
of that which was not himself, or to put himself and
the universe into a set of formulas, I lose sight of him.
I am glad to know that opponents rose up to vindicate
what he disparaged. I am glad to believe that he was
restless within the walls which he had raised around
him. He belongs, as I said, emphatically to my opening Lecture for this reason. I wanted not only to give
you an example of a great egotist; but to shew you
why I have pleaded for egotism. It is that each of us
may reverence his own life and the life of his fellow-
man above all theories that any have formed about him
or them. It is that we may study the problems of life
seriously and truthfully, whether we can make out a
theory about them or no. It is that in studying these *Use of*
Fichte's
problems we may profit by the lessons of those with *example*

whose dogmas or conclusions we may the least agree. When I speak of the Conscience I shall not turn to Fichte. I think our English writers will give us more light on that subject. But I doubt whether we shall be able to use that light, coming to us as it does in many broken rays, if we do not take our stand upon that ground to which Fichte was led by his stern experiences. Think of the word I, and you will be able to enter upon the study of the word Conscience with some hope of a satisfactory result.

How an
able teach-
er who
aims at
making a
System of
Morals
may assist
those who
dread Sys-
tem.
I have alluded to one deviation which I am making from the course that was marked out by Dr Whewell. What I have just said—indeed the whole of this Lecture—will indicate another, it may seem to some a more striking difference, from him. He avowedly endeavoured to construct a system of Morality. I have declared that I have no such object, that I shall even strive diligently against the wish to pursue such an object. I am not the less rejoiced that he made the attempt, and made it with his characteristic vigour and courage, because I do not aspire to imitate it. He has added very much to the stores of our moral experience, and whilst pleading for System, he has furnished us with a series of warnings against the perils of System such as no one could have given who did not bring to the study of Morals a great knowledge of physics and the methods of physical investigation. These warnings I hope never to forget. He has urged us to see in familiar words the recognition of permanent and imperishable truths; he has bidden us not be content with the current notions of these words, but carefully sift them that we may discover their radical force; he would have us proceed step by step in our enquiries;

he says we must not allow affected respect for feelings
and emotions to be an excuse for vague undigested
thoughts.   In the second of his lectures on Systematic
Morality he asserts with great force and eloquence the
maxims which I have been trying to maintain this
morning, that the moral student is as much occupied
with realities as the physical student, and that he has
as wide a field to examine.   'He has' (I must quote
his words, for I would gladly take them as the motto
for this Course of Lectures) 'for his region of thought
everything about which other men think most eagerly,
all that occupies the mind of the historian, the poet,
the tragedian, the comedian, the advocate, the statesman, the poor, the rich, the recluse, the man of the
world; he has to consider not only all the means which
they have to gain their purposes; but he has also to
weigh their purposes against each other; to compare
the ends of life according to each view; to decide how
far each lies in the road to the far end, the true aim of
human life....For the *microcosm*, the little world of
man, is really not less than the *macrocosm*, the great
world of Nature.'

LECT. I.

*The sphere
of the Mo-
ralist.*

*Whewell
on System-
atic Moral-
ity, p. 48.*

LECTURE II.

THE WORD 'CONSCIENCE'.

MANY definitions of the Conscience are to be found in books of Philosophers, many accounts of its operations. We may consider some of these in due time. I should be sorry to neglect them, for each thoughtful man will supply some hint which may make our thoughts clearer. But, as I said in my last Lecture, we must begin with asking ourselves what meaning we have given to the word and do give it in our ordinary discourse. We are using it on the most vulgar occasions. We say that a tradesman who sends in an extravagant bill, or adulterates the food which he sells, has no conscience. And yet we do not really admit that he or any man is without a conscience. We appeal to it as if we thought it was in him, and could respond to the demand we make upon it.

I observed in my last lecture that the adjective Conscious is inseparably connected with the word I. Nothing, I said, which we taste or smell or handle would suggest it to us. I am conscious of the taste of the orange or the smell of the rose. I never dream that the orange or the rose is conscious. I *know with myself* what impression I have received from the rose or the orange. The difference of the effect of sights or scents on different men or women, as on different classes of animals, may depend on peculiarities of their bodily structure; but when you have taken all account of these, if you understand them ever so perfectly, you will have to say at last, 'It is I to whom the pleasure or the pain comes which is brought to me through any sense.' If I were not there the words pain and pleasure would carry no signification with them. I can only tell anything about either, because I am conscious of it.

Dr Whewell remarks that the word conscious has been far too much restricted by some moralists; that I have a right to say, 'I am conscious that two straight lines cannot enclose a space.' Assuredly if I am not conscious of that truth it is not one for me; I have taken no hold of it. And yet we all feel that in general we are adopting a pompous and unnecessary phraseology if we introduce the word conscious in either of these cases. It is enough to say, and therefore it is better to say, 'I taste or smell,' than 'I am conscious of a taste or smell.' Dr Whewell would not have been pleased with any pupil in his Mathematical Class Room who, instead of repeating the postulate as his fathers did before him, improved it by speaking of certain internal convictions which he had about it.

I am conscious of the truth of propositions.

But there are some cases in which we cannot dispense with the word, in which none other would serve us so well. Œdipus meets Laius on a cross-road going to Thebes. There is an encounter. Laius is slain. Is Œdipus conscious of what he has done? Of course he knows that he has killed a man who would have killed him. He meant to do that. But is he conscious—does

When this word becomes necessary.

he know with himself—what sort of act he has done: is he aware that he is a parricide? The story which the genius of Sophocles has so wonderfully unfolded is the story of the awakening of this Consciousness, of the discovery to Œdipus of what he has done, of what he is. And this Consciousness is fresh and alive years after, when he himself is a father and a king. The act done so long ago is with him then. It has become a part of his own existence.

The moment I pass from the consideration of the things with which I have to do to the consideration of that which I am, this problem confronts me; it is this conscience which binds the different parts of my existence together, which assures me that the past still belongs to me. It seems very terrible. But banish it, and there is no drama, no biography, no history: human existence becomes the dreariest blank; men only brutal. There is, however, a Consciousness which is not grand or terrible, which we are wont to connect with what is petty and ridiculous. We say about some picture of a man or woman or child, How self-conscious he or she is! We mean that the person has been thinking what attitudes would be most becoming; how it would be best to appear when other people should see the likeness. This way of *knowing one's self* we pronounce very disagreeable, and worse than disagreeable; it implies insincerity, and must lead to greater insincerity.

We certainly do not mean this, or anything approaching to this, when we speak of a *conscientious* man. Not this, even the reverse of this. And yet we do suppose the conscientious man in some sense to take account of himself, to be aware of what he is doing.

The Consciousness which is awful.

The Consciousness which is vain and trivial.

We do not always use the epithet 'conscientious' as one of strong commendation. We may not like the person on whom we bestow it. There may be something like a sneer or a curl of the lip when we observe 'That man is always thinking what he ought to do or ought not to do.' Such surly judgments, hastily thrown off, are often of great value. They indicate, better than formal explanations, what force we give to the words which we utter most frequently and familiarly. I am not sure that if we sought long we should find a more exact account of a conscientious man than this, He is one who is always considering what he ought or ought not to do ; or whether there is a more exact description of the Conscience than this, It is that in me which says, I ought or I ought not.

How we may get a popular definition of the Conscience.

If we adhere strictly to this expression on which we have stumbled, we shall be able to recognize a fact which is of quite infinite importance to us. We shall clear away difficulties which eminent men have created in their eagerness to magnify the conscience, as well as objections which other eminent men have raised against the acknowledgment of it. The fact is this. However we may account for it each of us does say 'I ought' and 'I ought not.' We cannot weed those expressions out of our dialect or out of the dialect of any civilised nation. Like the word I they have established themselves in language ; it could not exist without them. How is that? Do you think it would be so if *we* could exist without them, if the *I* and the *ought* had not some very close affinity? We need not perplex ourselves with the question how soon a child begins to say I 'ought.' We know it does not at first say I. It describes itself in the third person. It learns,

This popular definition a strict and available one.

The I and the ought inseparable.

some tell us, to say I by imitating those who are around it. Be it so; that may be the way in which it acquires the *sound*. The question for practical people is, what the sound signifies to the child. *What* is imitated in the use of the word? To what account *Does* does the little mimic turn its new possession? And so *imitation account* about the *ought*. That sound may also be caught from *for either?* neighbours old or young. When caught how does it work? Is it a disease which can be cured by certain skilful medicines, or is it to be cherished as necessary to health and life? At all events, however you may have come by the word, frankly own to yourselves, each of you, that you have it; that you cannot part with it. You must use it to denote your desire to be rid of it. You must say 'I *ought* not to be troubled with this ought.'

And steadily remember that the I and the ought are twin words. Like the *Siamese twins*, they are not without violence or risk of death to be severed from each other. I impress that remark upon you because it will save you many confusions hereafter if you *I impute a* thoroughly take it in. I said that you complained of *Conscience to another* the want of conscience in the shopkeeper who charged *because I* you more than you thought was reasonable for articles *am con-scious.* you had purchased of him. You ascribe a conscience to him because he calls himself I, just as you do. And you cannot suppose that he is like you in that respect without supposing that like you he says to himself 'I ought and I ought not.' But I am only *conscious* of that which passes in myself; as he is only conscious of that which passes in himself. There is no doubt in some persons a very wonderful apprehension and divination of that which others are thinking, imagining, purposing. Those who really have that gift,—who do not merely fancy they have it and make all kinds of false, suspicious, and illnatured guesses about their neighbours—we call men and women of genius. Sympathy has much to do with genius, perhaps is the essence of it. But it cannot exist, I apprehend, except in a person who has a lively consciousness of what is passing in *him*. He is awake to that, and so can make more than a guess at what is passing in me. This divination therefore does not interfere with my maxim or even offer an exception to it. The act of conscience is an act in me. It means 'I ought or I ought not.' I may pass judgment on other men's acts; but that is another process; I am abusing terms and what the terms represent if I identify it with the Conscience.

Perhaps you will say to me 'What! if I see my friend pursuing a course of conduct which I am sure will ruin him, is it not my conscience which bids me warn him of his danger, though I know he may quarrel with me, even hate me for doing so?' Yes, I fully admit that it is your conscience which bids you warn your friend. What I affirm is, that the conscience does bid *you*, and no one else. When you speak to him you try to arouse *his* conscience. You will effect nothing for him unless you arouse it. And therefore it is of great practical importance to remember the distinction which I have drawn. Many hard pharisaical censures, which lead to no result, are the consequences of our forgetting it, as well as the omission of many counsels which would benefit our neighbours because they would be the fruit of our experience of ourselves.

And thus another perplexity may be taken out of our way. 'What must we call the Conscience? Is it

LECT. II.

I cannot transfer my Consciousness to another.

I can only call it forth in him.

a special faculty? Is it a faculty in all men or only in some men?' Butler describes it as a faculty of human nature. Dr Whewell demurs; it is according to him only an exercise of the Reason. Which opinion are we to adopt?

Just because I hold the fact of the existence of a conscience to be one in which each of us is deeply and practically interested, I decline to enter into these controversies between learned men. If I called the conscience a faculty, I am not at all sure that I should understand my own meaning; I certainly should have no right to expect you to understand me. A faculty should from its derivation have reference to doing; when we speak of a man of considerable faculty, we understand one who can readily turn his hand to any work which is committed to him. There is nothing in the 'ought' or 'ought not' of the conscientious man which intimates that he has any peculiar capacity of doing. I do not think that I remove the objection or gain any additional clearness by introducing the words, *our* nature or *our* mind. I rather incur the risk of losing that which I have dwelt on as most characteristic of the word Conscience, its adherence to the singular pronoun. And as I have not yet tried to explain what I mean by Nature or Mind or Reason—supposing I am able hereafter to offer any such explanations—it would be very much out of order to thrust in such phrases, as if we knew all about them at the outset of our enquiry. It was almost inevitable that Butler, following that method of which I spoke in my last lecture, should begin with assuming Human Nature as the basis of his remarks on the Conscience. He has behaved with perfect honesty. He has been at great pains to explain what Human Nature signifies and does not signify, in his acceptation of it. We owe him much gratitude for this service. Whether we are satisfied with the explanation or not, it throws light upon a number of difficult points which may come under our notice in future lectures. But that egotistical rule which I am trying to follow does not allow me to meddle with any of these problems at present. According to that rule the question, ' What am I,' takes precedence of all that concern my or our nature ; if so, it will also take precedence of all questions about my mind or our mind, my reason or our reason. We are not then in a condition to decide whether Butler is right, or Dr Whewell is right, or whether both are wrong, or whether there is some way of reconciling them, so that neither may be wrong. But we may thankfully accept their joint testimony in support of a fact which each of them had realized in himself, and which each of us may realize in himself.

I am not the least afraid of bringing the question whether there is a conscience to this test. I am only afraid lest our decision about it should be embarrassed by the introduction of other questions to which the test cannot be applied. If I am told there is a Conscience in Human Nature, I begin to ask whether there are not the widest conceivable differences between the persons to whom this Nature is attributed, and whether what is true about one may not be untrue about another. Especially when this Conscience is credited as it is by Butler with the grandest functions, when it is appealed to as the highest of all authorities, the question will suggest itself, Do you say that of every man's Conscience, or of some particularly exalted Con-

LECT. II.

Why we cannot start from it.

The question; Whose Conscience do you mean ? How treated

(a) *by Dr Whewell,*

science? Dr Whewell was aware that Butler had laid himself open to cavils of this kind. He tried to avoid them. "We cannot," he said, "properly refer to our "Consciences as to an ultimate and supreme authority. "It has only a subordinate and intermediate authority "standing between the supreme law to which it is "bound to conform, and our own actions which must "conform to it, in order to be moral." He adds a little further on, "As the object of reason is to deter-"mine what is true, so the object of Conscience is to "determine what is right. As each man's reason may "err, and so lead himself to a false opinion, so each "man's conscience may err, and lead him to a false "moral standard. As false opinion does not disprove "the reality of truth, so the false moral standards of "men do not disprove the reality of a supreme law or "rule of human action[1]."

This language is moderate and cautious; yet it has provoked a criticism which I will read to you from the 15th chapter of Mr Bain's volume on the Emotions and Will.

(b) *by Mr Bain.*

His objection to a standard Conscience.

"What then," asks Mr Bain, "is this standard? "Where is it to be found? Until it is produced we "have nothing to discuss, affirm, or deny. Is it some "model conscience like Aristotle's serious man (ὁ σπου-"δαῖος), or is it the decision of a public body authorised "to decide for the rest of the community? We have "no difficulty in deciding what is the standard of truth "in most other matters, but what is the standard con-"science? That *must* be got at, or morality is not a "subject to be reasoned or written about."

---

[1] *Elements of Morality,* Vol. I. p. 161, 2nd Ed.

"Dr Whewell (he continues) appears to presume
" the existence of certain moral ideas without reference
" to any individual mind whatever, concerning every
" one, and yet originating with no one. He sets up for
" morality a standard having a degree of independent
" existence, such as hardly can be conceived, and which
" does not exist with reference to anything else. We
" have standards of length, of measure, of weight,
" which even although embodied in material objects,
" can hardly be said to have the independence here
" contended for. In constructing the imperial yard,
" gallon, or pound weight, a certain number of persons
" concur in adopting a definite unit, and these persons
" being either themselves the governing body of the
" nation, or being followed by the actual governing
" body, give the law or so dictate the standard for
" themselves and all others. It is quite true that indi-
" viduality is controlled or overruled in this matter,
" but not by abstract, unseen, unproducible power. It
" is one portion of the community agreeing upon a cer-
" tain choice and the rest falling in with that. Every
" dealer must bring his weights and measures to be
" tried by the authoritative standard, but he is at no
" loss to say who are the authors and maintainers
" of that standard. So with Time. When we are
" called upon to adapt our watches to Greenwich time,
" it is not a standard beyond humanity. The collective
" body of astronomers have agreed upon a mode of
" reckoning founded upon the still more general recog-
" nition of the solar day as the principal unit. At
" Greenwich Observatory, observations are made which
" determine the standard of this country; and the po-
" pulation in accepting that standard know or may

"know that they are following the Astronomer Royal "with his staff, and the body of astronomers generally." pp. 291, 292.

Whether these illustrations from pounds, gallons, and watches, confute or confirm the doctrine of an immutable moral standard which Dr Whewell asserted— whether the arguments from the weight of tradition, of professional observers, of mere numbers, tend to prove the impossibility or the necessity of such a standard,— whether Mr Bain is himself less or more chargeable than Dr Whewell with appealing in his treatment of *Difficulty* the Conscience to "an abstract, unseen, unproducible *if we as-* power,"—are questions which may all come before us *sume even* *a partial* in due time ; the last I shall have to consider in the *authority* *in the Con-* next lecture. Here I am constrained to admit that *science.* even a statement so qualified, as that in the *Elements of Morality*, does lay the author of it open to the charge of imputing an indefinite authority to *the* Conscience, while we are not told in what particular person it dwells. But now supposing that 'I ought and I ought not,' are the formulas of the Conscience, does it strike you that we must produce a model Conscience before we can affirm that each of us so far as he is an I uses *If the Con-* those formulas ? Of course Mr Bain is at full liberty to *science* say 'I decline to reason or write about your doctrine of *means 'I* *ought'* a Conscience, unless you do that.' No British subject is *the vul-* compelled to write or reason about a subject except on *garest in-* *stance is* his own terms. But if the point to be ascertained is *the best.* whether that which I call a fact is a fact or a fiction, one would fancy that the vulgarest specimen of our race would supply a much better test than some person of rare excellence. After thinking much who might serve the purpose of an experiment most effectually, I

can remember no one whom on the whole I should prefer to Mr Tennyson's *Northern Farmer*.

You will not complain, I hope, that he is a fictitious character. He is real enough. He is very strictly
an individual. Yet he could not have been described
to us by any writer who had not taken a careful observation of his class. We at once recognise him as a
member of our own tribe; an Englishman to the very
bone; one whose brutality we cannot put at a distance
from us and ascribe to any people as being more characteristic of them than of us; one who has a manliness breaking through the brutality, which as patriots
we may think is also not uncongenial to our soil.
There is no doubt about the lower stratum. The tastes
of the Northern farmer are altogether animal; he has
no dream of what Mr Arnold would call culture; his
thoughts about what will become of himself when he
leaves the world, or how the world will go on without
him, are equally bewildered; his moral standard has
certainly not been fixed by any body of men answering
to those who have determined so satisfactorily the
standard for the gallon or the time-piece. How is it
that one who has all these tendencies and inclinations
can be a subject for art, that we are able to contemplate him without utter disgust? A Conscience is
there. We are not in the presence of a mere drinker
of 'yüale.' Even about that there is a rule from which
he cannot depart. And he has stubbed Thorneby
waste, because he has a duty to the land. He has
gone to church Sunday after Sunday, not because he
understands what the parson has said, but because the
parson, being a parson, ought to say it, and he ought
as farmer to hear. He has too a sense of having

The Northern Farmer.

His bru- tality and humanity.

Tokens of a Con- science.

3—2

done something which he ought not to have done. He thinks he may have made compensation for his wrong doing; but he is not at ease about it. He recurs to it, tries to balance it against good deeds. An I is there; the past cannot be left behind; it is with him on his death-bed. We have encountered a man

Every-thing in this poem depends upon the ought.

like ourselves in his degradation and his dignity. The strength which we disguise under flattering phrases about Anglo-Saxon muscle and toughness lies in the ' owt.' That rises out of the coarse nature of the farmer

It is the same in every high-er instance.

as out of a prison-house or a grave. But it is the same which spoke forth clearly, musically, effectually in Christopher Columbus, when he determined that he ought to cling to his belief in a new Continent if all the wise heads in Europe derided him, if all the crowned heads trifled with him; in Martin Luther, when he said that he ought to go forward to the Diet though there was as many devils in Worms as there were tiles on the houses; in John Hampden, when he said that he ought not to pay the forty shilling tax of ship-money, if the resistance to it involved him in ruin, even if it ended in a civil war for his country. How different the standard of any one of these men was from that of the Northern farmer, I need not stop to explain; how different the sense in each of the power which could enable him to follow that standard. But the Conscience of an obligation, involving some effort, endurance, sacrifice, dwelt in them all; the presence of this light is most conspicuous in the farmer from the darkness of the ground which throws it back.

The pendant to this portrait.

But can we find no picture which stands in direct contrast to this one, and which may teach us what the effect on a man would be if the Conscience were—not eliminated from it,—but reduced to the smallest possible force and vitality? Modern literature in this case also is most helpful. You know the story of Romola probably better than I do. You will remember therefore the full-length and admirable portrait of the young Greek, Tito. With a perception of all sensual delights as exquisite as ever belonged to his race when it was in the fullness of its glory, with the accomplishments which made it the teacher of Western Europe in the 15th century, with energy for all the intellectual pursuits which were so dear to the Italians of that day, failing in no subtlety of mind or grace of person or aptitude for affairs, able to attract the admiration of the wisest statists, and to win the heart of the noblest woman, what is there deficient in this man? This only. The words 'I ought' and 'I ought not' have vanished from a vocabulary rich in the spoils of all languages capable of expressing every delicate and refined apprehension. That is his one want, and for that—it is a victory of genius for which we cannot be too thankful —the authoress of Romola has compelled us to regard him with a contempt and a loathing which it is impossible to entertain for the Northern Farmer.

This character also I dare not call fictitious. It is true in all its essentials, even in its details. The maxim of Tito, 'Seek all the pleasure you can get, avoid all the pain,' is the maxim on which thousands of young men in England, with or without the refinement of the Greek, are trying to act. Most of them trouble themselves little about philosophy. . There are some who think that they can plead the authority and sustain themselves by the arguments of an eminent philosopher, not a Greek, but an Englishman; not of the 15th cen-

The refined Greek.

His maxim of life widely accepted in modern England.

tury, but of the 19th. Of him I must say a few words.

Mr Jeremy Bentham was, I should imagine, more utterly unlike Tito in his conception of the purpose for which he existed than even the Northern Farmer. He scorned delights and lived laborious days. Instead of devoting himself to the luxury either of a sensual or an intellectual life, he toiled for the improvement of prison discipline, for the overthrow of prejudices about transactions between the lender and the borrower, for the removal of abuses in various departments of legal administration. With great eagerness for the assertion of a general theory, he never excused himself from the trouble of entering into the minutiæ of practice. The greatest happiness of the greatest number was his watchword; he showed that he sincerely valued this object above all his private interests. He was, moreover, thoroughly an I. He defied public opinion in his opinions, and in his mode of presenting and enforcing his opinions. He worked on in his own way; severe, even fierce, in his censures and contempt of that which he supposed to be mischievous and foolish; resolute in his assertion of what he believed to be useful and logical.

What possible plea can those who have adopted the Tito scheme of life find for claiming Mr Bentham as their ally? The smallest plea imaginable if they studied his example, and tried to frame themselves upon that; a very tolerable plea, I think you will admit, when you read these opening passages of his *Principles of Morals and Legislation.*

" Nature has placed mankind under the government " of two sovereign masters, *Pain* and *Pleasure.* It is

"for them alone to point out what we ought to do, as
"well as to determine what we shall do. On the one
"hand, the standard of right and wrong, on the other
"the chain of causes and effects, are fastened to this
"throne. They govern us in all we say, in all we do,
"in all we think; every effort we make to throw off
"our subjection to them, will serve but to demonstrate
"and confirm it. In words a man may pretend to
"abjure this empire, but in reality he will remain subject to it all the while.

"The principle of Utility recognizes this subjection,
"and assumes it for the foundation of that system, the
"object of which is to rear the fabric of felicity by the
"hands of reason and of law. Systems which attempt
"to question it, deal with sounds instead of sense, in
"caprice instead of reason, in darkness instead of
"light.

*   *   *   *   *

"The principle of Utility is the foundation of the
"present work; it will be proper therefore at the out-
"set to give an explicit and determinate account of
"what is meant of it. By the principle of Utility is
"meant the principle which approves or disapproves
"of every action whatsoever, according to the tendency
"which it appears to have to augment or diminish the
"happiness of the party whose interest is in question;
"or, what is the same thing in other words, to promote
"or to oppose that happiness. I say of every action
"whatsoever, and therefore not only of every action
"of a private individual, but of every measure of Govern-
"ment. By Utility is meant that property in any
"object, whereby it tends to produce benefit, advan-
"tage, pleasure, good, or happiness (all this in the

*Every sys-
tem which
does not
own their
supremacy
nonsensi-
cal.*

*Pleasure,
Good,
Happiness,
synony-*

" present case comes to the same thing), or (what comes
" again to the same thing) to prevent the happening of
" pain, evil, or unhappiness to the party whose interest
" is concerned : if that party be the community in
" general, then the happiness of the community; if
" a particular individual, then the happiness of that
" individual.

" The interest of the community is one of the most
" general expressions that can occur in the phraseology
" of Morals.   No wonder that the meaning of it is often
" lost.   When it has a meaning it is this: The Com-
" munity is a fictitious body composed of the individual
" persons who are considered as constituting, as it were,
" its members.   The interest of the Community then is,
" what?—the sum of the interests of the several mem-
" bers who compose it.

*How we
find out
what is the
interest of
a Commu-
nity.*

" It is in vain to talk of the interest of the Com-
" munity without understanding what is the interest of
" the Individual.   A thing is said to promote or be for
" the interest of the individual when it tends to add to
" the sum total of his pleasures ; or, what comes to the
" same thing, to diminish the sum total of his pains."

" An action then may be said to be conformable to
" the principle of Utility, or, for shortness' sake, to
" Utility (meaning with respect to the community at
" large) when the tendency it has to augment the hap-
" piness of the community is greater than any it has to
" diminish it.

I omit two or three sentences which refer specially
to maxims of Government; then we come to this:

" Of an action that is conformable to the principles
" of Utility one may always say either that it is one
" which ought to be done, or at least that it is not one

"that ought not to be done. One may say also that it
"is right it should be done; at least that it is not wrong
"it should be done; that it is a right action; at least
"that it is not a wrong action. When thus interpreted,
"the words *ought* and *right* and *wrong* and others of
"that stamp bear a meaning: when otherwise, they
"have none[1]."

Surely a disciple of Tito has a right to exclaim,
when he reads these sentences, 'I am the true Ben-
'thamite. You who boast of that name and yet spend
'your lives in seeking for the reformation of what you
'deem abuses, even if you can plead the precedent of
'Mr Bentham himself, are utterly inconsistent men.
'You defy the vengeance of those deities, Pleasure and
'Pain, whom I, in accordance with your creed, acknow-
'ledge as my sovereigns; the one to possess the service
'of my life, the other to be induced by all possible
'bribes to leave me alone. You, after all, are mimick-
'ing the young Hercules in the fable: I am convinced
'that he was a fool.'

Many men of this sort however, instead of claiming
to be Mr Bentham's followers, call him a hard dogma-
tist; perhaps hold that their fine sentimentalism, or
their religious faith, gives them a right to speak scorn-
fully of one who merely cared for Utility. His hard-
ness seems to me far better than their softness—the
barest Utilitarianism which is in earnest, than a Sentiment and a Religion which are only an excuse for
self-indulgence and contempt.

I will not point a moral against others, and avoid
the application of it to myself. As I have pleaded for

[1] Bentham's Works, Vol. I. *Principles of Morals and Legislation*, c. I.

egotism I will commit a flagrant act of egotism, very humiliating to me, I hope of some good to you. I remember what no other single person in the world will remember, that when I was an Undergraduate in this University I wrote a foolish parody on a book of Mr Bentham, who was then living. It was the easiest thing possible to travesty his style, which was full, especially in his later days, of obvious peculiarities, very interesting to a real student of thought and language, merely tempting an idler such as I was to ridicule. I do not suppose so silly a composition did harm to any one but the writer. A gnat's sting may annoy a giant, so it might have given a moment's distress to the old man, if he had met with it; I trust as scarcely any one else read it that he never did. But slight as may have been the consequences of the act, my conscience says distinctly, 'I ought not to have done it.' I shewed, by doing it, that I was wanting in reverence for grey hairs, and for the continuous effort of a man through a long life, at the risk of pain, at the cost of pleasure, to effect what he thought good for his fellows. If I had not been more a victim of his theory than he was, I should have paid greater honour to him.

An act may be wrong without reference to the pain which it inflicts.

I make this confession because the recollection of an incident, in itself so trifling, illustrates one of the most serious and awful problems of the Conscience. Its records are permanent. Acts that to others are dead, still live for the doer of them. Coleridge tells the story of an ignorant servant girl who, in the delirium of a fever, repeated sentences of Greek and Hebrew, which she had heard her master repeat years before whilst she was sweeping his study. He deduces this lesson from the tale. "It may be

The testimonies of the Conscience imperishable.

"more possible for heaven and earth to pass away, than
"that a single act, a single thought, should be loosened
"or lost from that living chain of causes, with all the
"links of which the free-will, our only absolute self, is
"co-extensive and co-present. And this, this perchance
"is that dread book of Judgment, in the mysterious
"hieroglyphics of which every idle word is recorded."

LECT. II.

Biographia
Literaria,
2nd Ed.
Vol. I. p.
119.

LECTURE III.

THE CONSCIENCE AND ITS MASTERS.

THE conscience in me says I ought and I ought not; so far we arrived last week. There is no difference about the question whether these words 'ought' and 'ought not' do exist in our language, whether there are not equivalent words in the language of every civilised nation. There is no difference about the question whether they are deeply fixed in human speech; no one seriously dreams of extracting them out of it. Nor, I believe, if we understand one another, will there be much hesitation in admitting the maxim for which I have been contending, that none of the things I see or handle suggest the word; that the moment I speak of myself, it starts forth full armed.

That is the explanation of an opinion to which I alluded in my first Lecture. A very eminent writer on Ethics, Sir James Mackintosh, says that other sciences are conversant with what is; that the science of Ethics is conversant with what ought to be. The distinction was plausible in itself even without considering the authority from which it proceeded. Yet if we accepted it, Ethics seemed transferred from the real world in which we dwell to some other imaginary world. In that case I was sure we should get no serious attention for them in this busy practical age. Dismissing therefore that opinion, without examining what might be the arguments for it, we asked whether there was no other difference between this study and those with which we are engaged elsewhere. We lighted upon this. We could not find that the question ' What am I ?' is considered by any teachers, though it is continually suggested by the business of the world, as well by every debate in the schools. To grapple with this question seemed to us the function of the Moralist. If so, he cannot be less immediately occupied with that which is—with existing facts—than any physical student. His business cannot be carried on in some distant Atlantis, nor can he be engrossed in the search for one. Nevertheless an acute thinker like Sir James *How it* Mackintosh, who was also a man of the world, was not *may be* likely to throw out a hint which had no substantial *defended.* worth. In pursuing our own course we have discovered the worth of it. The ought does not belong to things —it does not suggest some vague possibility for *their* improvement—it is linked inseparably to me. It may be that when I use it most emphatically I am least inclined to imagine some different condition from that in which I find myself. Perhaps I ought to be acting more in conformity with this state than I do act; perhaps I ought not to be doing so many things which are inconsistent with this state.

This was unquestionably the doctrine of a writer *Butler's* for whom Sir James Mackintosh entertained a very high *dislike to* admiration, Bishop Butler. I have already referred to *any con-* those discourses of his on Human Nature, which occupy *ceptions of* *an order* so conspicuous a place in the list of subjects for the *which we* *frame for* *ourselves.*

Moral Sciences Tripos. I have spoken of them as especially bearing on this question of the Conscience. If
you would understand them you should be aware of
the intense dislike which Butler felt for all schemes by
which an Order made out of our fancies is substituted
for the one in which we are placed. His other great
work, the *Analogy*, is full of vehement even scornful
expressions towards those who fashion worlds for themselves, and are not content patiently to examine the
characteristics and indications of that wherein they are
sent to live and work. He exhibits precisely the same
temper in these discourses. He seeks to find out what
human nature is, not what it might be or ought to be.
Though a preacher, he is anxious to exclude all notions
of divinity which would interfere with this design.
And therefore the office which he assigns to the Conscience is primarily that of warning us that we should
not do acts which disturb the harmony of this Nature,
—what Shakespeare calls 'unproportioned acts.'

What is conformity to Nature?

That is Butler's principle. He demands a Conscience to exercise a control over our thoughts and
acts, to declare which are and which are not consistent
with the Order or Constitution of our Nature. But
then Mr Bentham tells us that according to this Order
or Constitution of Nature, Pleasure and Pain are our
Sovereign Masters. And though we may not understand
this lofty phraseology, we are wont to say in plain
prose that we find it natural to take what we like and
to reject what we dislike. If that is what Mr Bentham
means, I should be afraid to oppose to him some general theory of what is natural, even if there were ever so
much to urge in favour of it. I would rather at once
give up the dispute with him so far as it is a verbal

Concession to Ben-tham as to the word Nature.

one, and admit that if my Conscience tells me I ought not to take what I like and to reject what I dislike, my Conscience is bidding me not stoop to my nature, but resist it.

Do I then give up what I take to be Butler's meaning in these statements respecting human Nature, because I find myself puzzled and entangled by the terms which he has chosen? No; for I recur to my old question, 'What am I?' There are a few simple answers to that question which shew me that there is an Order in which I am placed, a real order, not an imaginary one—not an order which might be desirable but which exists. I *am* certainly a son, I *am* a brother, I *am* a citizen. Perhaps I *am* a husband, perhaps I *am* a father. And if the enjoyment of any pleasure or the avoidance of any pains leads me to acts which are inconsistent with any of these positions, my Conscience says 'I ought not to enjoy that pleasure, I ought not to avoid that pain.' Let the enjoyment or the avoidance be as natural as it may, it involves a departure from the order in which I am placed. I care nothing about ideals or possibilities. It is a violation of my actual state; a disturbance and interruption of that.

Let us see then to what we have come. Bentham tells us that we are under certain obligations. So far we are agreed. In using the words ' I ought,' I confess that I am under an obligation. Next, he says the obligation is not one of mere force. I am not moved as a stone is moved, by external violence. So far also we are agreed. Thirdly, he says that there are certain influences of pleasure and pain acting upon me, and that it is natural for me to yield myself to these influences. Once more, there is no difference. I confess these influences. I feel the force of them; I am not angry that they should be called natural; it does seem to me natural to bow before them. But here our strife begins. You tell me that I must yield to these motives; that when I use the word *ought* I only mean, if I mean anything, that I do what they tell me. I say I mean something when I use the word ought, and that I never did mean that; I say no one has meant that by the word; no one less than Mr Bentham.

Ought and ought not involve a conflict with Pleasure and Pain.

The word signified to him what it signifies to me, what it signifies to every one, precisely the reverse of this; it is a self assertion, a denial of the claim of external powers to rule me. Pleasure and Pain are not things which I can see or touch or taste; they are secret influences which come to me through my sight or touch or taste. I cannot find them by dissecting or analysing the things through which I receive them. If I were not, they would not be. They have no business therefore to set themselves above me. Every time any man or woman or child says 'I ought,' it says 'I am under an obligation which is not to you.'

Nature and human order.

To what then? If we said to Nature, we should retract our previous concession. Moreover we should incur the peril of Mr Bain's denunciation against 'those who set up abstract, unseen, unproducible powers.' But if I shew by broad patent facts that I am in a certain order—an order which affects me at every moment—an order into one part of which I entered at my birth, parts of which I have deliberately adopted,— it is not a great assumption to say, In this order I ought to abide; its influences, like those of Pleasure and Pain, are invisible, but they are just as real. And if they come into conflict, as we know that they do

continually, my obligation to the one may be an obli- |
gation to resist the other.

Obligation to an Order or a Constitution may not sound very practical language. Translate it as quickly as you please into obligation to fathers and mothers, to brothers and sisters, to a wife, to your Queen and country. Change as soon as you will the long word Obligation into the shorter homelier word Duty. I shall never object to such alterations; the mother tongue is always sweeter, often more distinct and definite, than the tongue of philosophers. But happily when we speak of persons we cannot forget the affections which we have for them. How precious these are, how closely they are intertwined with the roots of our social existence, I hope to shew you when we come in a future Course of Lectures—that on Moral Philosophy—to speak of the Family and the Nation. But there is a danger of treating those affections as if they created the Order which calls for them. If we fall into that mistake, the affection will become merely a part of our pleasures or pains. As long as we like a person we shall suppose we are bound to him; our dislike will dissolve the tie. We shall live in a circle of what are called in the cant of our day *elective affinities;* the grand old name of Relations will be treated as obsolete. That you may escape this danger, I dwell upon this fact—that we are in an order; that relations abide whether we are faithful to them or neglect them; and that the Conscience in each of us affirms 'I am in this order, I ought to act 'consistently with it, let my fancies say what they ''please.' The necessity for such firm and distinct language becomes more evident to us the older we grow and the more we notice the habits and doctrines which

Practical view of this order.

Affections correspond to it; do not create it.

Elective affinities and Rela-tions.

are prevalent amongst us. The reverence for parents, the sanctity of the marriage vow, the permanence of friendships, are all in peril from the confusion between likings and affections. Those who resolutely draw a distinction between them will have their reward. They will find that the conscience protests not against the fervency, but against the coldness, feebleness, uncertainty of our affections.

The greatest number.

There is another point, closely connected with this subject of Duty or Obligation, which is suggested by the passage that I read to you last week from Mr Bentham's Treatise on Morals and Legislation. He sets before himself the greatest happiness of the greatest number of people as the object which individuals and governments are to seek. I have said already that I believe he did seek after that object; when I speak hereafter of the ideals which have had an influence in raising men's thoughts above narrow and partial interests, I shall hope to do justice to that ideal. Here, as I have told you, my business is not with ideals, but with the questions, What am I? what has this word 'ought' to do with me? These questions can never be answered whilst we are busy about numbers, whilst we are losing ourselves in a crowd. Mr Bentham was

Each and all.

aware of this fact himself. He says, you may remember, "It is in vain to talk of the interest of the Com-"munity without understanding what is the interest of "the individual." A little while afterwards he discusses

Principles of Morals and Legislation, c. II. Works, Vol. I. p. 12.

an objection. Mr Bain says of Dr Whewell's doctrine of the Conscience, that it makes a man a judge in his own case. Mr Bentham foresees that his doctrine is open to the same complaint. "It may be said every "one will be constituting himself judge of this utility;

LECT. III.

"every obligation will cease when he no longer per-
"ceives that it is his own interest." He replies, with
his usual promptness and decision, "Every one will
"constitute himself judge of his own utility; this is,
"and this ought to be, otherwise man would not be a
"reasonable being. He who is not a judge of what is
"reasonable for himself is less than an infant, is a fool.
"The obligation which binds men to their engagements
"is nothing but a feeling of an interest of a superior
"class, which outweighs an inferior interest. Men are
"not always held by the particular utility of a par-
"ticular engagement, but in the case in which the en-
"gagement becomes burthensome to one of the parties,
"it is still upheld by the general utility of engage-
"ments, by the confidence which each enlightened man
"wishes to have placed in his word, that he may be
"considered as trustworthy, and enjoy the advantages
"attached to probity and esteem."

Every man his own judge of what is useful and mischievous.

Grounds of honesty.

How we are tossed back in these sentences, from
the Community to the individual, from the individual
to the Community! "It is vain to speak of the interest
"of the Community without understanding the interest
"of the individual." "He who is not a judge of what
"is reasonable for himself is a fool." And yet the reason which a man has for being faithful to his engagements is, that he wishes to have faith placed in his
word (of course by the Community to which he belongs), that he wishes to be considered (of course by
that Community) as trustworthy, and enjoy the advantages attached (of course by that Community) to probity and esteem.

Evasions and ambiguities in these state-ments.

One is absolutely sure that these motives did not
govern Mr Bentham. He wished to speak true words,

They do not imply any dis-

4—2

not to have credit for speaking them; not to be considered trustworthy, but to be trustworthy; not to have
the votes of men on his side, but to deserve them, and
to maintain his cause without them, if they were all
against him.　But this bewildered language in a writer
who especially desired to be precise—this suggestion of
insincerity in one who continually denounced insincerity in his neighbours, and certainly strove to be clear
of it in his own acts—is inevitable, it seems to me, if
the solemn 'I ought' and 'I ought not' of the Conscience is explained away as the result of some external
influence.

I should not do justice to that mode of accounting
for its operations, if I confined myself to Mr Bentham.
Since his time Mr Bain has elaborated the same doctrine more completely, and in language far more august
and imposing.　There are several passages on the subject in his work on the Emotions and the Will.　I
quote the one in which he has summed up his decisions.

*Resolu-
tion of the
Conscience
into the
fear of
punish-
ment.*

"I have given it," he says, "as my deliberate opi-
"nion that authority or punishment is the commence-
"ment of that state of mind recognised under the va-
"rious names Conscience, the Moral Sense, the Senti-
"ment of Obligation.　The major part of every Com-
"munity adopt certain rules of conduct necessary for
"the common preservation or ministering to the com-
"mon well-being.　They find it not merely their in-
"terest, but the very condition of their existence, to
"observe a number of maxims of individual restraint
"and of respect to one another's feelings on such points

"as person, property, and good name.　Obedience must
"be spontaneous on the·part of the larger number, or
"on those whose influence preponderates in the Society;

"as regards the rest, compulsion must be brought to
"bear. Every one, not of himself disposed to follow
"the rules prescribed by the Community, is subjected
"to some infliction of pain to supply the absence of
"other motives; the infliction increasing in severity
"until obedience is obtained. It is the familiarity with
"this *régime* of compulsion and of suffering, constantly
"increasing until resistance is overborne, that plants in
"the infant and youthful mind the first germs of the
"sense of obligation. I know of no fact that would
"prove the existence of any such sentiment in the pri-
"mitive cast of our mental constitution. An artificial
"system of controlling the actions is contrived, adapted
"to our volitional nature, the system of using pain to
"deter from particular sorts of conduct. A strong line
"of distinction is drawn in every human mind between
"actions that bring no pain, except what arise out of
"themselves, as when we encounter a bitter taste or a
"scalding touch, and those actions that are accompanied
"with pains imposed by persons about us. These ac-
"tions, and the circumstances attending them, make a
"deep and characteristic impression; we have a peculiar
"notion attaching to them, and to the individual per-
"sons the authors of the attendant pains. A strong
"ideal avoidance, not unmixed perhaps with the per-
"turbation of fear, is generated towards what is thus
"forbidden by penalties rising with transgression. The
"feeling drawn out towards those that administer the
"pain is also of the nature of dread; we term it usually
"the feeling of authority. From first to last this is the
"essential and defining quality of the Conscience, al-
"though mixed up with other ingredients. As Duty is
"circumscribed by punishment, so the sense of obliga-

LECT. III.

fractory members.

Treatment of the re- fractory.

Ideal avoidance.

Authority and Dread.

Education.

How the flogged become floggers.

The sentiment of the forbidden.

The subordinate motives.

"tion has no other universal property, except the ideal
"and actual avoidance of conduct prohibited by penal-
"ties. This discipline indoctrinates the newly intro-
"duced member of Society with the sentiment of the
"*forbidden,* which by and bye takes root and expands
"into the sentiment of *moral disapprobation;* he then
"joins with the other members of the Community in
"imposing and enforcing the prohibitions that have
"been stamped and branded in the course of his own
"education. Duty then may be said to have two prime
"supports in the more self-regarding parts of our na-
"ture—the sense of the common preservation and well-
"being operating upon a preponderating majority, and
"the sense of punishment brought to bear upon indi-
"viduals (who must be the smaller number) not suffi-
"ciently prompted by the other sentiment. Order
"being once established in a Society, that is to say, the
"practice of obedience being habitual to the mass of
"the Community, it is only necessary to apply a dis-
"ciplining process to the young to prepare them for
"the same acquiescence in the public morality. The
"imposition of penalties begets at once the sense and
"avoidance of the *forbidden* and the awe of authority,
"and this, as a general rule, is retained through life as
"the basis of the individual Conscience, the foremost
"motive to abstain from actions designated as wrong.

"It is not implied" (he goes on) "that Conscience
"is never anything else than the actual and ideal
"avoidance and dread of punishment. Other elements
"concur sometimes so largely as to obliterate in the
"view the primary germ and characteristic type of
"the faculty. There are motives that supersede the
"operation of punishment in a variety of instances;

"as when we contract a positive sentiment of good will "towards those whom the law forbids us to injure. " Even then we do not lose the strong feeling implanted "in us respecting the forbidden and the authoritative; " we simply are no longer in the position of being moved " by that alone. Our tender feelings, our sentiments " of the fair, the equal, and the consistent, if liberally "developed and well directed, impel us, as it were of "our own accord, to respect those interests of our " fellow-beings that are protected by the enactments " of Society. Moreover, as already said, there is a "certain maturity of the well-disposed mind at which " we enter the company of the majority, spontaneous " in its own obedience from a recognition of the common "safety, and compelling the dissentient minorities by "force or punishment. At this stage the Conscience, "which was at first derived or implanted, is now in- "dependent or self-sustaining. The judgment of the " individual approves of the common prohibitions against "falsehood, injustice, breach of bargains, and other "injuries, as prohibitions essential to its own security, "in company with the rest of the Society, and Con- "science therefore passes into a higher grade of the "prudential motive." *Emotions and Will*, 2nd Edition, pp. 481—483.

Entering the company of the Majority.

The perfected man.

Here the Community stands forth in its full grandeur. Mr Bentham is in general much more direct and straightforward than his successor. Throwing off philosophical conventionalities, he can talk in plain English of a man being a fool. But he falls into vagueness and contradiction because he cannot give up the claims of the individual to be heard; he puts those claims higher than any one who recognises a Conscience

Comparison of the two writers.

would dare to put them. Mr Bain is free from any such perplexity. The work of the community is deliberately to coerce the individual by punishment (which Mr Bain identifies with authority), till in the maturity of a well-disposed mind he enters into the company of the majority. Mr Bain has therefore not the slightest objection to a Conscience. So far from disliking it, he values the Conscience as that in each man which leads him to tremble at the decrees of a majority. It has nothing to do indeed with 'the

primitive cast of our mental constitution.' But by cultivating 'a strong ideal avoidance' 'of the pains imposed by the persons about us, not unaccompanied perhaps with the perturbation of fear,' the 'newly introduced member of society is indoctrinated with the sentiment of the *forbidden*.' And thus having his own Conscience properly corrected and shaped under this discipline, 'he joins with the other members of the community in imposing and enforcing the prohibitions that have been stamped and branded in his own education.' My excuse for repeating expressions which I have just read to you is that I fear you should lose them in the multitude of eloquent phrases by which they are encompassed, and that, as they are exactly opposed to what I have been saying respecting the Conscience, you ought to have the opportunity of carefully weighing them.

You will judge from what I have said already that I am not at all anxious to debate the question whether the Conscience belongs to the primitive cast of our mental Constitution. Some—probably Mr Bain—would seek for that primitive cast among savages. I have contended that the words 'I' and 'ought' do not belong to the vocabulary of savages as they belong to the vocabulary of civilized men. Again, no one I suppose would dispute the assertion that the parent or teacher of a child exercises an authority over it which is external to it. Nor should I, or any one I know, say that punishment is not one of the instruments of this authority, or that it may not be used for the purpose of awakening or cultivating the Conscience. That the community of which a parent or a teacher is a member is deeply concerned in the question, *how* he exercises this authority, *how* and to what end he wields this punishment, is a belief which I think we should all entertain, even if it had not received Mr Bain's imprimatur. But in that 'how' and 'to what end' lies a tremendous controversy. The distinction of the civilized man from the savage is, as it seems to me, that he is not to the same extent the victim of external influences, that he rises above them and tries to rule them. The external authority of the parent or teacher I maintain is useless unless he appeals to that which is within the child, is mischievous unless it is exerted to call that forth. The external authority must become an internal authority, not co-operating with the forces which are seeking to crush the I in the child but working against those forces, working to deliver the child from their dominion. The punishments therefore which are the weapons of this authority but never can be confounded with it, must be directed expressly to *this* purpose. If the child stoops, as it will stoop continually, to the attraction of outward things which it has been forbidden to touch or taste because they will do it harm, punishments will remind it that to obey its teachers is better than to obey its inclinations.

The teacher will endeavour so to contrive his punishment that 'the sentiment of the forbidden' may always be accompanied with the sentiment of trust in the person who has forbidden. If the child is taught to have a dread of him as one who is an inflicter of pain, not to have a reverence for him as one who cares for it and is seeking to save it from its own folly—if the child is instructed carefully to separate the pain which rises out of its own acts from the pain which the parent inflicts so that it may associate the pain with him rather than with them—then all has been done which human art can do to make it grow up a contemptible coward, crouching to every majority which threatens it with the punishments that it has learnt to regard as the greatest and only evils; one who may at last, 'in the maturity of a well-disposed mind,' become the spontaneous agent of a majority in trampling out in others the freedom which has been so assiduously trampled out in itself. A parent or a teacher who pursues this object is of all the ministers of a community the one whom it should regard with the greatest abhorrence, seeing that he is bringing up for it, not citizens, but slaves.

I do not deny that Mr Bain can appeal on behalf of his view of Society and Education to a number of precedents in past days—to a vast body of opinion in our own. If it were not so I should not care to speak of his theories; for theories go for very little, except so far as they condense and formulise the tempers and habits which shape the talk of drawing-rooms, the debates in parliament, the lessons in primers and story-books, the transactions in counting-houses and shops.

There has been a disposition in many—from very different even opposite motives—to say that our soldiers and sailors must be drilled according to the maxims of Mr Bain's education that they may have a merely public Conscience. "What would become of us," it has been asked, "if each of them felt himself to be an I ; said for himself, ' I ought and I ought not' ?" My answer is this, I know not what would have become of us in any great crisis if this personal feeling had *not* been awakened ; if every man had not felt that *he* was expected to do his duty ; if duty *had* been understood by each sailor or soldier in Mr Bain's sense as the dread of punishment ; if the captain who asked for obedience had been just the person towards whom that slavish dread was most directed. Unless the obedience of our sailors and soldiers had been diametrically the reverse of that sentiment which Mr Bain describes, I believe there is not a regiment which would not have turned its back in the day of battle, not a ship which would not have struck its flag. The charm of the captain's eye and voice, of his example and his sympathy, this, as all witnesses whose testimony is worth anything have declared, has had an electrical influence upon hosts which could enable them to face punishments from enemies considerably more terrible than any which the most savage vengeance could devise for desertion. It is not the thought of what a majority will say or do that can stir any individual man to stand where he is put and die. It is that he has been aroused to the conviction, ' I am here, and here I ought to be.'

That is not sentiment but plain sense ; an adherence to facts known and confessed, a refusal to exchange facts for grand and empty generalisations. There are indeed cases, extreme cases, Mr Bain admits, when

'Conscience passes into a high grade of the prudential motive.' Let us look at one of these extreme cases. A set of soldiers, rough men of the ordinary English type, are off the Cape on board the ship *Birkenhead*. I shall spoil the story. The Professor of Poetry in the sister University shall tell it for me.

Right on our flank the crimson sun went down,
　　The deep sea rolled around in dark repose,
When, like the wild shriek from some captured town,
　　A cry of women rose.

The stout ship Birkenhead lay hard and fast,
　　Caught, without hope, upon a hidden rock;
Her timbers thrilled as nerves, when thro' them passed
　　The spirit of that shock.

And ever like base cowards, who leave their ranks
　　In danger's hour, before the rush of steel,
Drifted away, disorderly, the planks,
　　From underneath her keel.

Confusion spread, for, though the coast seemed near,
　　Sharks hovered thick along that white sea-brink.
The boats could hold?—not all—and it was clear
　　She was about to sink.

"Out with those boats, and let us haste away,"
　　Cried one, "ere yet yon sea the bark devours."
The man thus clamouring was, I scarce need say,
　　No officer of ours.

We knew our duty better than to care
　　For such loose babblers, and made no reply,
Till our good colonel gave the word, and there
　　Formed us in line to die.

There rose no murmur from the ranks, no thought,
　　By shameful strength, unhonoured life to seek;
Our post to quit we were not trained, nor taught
　　To trample down the weak.

So we made women with their children go,
    The oars ply back agen, and yet agen ;
Whilst, inch by inch, the drowning ship sank low,
    Still under steadfast men.

What follows why recall ? The brave who died,
    Died without flinching in the bloody surf ;
They sleep as well, beneath that purple tide,
    As others, under turf.

I need not tell you that these soldiers as little dreamed of doing a great or meritorious act as of escaping punishment. They simply did what they ought to do. Their business was to go to the bottom, and they went.

I have spoken of our own times, for they concern us most. But I said, Mr Bain had also precedents of other days in his favour. Inquisitors and persecutors of all ages have attempted in different ways to act upon his maxim. They have thoroughly understood that identification of authority with punishment, which he perhaps has been the first openly and in terms to proclaim. By punishment to bring a reluctant minority into conformity with the will of a majority has been their expressed and deliberate purpose. To cultivate a Conscience in the young which should begin with a dread of transgressing the decrees of the majority, which should at last acquiesce in them naturally and enforce them upon other men, has been the aim of their policy. And having had great and wonderful success in putting down recusants by force, and in reducing nations to servility, they have looked forward with a certain dim anticipation to a period when the higher grade of the prudential motive shall be attained, when no man who has thoughts unlike

Anticipation of Mr Bain's doctrine in the practice of Inquisitors.

those of the majority shall utter them, when very few indeed will have any thoughts to utter.

These inquisitors and persecutors of old times, Mr Bain will tell us, appealed to 'an abstract, unseen, unproducible power;' he acknowledges no such power. He would do himself great injustice in saying so. *Society the most frightful of bugbears.* No power that I ever heard of is so 'abstract, unseen, unproducible' as the Society which is put forth to terrify and crush each man who dares to claim a distinct existence. Where is it, what is it, who brought it forth? Parents, Schoolmasters, Legislators, are its agents. It remains full of ghostly dread, gathering into itself all that is most tremendous in the phantoms which we boast that modern enlightenment has driven from our nurseries. When Mr Bentham speaks of a Community he says that 'it is a fictitious body composed of the individuals who are *considered* as constituting *as it were* its members.' A man who abhorred fictions and figures of speech falls into these strange expressions, because he cannot quite divest himself of the old belief that a community is a body, real and not fictitious, consisting of individuals who are its actual members. There is in his phraseology the after-glow of a sun which has set. No such parting radiance disturbs the heaven of Mr Bain. He is haunted by no old recollections of a body and its members. Whether the Community be fictitious or real signifies little to him. It serves equally, in either character, to extinguish the individual.

And therefore it may be quite necessary, in order to avoid the terror of these 'abstract, unproducible powers,' that we should face the question whether the Conscience bears witness of any actual living super-

LECT. III.

*The De-
monology
of modern
Philoso-
phers.*

human power to which it owes homage. Do not start at the word 'superhuman,' as if I were bringing it forth out of some cavern of divinity. Butler, we have seen, did his utmost to confine the Conscience within the limits of human nature. The experiment was an interesting one, most ably conducted. But it involved him in evident perplexities. It laid him open to the charge pressed by Mr Bain against Dr Whewell, who tried to present Butler's statements in a modified form, that he either invented an ideal Conscience, or made every man a judge in his own case. Mr Bentham escapes that danger by erecting Pleasure and Pain into two *superhuman* powers, to which man must needs be in subjection; they themselves, it would appear, paying a feudal homage to another Power called Nature—obviously not *Human* Nature in Butler's sense, but a very awful, mysterious, 'unproducible' deity. Equally *superhuman* is that Society which creates a Conscience by the infliction of punishments, the remembrance and expectation of which keeps its subjects in habitual prostration. Such opinions, which are specially the opinions of our day, leave one who is discussing the question of the Conscience no choice. He is hemmed in by superhuman influences of *some* kind. If those which great philosophers bid us tremble at appear to him of a very oppressive kind, ministering to weakness, to superstition, to slavery, he must ask if there is no other which may be stronger than these, which may be a deliverer from them?

Though in this course of Lectures I may do little more than raise that question, I must observe here that it could never less be evaded than in this England of the 19th century. The superhuman is not banished,

*Some
superhu-
man power
the con-
fessed
master of*

as we have seen, from the speculations of its most approved sages; it is certainly not banished from the entertainments of its most refined and most sceptical triflers. That which is not allowed a place in our inmost conviction will float about us in phantastic shapes, which we dare not ask whether they bring with them airs from Heaven or blasts from Hell. The Conscience will make cowards of us all, if it does not lead us to the source of courage.

LECTURE IV.

CASES OF CONSCIENCE..

I HAVE found myself already in conflict with two eminent philosophers of this century on the subject of the Conscience. I should not have plunged into such disputes if they had only concerned certain Moral Systems. But the assertion of Mr Bentham that Pleasure and Pain are the Sovereigns of mankind,. the doctrine of Mr Bain that the Conscience is to be trained by punishment till it bows before the decrees of a majority, involve questions which affect every act of our lives. A number of those cases of Conscience with which the Casuist professes to deal, and which, whether he deals with them or not, perplex our conduct and distract our thoughts, take their rise in the demands: Ought I or ought I not to obey the commands of this Pleasure or this Pain, or of this Nature which appears to be their Mistress? Ought I or ought I not to obey the commands of this Society, this Majority, which is able to enforce its decrees by terrible penalties, and which has various bribes for bringing me into sympathy with it? I cannot, as I said last week, avoid entering on a third enquiry, Ought I or ought I not to perform certain services, to offer certain sacrifices, at the bidding of some

M. C.   5

invisible divinity? I might comprehend this enquiry in the other two, for Pleasure and Pain, Nature and Society, as Mr Bentham and Mr Bain set them forth to us, *are* invisible powers, whatever visible forms they may assume. Still we shall find that for practical purposes it is convenient to speak of Cases of Conscience under each of these three heads.

I. Those which turn on the words Pleasure, Pain, Nature.

I. I begin with those which concern Pleasure and Pain. Mr Bentham appears to have thought that there are but two ways in which this subject can be contemplated. He himself, the champion of the principle of *Utility*, maintains that it behoves us to seek the greatest amount of pleasure which it is possible for us, being such creatures as we are, to enjoy, the least amount of pain which, being such creatures as we are, it is possible for us to suffer. Another set of men are champions of what he calls the principle of *Asceticism*. These, he says, 'approve of actions so far as they tend 'to *diminish* the happiness of the persons whose inter-'est is in question, disapprove of actions so far as they 'tend to augment it.' Whether there are any persons who would acknowledge this to be a fair statement of their objects, I greatly doubt; most will say that the description is an ugly caricature, not a faithful portrait.

Utility and Asceticism.

But since there are two or three kinds of Asceticism, which may present themselves to us in our own experience, and may give rise to cases of Conscience, I shall avail myself of Mr Bentham's word for the sake of enquiring what it means, and how it may concern us.

1st Form of Asceticism.

Pleasures

(1) Mr Bentham's specimens of the Ascetic are the Stoic of the old world and the Monk of Christendom: men of both these classes, he says, have dis-

approved of pleasure as such, and have approved of pain as such. Now there is a sense, as I have observed already, in which Mr Bentham himself was an Ascetic as much as any Stoic or any Monk. Pleasures offered themselves to him, and he deliberately chose pains in preference to them. He may have posted his books carefully—may have calculated accurately that he should have so much more pleasure on the whole, if he endured some immediate trouble and annoyance: he may even have thought that he secured some pleasure at the moment which, either from the quality of it, or from the intensity of it, outweighed the pain of that moment. All this is possible; but whatever the previous processes that went on in him were, when the pleasure actually stood before him inviting him to partake of it, he must have assumed the position of an Ascetic. Do not· forget this. The reasons of his conduct may have been of one kind or another; his actual conduct was that of a man who would be stigmatised by the habitual followers of pleasure as an Ascetic. For an Ascetic, to all intents and purposes, every man must be who has a work to do, and who determines that it shall be done, let the inducements to abandon it or neglect it be what they may.

Take another instance from a man who will not generally be suspected of an over amount of conscientiousness. Napoleon the first, when about 15 years of age, was in the military school at Paris. He complained to the superintendents of the school about its arrangements. What do you suppose were his objections to them? He said the fare of himself and his brother scholars was too luxurious. It could not prepare them for living in poor households, still less for

LECT. IV.

abandoned, pain accepted for the sake of work.

Asceticism of Mr Bentham.

Asceticism of Napoleon.

5—2

the hardships of the camp. He urged that instead of having two courses a day they should have ammunition bread and soldiers' rations, and that they should be compelled to mend and clean their own stockings and shoes. Here you have a young Ascetic; so assuredly he would have been considered at the school; so he was. He chose what was painful in preference to what was pleasant. And because he did so, he was able hereafter to trample upon those peoples and monarchs who accounted pleasure the end of life, whose greatest desire was to avoid pain. No Alpine snows, no armed men could withstand him. Only when he encountered men who had learnt, as he had learnt, to claim dominion over circumstances, to endure suffering for the sake of a higher end, could that strength, which he had won through his Asceticism, be broken.

The fruits of it in his case.

2nd Form of Asceticism.

(2) Napoleon was no theorist; he hated theories. He wanted to be independent of his own inclinations that he might exercise power over other men. The Stoical *theory* was deduced from an observation how much power a man possesses who is not the victim of pleasures or of pains. The endurance of pain, the contempt of it, seemed to the Stoic the signs of a man. He exaggerated the notion, till pain itself acquired a glory in his eyes, till he thought himself grand for hating pleasure. Such pride involved contradiction. Pleasure was not his master, what was? To be simply his own master, to be alone in the world, was a poor result of his victory. Men might say with great reason, 'It is better to eat, drink, and be merry, than merely 'to dwell in this magnificent self-sufficiency.' The Asceticism of the Monk had a different ground. It was associated with the belief that the best man is he who

Pain becoming elevated into a good.

The Stoic.

The Monk.

can bear pain for his fellows. But it often passed, like the Stoical doctrine, into a notion that pain had some virtue or excellence of its own. Out of this arose a greater contradiction than in the former case. He who was to be a sacrifice for others began to think how much glory his pain could bring to him.

(3) This is the second form of Asceticism; that form under which it presented itself to Mr Bentham as the direct antagonist of his principle of Utility. There is a third form which is, as it seems to me, not opposed to that principle, but a developement of it. A man believes that by enduring pain he may save himself from pain in a future state, may even perhaps obtain pleasure in a future state. He calculates, as Mr Bentham would teach him to calculate, how he may secure the least amount of pain, the greatest amount of pleasure, possible. His calculation may take in elements which Mr Bentham would exclude; their fundamental axiom is the same.

(*a*) In each of us there will arise cases of conscience into which one or another or all three of these ascetical notions may enter. Every one has some work to do. Every one has inducements to forsake that work for things which, whether pleasant to others or not, are pleasant to him, which no sophistry can persuade him are not pleasant. Mr Bentham's assumption that what is pleasant is natural, that Nature has appointed it for us, commends itself to his judgment. Only there is something in him which says I ought not. The agreeable thing will hinder me from doing the thing which I am occupied with. The agreeable thing accepted to-day will make me weaker to-morrow, less capable of determining my course, more the victim of

3rd Form of Asceticism.

The calculations of the Utilitarian associated with immortality.

Cases under the first head.

the impulses and impressions that come to me from without.

Some men get rid of this troublesome remonstrance easily; 'I like it' drives away 'I ought not' speedily. Some at once, as Napoleon, take the ascetical course. *Struggle between 'I like' and 'I ought not.'* They have a distinct object before them, nothing shall tempt them to forget it. A great number, perhaps the greatest number of men, touch neither of these extremes. They hover between Nature and Conscience. They cannot silence the 'ought not.' But they ask themselves *why* they should pay heed to it, *why* they should not take this or that pleasure which it seems to prohibit, undergo this or that painful effort which it seems to enjoin? 'What is this restraining, tormenting 'voice? From what cavern does it issue? Do I clearly 'catch its messages? Are they indeed saying, Avoid 'this and this? Do this and this'? Here begin cases of Conscience. The man consults himself or consults some friend or some professional Casuist about these *The former highly argumentative.* points. 'May I indulge my own taste or fancy? If 'not, why not? If it is not bad for that man, why is it 'for me?' What answers the Casuist may make to these enquiries I am not now considering. I am only tracing the cases which come before him to their sources, and showing you that they are not imaginary, but such as enter into the transactions of every day, and are mingled with the threads of each man's existence. One remark I would make in reference to them here. You may have thought me pedantical or fanciful for insisting that the Conscience should be contemplated in each particular man, that it should never be treated as something general or belonging to a number of men. But when these cases present themselves to us, the danger of departing from that maxim becomes apparent, even if adherence to it is troublesome. The habit of measuring ourselves by others is one into which we slide most easily, and which involves continual unfairness to them, still greater to ourselves. I ask why I may not indulge in extravagances in which a man of twice or thrice my means indulges freely; why I may not eat or drink what a man with twice or thrice my strength or my labour perhaps needs. I cling therefore to the '*I* ought' and the '*I* ought not;' that will not interfere with the discovery and acknowledgement of laws by which we are all bound; it will prevent me from assuming the practice of this man or that as the standard of mine, or my practice as the standard of his.

(*b*) The first form of Asceticism, that which Mr Bentham and Napoleon practised, may then be very needful for you and me; we may not be safe if we discard it. Shall I tell you how we become involved in the second? in that kind of Asceticism I mean which treats pain as a positive good, pleasure as a positive evil? We do not drop into Stoicism naturally. A few may have some bias to it from education; in general when it is enforced in childhood there is a reaction against it in later years. A few may be drawn into it by the arguments or the example of others; more attractive arguments and examples will probably in a little time break the force of those; the Stoic may soon be turned into an Epicurean. The doctrine is much more commonly embraced by one who has for a long time acted on the maxim that pleasure is the supreme power which he must obey. He has had some stern and clear intimations of the effects which come from subjection to this ruler. A violent quarrel with himself is the consequence; with himself or with the tendencies to which he has passively yielded. He gnashes his teeth at the things which have been the occasion of his distress and humiliation; he calls them by hard names; he denounces pleasure as pleasure; he greedily seizes upon pain as if by enduring it he could take some revenge upon himself for that avoidance of it in times past which now seems to him feeble and cowardly. Cases of Conscience involving this kind of Asceticism are very numerous. The symptoms which they disclose are hard for the patient himself to deal with; they may be much aggravated by the prescrip-

tions of quacks. Mere abusive epithets, such as Mr Bentham indulges in, or the solemn announcement that we ought to seek the greatest amount of pleasure and the least amount of pain possible, will not touch even the surface of such cases.

(c) Still more embarrassing are those cases into which the third notion of Asceticism enters. Suppose a man rich and comfortable, who has never for a moment dreamed that there could be any maxim of life but that which Mr Bentham enunciates, who has habitually sought as much pleasure as he could get and avoided pain of every kind,—Or suppose an Irish labourer with dilapidated trousers and straw peeping through his hat, who yet to the extent of his means has wooed pleasure at wakes and fairs, sometimes inflicting a little pain with a shillelagh as a way of

diversifying the pleasure. Either of these awakens on a certain day to the feeling that there is something which he ought to have done, or ought not to have done. The past which he seemed to have left far behind him comes strangely back to him. His yesterdays claim to be part of him as much as the present moment: they may continue to put forth that claim for ages. He may *never* be able to shake them off. That would be dreadful. How can he banish the apparition? What can he do that it may not give him much more pain, and greater pain, than it is giving him now? Some one is tormenting him; seems to like tormenting him. Could he not make terms with the enemy? Could he not agree to suffer something now that he may have less weight of suffering hereafter? Could he not find, or could not some one find for him, a scheme of arrangements, compromises, compensations, by which he might be excused from part of the punishment which he dreads, and might also retain a certain tolerable share of the present pleasure which he is loath to part with? How many cases have occurred, and are occurring every day, of this kind, no words can tell; or what schemes of Casuistry have been devised to meet them. The precepts of Mr Bentham, diffused ever so widely, embraced ever so cordially, can have no effect in settling them. For as I said before, his precepts have to all intents and purposes been adopted already by these troubled spirits. They are turning to the religious Casuist for help, because their Utilitarian adviser has failed to take account of a disturbing force in them which makes his medicines ineffectual. 'You can of course call me an Ascetic 'if I resort to plans plausibly and skilfully devised 'for supplying the defect in your system: for avoid'ing a pain which I actually feel, and which, upon 'your own showing, I ought to account the great and 'only evil, for obtaining as much pleasure as I can 'under the conditions in which I find myself. Some 'may call my calculations ignominious; you cannot. I 'learnt the need of them in your school.'

II. Social Tyranny.

II. I pass to that class of Cases which has reference to Society. Whether the Education which Mr Bain speaks of—the education which shapes each man's wishes, purposes, convictions, according to the wishes, purposes, convictions of a majority—is desirable or not, there can be no question that such an education exists, that it is working very extensively and with great

Popularity of Mr Bain's notions on this subject.

power. The philosopher has here also generalised from the practice which he sees around him; his doctrine is certain to meet with favour for precisely the same reason which secures favour to Mr Bentham's doctrine respecting Pleasure and Pain; it represents accurately what a number of men in various quarters are actually doing or striving to do.

To appreciate their work or their endeavour we must recollect that the grand word *Society* or *Community* really represents a number of different Societies or Communities, each of which is acting upon a certain

Example from Trade Maxims.

number of individuals. For instance, in every trade there is a community aiming to train the notions of those who belong to it in accordance with the notions which it has inherited or which it has adopted. The Conscience of the individual who engages in the trade is formed, Mr Bain would say, by the majority of those who have entered into it already; punishments, such as exclusion from the intercourse or sympathy of his fellows, make him feel the great inconvenience of adopting any maxims or practices unlike those of the

How they become ' branded' into the young.

majority. The younger members by degrees rise to their share of government and enforce the same rules upon their pupils and successors. A great number

attain that 'high grade of the prudential motive,' at
which conformity becomes no longer a difficult effort,
the result of terror at a rod continually suspended over
them, but means the ready submission to a rule which
they feel to be convenient, and which they have the
pleasure of making others feel to be inevitable. All
that is, no doubt, true. Mr Bain himself allows for
occasional exceptions; a few men like to be independent, to choose a way of their own. He does not deny
that there is a certain amount of benefit to be derived
from these anomalous individuals. He does not en-
courage their growth; all the processes of his discipline
tend to discourage it. But if they start up in spite of
the discipline they may perhaps be turned to some
account. However dangerous, an optimist will hope
that their existence may at last turn to the benefit, not
the mischief, of the Community.

Now when I speak of Cases of Conscience in respect
to Society, I mean this; that every man whatsoever
who has been brought under this kind of discipline not
only feels tempted to rebel against it, for the reason
which Mr Bain supposes,—because it thwarts his incli-
nation, because it restrains some of his enjoyments,—
but for another very different reason; because it pre-
scribes acts to him which, though they are agreeable to
him, though the punishment for not doing them is
very severe, yet something tells him that he ought
not to do. I say that there are moments when such
qualms come over every one; and further that those
individual men in whom they become most strong are
not those who find their luxury in arrogant independence, but are those who have the liveliest sense of
their obligations to their fellowmen, the greatest desire

LECT. IV.

*The occa-
sional pre-
ference for
individual
opinion.*

*The con-
tinual pro-
test of the
Conscience
in each
man,*

*a protest
for Law
not for
Indepen-
dence.*

that the laws of the Nation to which they belong may be not violated, but maintained.

Consider that instance of trades to which I referred just now. A man finds a custom established in the trade to which he has been bred, the trade by which he is to get his living, which directly interferes with the observance of a contract recognised by the law of the land between the tradesman and his customers, at all events interferes with what he knows to be the understanding of the customer when the article is bought. *The fear of punishment not on the side of Law but of the social Tradition.* There is the smallest possible fear of his ever coming within the reach of the law; there are a hundred ways of evading that, a hundred reasons why any person who discovers himself to be injured, if he does discover it, may not wish to trouble himself with a lawsuit. The reputation he might get with the customer, if he knew —which is unlikely—that a maxim of the trade had been broken through in his favour, would not be the weight of a feather against the loss of credit and caste with those who surround him. Those for whom he has most respect—men much better than he counts himself—have gone on in these practices for years; they will be grieved if he adopts any other. It will seem to them, it seems to himself, a pharisaical exaltation of his own opinion against theirs. And yet the voice in him says, I ought not to do it. Here is a case of Consci- *Order and Tradition; which is to conquer?* ence. A whole world of Casuistry rises out of that struggle between the opinion of the majority and the 'I ought not' of the single man. But the 'I ought not' is not working against an Order, but with an Order. It is protesting against a disorder, which however long it has been sanctioned, however many votes concur in the support of it, is a disorder still, and will prove itself to be so more and more, the longer it exists.

I dwell upon this instance of Contracts which have reference to Property, because we are told again and again that these depend for their security simply upon the punishments which enforce the observance of them, or upon the opinion of their usefulness which those punishments create, or upon a general experience of the disadvantages arising from the violation of them. No country furnishes so good a test of this principle as the England of the present day. We are a commercial people. Punishments have been especially devised to support the fidelity of pecuniary engagements. They have been suggested by mercantile men. They have passed under the revision of lawyers. They have been accepted by parliaments. They have been enforced by the strongest public opinion. Seldom is there much compassion felt for a fraudulent debtor; still less for one who has been a trustee of others' money and has converted it to his own purposes. The newspaper press strengthens and supports the severest judgment of on-lookers and sufferers. It would seem as if commercial crimes in this country were prohibited by every motive which could act upon reasonable beings. And yet which of us has not heard complaints that they are on the increase? And which of us has not heard those who dwell most on the force of punishments and of public opinion—who laugh the bitterest laugh when a moralist speaks of any other—yet appealing in despair to the conscience of individuals, trying whether they cannot arouse that to sustain the weakness of the power which, according to their theory, should be in-vincible? To be sure when they explain themselves

Securities for com-mercial virtue in English Society.

Are they effectual?

LECT. IV.

The be-
liever in
the might
of opinion
begging
help from
the Con-
science.

they affirm that it is Opinion which gives effect to Conscience, that all they want is to create an Opinion against certain acts that are mischievous to Society. Wearisome and endless see-saw! From Opinion to Conscience; from Conscience to Opinion. You want Opinion to produce the effects of Conscience; the Conscience must itself create the Opinion. Oh learn to bear the scorn of the philosophers who talk to you in this fashion! The scorn is not for you, but for themselves. There is a Conscience in each of them, whether be owns it or not. Give him credit for it; appeal to it; let him keep his theory along with it, if he likes, and if he can.

The prin-
ciple illus-
trated in
Trades
applicable
to all Pro-
fessions.

The cases which arise in the Conscience of a Tradesman or Merchant, and which often set him at variance with the customs and maxims of his class, are not more numerous than those which occur in the Conscience of the Lawyer, the Physician, the Clergyman. A man asks himself if he ought to do this, if he ought not to do that. Why? That he may have a way of his own? No! precisely because he fears that he has been following a way of his own which was not consistent with his position as Lawyer, Physician, Clergyman, with that which was due from him to his clients, his patients, his flock. A Conscience of Duty wholly apart from any punishments which may be inflicted on him for the neglect of it is awakened in him; he asks whether this duty has been done. Suppose some opinion or censure or even punishment has brought out that Conscience; still it is there. The opinion, the censure, the punishment has only called it forth—

Cases of
Conscience
most nu-

availed nothing till it was called forth. So here again is a multitude of cases, various as the circumstances and as the characters of individuals are various, but all of the same kind; all beginning with the discovery in each man that he has responsibilities, which no class, no majority of men, has imposed upon him, and from which no class, no majority of men, can release him.

The treatment of such cases—the methods which may or may not be effectual for settling them—I am not concerned with in this Lecture. But I may perhaps assist you in understanding better the cases themselves, if I wander for a moment beyond the limits of our own country. Suppose an American, living in one of what were then Slave States thirty years ago. He is brought up under that discipline which Mr Bain recommends for the formation of a Conscience. He is taught to consider the slave as a chattel. He has acquired all the habits which naturally and necessarily develope themselves out of such a belief, when it has become a belief. He perceives the absurdity—the intense absurdity—of treating a *thing*, a chattel, as capable of rights, as able to form contracts. Perhaps some religious notion about the doom of a race helps to strengthen what would else have been merely the tradition of a Society. Suddenly the question presents itself to him, ' Is the ' premiss, from which the conclusions I have accepted ' logically follow, a correct one ? Is this creature a chat-' tel ? Do I stand in no relation to him? If not, clearly ' I have no duties to him; he has none to me. If there ' is a relation that must involve duties.' Out of this doubt cases of Conscience have proceeded, which cannot be treated with indifference, for they have produced a revolution in an immense Continent. What I want you to notice is the turning-point in these cases. A Society has organised itself on the ground of *Property*.

LECT. IV.

*ference to
Property.*

.

*The pos-
sessor dis-
covering
his own
dignity as
a man.*
We are *possessors;* as such we are bound to each other. These creatures are simply *possessions.* The Society has taught its members to look upon each other in this light, to fraternise on this ground. The discovery of which I have just spoken does not merely affect the Negro. Are there not *relations* between those who have called themselves the superior race? Are not these Relations a deeper ground of Society than Property can ever be? By acknowledging the manhood of the black they obtain a new conception of their own.

You will perceive that the question when it takes this form may lead to cases of Conscience affecting many beside the slave owners in North America; it may issue in a different belief respecting the foundation of Society in all countries.

Before I leave this division of my subject I will say a word about the Prudence, of which Mr Bain has written at great length. He connects it with his idea of the Conscience. So do I with mine. Prudence is the contracted form of Providence. It means foresight. Now foresight I believe will never be found to exist without reflection or retrospection. The man looks before and after. Till he learns to say 'I,' and thence 'I ought,' he will exercise no retrospection; he will therefore exercise no prudence. Whilst he is the slave of present impressions, still more whilst he is under the dread of punishments that a majority may inflict on him, he cannot look forward; he dares not. This is a very old opinion, inculcated by those who have been most devoted to the cultivation of prudence. You in

*Miss
Edgeworth
a teacher
of pruden-
tial
morality.*
these days do not know much of Miss Edgeworth's tales, or her books of Education. Many of us old men were nurtured upon them. In these works what is

called heroical morality, as well as what is called spiritual morality, was passed over; they were almost exclusively devoted to the formation of prudent habits. But so far was this accomplished lady from encouraging boys or girls to follow the will or habits of a majority, that she evidently desired above all things to teach them the danger of that subjection. She would have each one of them learn to say 'I ought' and 'I ought not;' on no other terms did she see any chance of making them prudent. To 'that higher grade of the prudential motive' which a man or woman reaches who has utterly accepted the yoke of Society and determines to follow it wherever it leads, Miss Edgeworth never aspired. Amidst many defects which I have since discovered in her education I cannot say how grateful I am to her for teaching us that we should labour diligently *not* to seek that elevation.

But a vigorous protestant against the morality which consists in submission to the will of a Society.

III. I come to the last class of cases of which I proposed to speak. I can illustrate it best by a familiar instance. The Greek fleet is stayed at Aulis by contrary winds. An acknowledged prophet declares that nothing will change the wind but a Sacrifice. No Sacrifice will avail but the daughter of Agamemnon. A power which is declared to be divine, which the opinion of the Greeks holds to be divine, imposes the command. It is obeyed.

The Conscience in conflict with the religious maxims of an age.

> Nam sublata virum manibus tremebundaque ad aras
> Deducta est; non ut solemni more sacrorum
> Perfecto posset claro comitari hymenæo,
> Sed casta inceste nubendi tempore in ipso
> Hostia concideret mactatu mœsta parentis.

Whether the story is true or not, even if it and the whole Trojan war are to be consigned to the region

The sacrifice of Iphigenia.

M. C.   6

of fable, it bears witness of facts that were characteristic of the age to which it was referred, and of many
later ages; of facts which belong to Greek history,
to Hindoo history, to the history of modern Europe.

Horror of Lucretius.

The poet who recorded the tale of Iphigenia so bril-
liantly felt as you know that it concerned his own
nation and his own time; otherwise it would not have
inspired him with such indignation, he would not
have uttered the passionate cry

Tantum religio potuit suadere malorum.

He believed that the religion of Rome in his own
civilised period might persuade men, if not to such a
sacrifice as that of Iphigenia, yet to very monstrous

His cry for an Order.

crimes. From a religion of this kind—from the worship of capricious and cruel gods—he fled to such
notions of physics as Epicurus could supply him with;
he thought he could discern the vestiges of an order
in the world which these notions of a divine government could not disturb.

This poet, then, who counted himself an Atheist
was demanding an Order; he was solemnly protesting
against that which seemed to him the transgression
of an Order. Powers which persuaded to evil deeds he
could not recognise, let the claims which they put
forth, let the terrors of public opinion which enforced
these claims, be what they might.

Will a knowledge of the Nature of Things supply the Order?

This I hold to be a protest of the Conscience, one
which the poet would never have made if there had
not been a Conscience in him. Because there was
that Conscience in him, I believe he could never have
been satisfied with those hints of an outward Order
which his Greek teacher offered him; no not if those

hints could have ripened for him into the actual discoveries of modern science. Still there would have been
the question, 'Is there not somewhere that which ought
to rule me?' still there would have been the answer,
'These things ought *not* to rule me.' As long as there
is that terrible 'I,' there will be the 'ought' linked to
it; there will be the demand, What am I? what therefore ought I to do? And in that is implied, as Mr
Bentham and Mr Bain no less than any other philosophers teach us, the further demand, 'What must I
obey?'

The ever-recurring question, What am I?

Vainly, therefore, are we told that if there is a
Conscience in each man that Conscience must be its
own standard, that the only escape is to suppose a
Conscience created by a Social Opinion. All such
propositions look very plausible upon paper; bring
them to the test of living experience and they melt
away. There is that in me which asks for the Right,
for that which ought to have dominion over me;
there is that in me which says emphatically, 'This is
'not that Right, this ought not to have dominion
'over me.' I may be long in learning what the Right
is; I may make a thousand confused efforts to grasp
it; I may try to make it for myself; I may let others
make it for me. But always there will be a witness in
me that what I have made or any one has made, is not
what I ought to serve; that is not the right, not what
I am seeking for, not what is seeking me.

Good and evil.

This class of Cases then lies beneath both the
others; they are derived from it; they enter into it.
The demands of Pleasure or of Nature upon me, the
demands of Society upon me, both suggest cases of
their own. But *the* case is that which the Roman poet

LECT. IV.

Ought I to murder a child at the bidding of Calchas?

has raised. There are powers which demand *evil* things of me. Ought I to acknowledge their demand? Very numerous are the cases which fall under this head, complicated in various ways, taking different forms in different times and places. But no one who speaks of Casuistry at all can dare to evade them, or must be hindered from handling them through fear of the censures which he may incur from one set of philosophers or another.

It is easy to tell me that in former days men believed in a number of evil powers, and that in our days we have cast off such dark imaginations. Whenever I read Macbeth with its blasted heath and its witch scenery, I feel certain that the story is essentially true; that no change of circumstances or of opinions has made it less real less tremendous for our time than for the time in which it was composed. I know not anything about stage hags, what they may be like, whether they are men or women. But suggestions do come to a man now as of old which he dallies with, which mix with dreams of ambition that he has been secretly cherishing, which seem to gain a wonderful encouragement from unexpected events, which are deepened by some counsellor less scrupulous than himself. And then come the opportunities for the crime, the first image of which

The legend of Macbeth true for all times.

> did unfix his hair,
> And made his seated heart knock at his ribs
> Against the use of nature.

The invisible taking visible shapes.

Before it is done the Conscience which has been resisted within presents itself in outward visible forms, the bloody dagger, the handle towards the hand which cannot be clutched. After it is done there rise before the imagination of the man ghastly figures which recal those whom he has put out of his way; an effort must be made to extinguish remorse by fresh crimes. The superstitions do not cease with the dark deeds, they become more fixed, more intense. 'There must be some 'rulers of my destiny; why should they not be evil 'rulers; why should these not be invoked?' But they cannot control the doom of their servant. Onward he goes to it. He hears that the Conscience of some *The end.* sharer in his crime which had seemed unmoved when his was quailing, has come forth in the hour of sleep; that there has been a damned spot on the hand which no water could wash out. And then having supped full of horrors, and being incapable of tasting any more, he can only say,

> Life is a walking shadow, a poor player,
> That struts and frets his hour upon the stage,
> And then is heard no more.

That is an ower true tale for the reign of Victoria as well as for the reign of Elizabeth or of Duncan.

And so a poet of the 19th century felt it to be. Do you know Lord Byron's Manfred? Have you read *Manfred.* that wonderful play of the Conscience? It has none of the variety of Macbeth; Byron had not Shakspeare's power of making us see a number of different men, each distinct in himself, each acting on the thought and life of the others. The interest is concentrated in the hero. For that reason it serves our purpose better. No one who reads it can believe it to be a mere work of imagination. There is a burning individual experience in every sentence. Count Manfred has come of *His circumstances.* an ancient line. His castle in the Alps. The monarch of mountains is continually before him. He revels in

The powers that obey him. What they cannot give.

the grand forms of Nature. But they have become, like everything else, an oppression to him. There is on him the burden of a great crime. He has power over spirits. They are ready to do his bidding, to give him any thing that he asks. He asks forgetfulness. That is the one thing they cannot give. What else is of any worth to him? The form of her whom he has injured rises before him. What he has done is clearer to him than ever before. He is on the edge of a precipice. Why may he not throw himself over it? What if he did? Will the vision depart? A chamois hunter saves him and brings him to his castle. At length the destined hour arrives. A priest visits him in his dying hours, a kindly well-intentioned man willing to use his knowledge and the powers of his office for the good of his fellow-creature. It is in vain. What are subordinate agents to him? He is face to face with the powers of good and of evil. Which is the stronger? Which is to prevail?

Spirits of darkness.

Lord Byron, you see, is as little able as Shakspeare to dispense with the aid of spirits. No poet will be able who speaks of the struggles of Conscience. Those struggles carry us into a region beyond the visible world. It may be a region of hags or of milder powers which can give us all blessings except the one we want, deliverance from the evil that haunts us. Is there any purer region, is there any better society, in which we might dwell? Is there any more effectual deliverer?

LECTURE V.

RULES OF THE CONSCIENCE.

I HAVE spoken to you of cases of Conscience. From these the Casuist derives his name. I come now to the Rules by which Casuists have tried to determine these cases.

What has suggested these rules? A man who is troubled with the questions, 'Ought I to do this? Ought I not to do that?' has just the same impulse to seek for advice as the man who is engaged in any controversy about property, or who is suffering from some bodily complaint. As I ask a Lawyer who has studied books of cases the judgments which have been delivered upon them the general maxims or the particular statutes which bear upon them, to tell me what is his opinion of the particular case which I submit to him—cannot I find one who will explain to me this debate which is going on within me, who will say what is the proper decision upon it? As I try to explain the pains I have suffered the symptoms which I have observed in myself, to a physician, trusting that his learning will suggest questions which may draw out clearer statements from me than I have been able to make, and that the same learning will suggest remedies for what he has discovered to be my disorder—cannot I, in like manner, make some one understand the influences which sway me to the right or to the left; cannot he make me understand them better than I do; cannot he put me on some method of dealing with them, so that I may not continue in restless embarrassment, or escape from it by some rash determination which I may lament hereafter?

The demand for such counsellors and prescribers has been great in all ages; the supply has answered to the demand. Some of them have been suggested to us by the circumstances of our birth, by the accident of

our position. A parent who does not identify authority with punishment wins the confidence of his child in his wisdom and in his affection. The less he tries to worm any secrets from him the more frankly they are told; the utterance of them is a relief for the present, the reproof and the warning which follow a help for the future. The friend, judicious or injudicious, to whom we ascribe great discernment or experience, is resorted to next; he may give us hints which will shew us the way out of a confusion, or he may make the confusion worse confounded; the knots of the conscience may be untied or cut by his hands,

or may be entangled hopelessly. And then comes the professional director of the Conscience, to whom is attributed in most countries of Christendom, by not a few men and women in our own, a divine capacity of penetrating into the sources of the derangements from which the Conscience is suffering, and of administering the medicines which it requires.

Are such advisers to be trusted in virtue of their personal sagacity or their official illumination? The

Lawyer points to the Statute book, to maxims which have been established for ages, to a series of judgments the result of careful investigations by able men. The Physician appeals to experiments upon the actual frame of man, to a science ever expanding which rests on those experiments. Has the director his books to which we may turn for the correction of his own private instincts ? Can he make us aware of the laws and principles by which his opinions on special cases are guided ?

The necessity for such books began to be very loudly proclaimed in that very bookish century, the 17th. It was affirmed that nothing could be more dangerous than to trust particular persons with the authority which they claimed to settle questions affecting the life of states as well as of individual men. He who could tell men what they ought or ought not to do, what should be their purposes as well as their acts, was exercising a dominion which no king or parliament could exercise, which might greatly interfere with the dominion that kings and parliaments had a right to exercise. It was found as a matter of fact that the influence of Confessors and Directors over the consciences of monarchs and statesmen, was such as affected in a number of ways the condition of nations; there was a complaint deep, sometimes loud, that it did not cultivate in them any special reverence for veracity and honourable dealing. Let us know what the maxims of these directors of the Conscience are, was the cry, what rules they lay down for the acts and life of men. There was, it must be owned, no tardiness in answering this cry. The volumes recording Cases of Conscience as well as solutions of the Cases and rules for the guidance of the Conscience which that age accumulated, would alarm you if I only enumerated the titles of a few, more still if you looked into them, far more if you were fairly to examine their contents. I do not enjoin any such task upon you, or recommend it. I do not think that would be a fair way of testing the question, whether Rules of the Conscience are ever likely to be found which will settle Cases of the Conscience. I who hold that none such ever have been found or will be found, should think I was taking an unfair advantage of you—that I was bribing you to support my opinion—if I drew my *Latin Ca-* examples of them from books written in Latin, by men *suistry not* of a different Church and a different Nation from our *a fair test* *of its* own, many of whom besides have earned a very evil *worth.* reputation through the denunciations of eminent divines of their own Church, sometimes of their own nation. But if I could light upon a set of Rules for the Conscience, drawn out with care and elaboration *Jeremy* by an English Churchman, who desired especially to *Taylor.* avoid the errors into which Casuists abroad had fallen, a man open to no suspicion of being dull or crabbed, a man whose character as well as his intellect has stood the trial of more than one century and commanded the admiration of the most opposite schools, those rules I should regard as offering safe materials for an experiment. Our illustrious Bishop Taylor fulfils all the *His style.* conditions which I have enumerated. He did not write in a hard scholastical dialect, but was master of the most copious and picturesque of English styles. He was so various in his ways of contemplating subjects, his erudition was derived from such a number of sources, that nearly every man whatever his opinions may be, whatever his education may have been, will recognise something in Taylor to countenance his theories and to meet his tastes. The Romanist, the Protestant, the most vehement defender of the right of men to speak out their thoughts let them be ever so much opposed to established doctrines, may each point to works of the Bishop in which his leading maxims are learnedly and eloquently enforced. Yet his mind did not vacillate either from feebleness or from self-interest. He yielded to the force of arguments, and could put them forth with the dexterity of a special pleader, also with an undoubted conviction of their soundness; his attachment to his own Church was strongest when it was in trouble and persecution. An intense sympathy with goodness, an indifference to everything which he could not connect with goodness or which he did not suppose ministered to it directly or indirectly, was his great characteristic; he could romanise or protest against Romanism, he could be tolerant or intolerant, just as he believed that the interests of goodness were furthered by one mode of thinking, by one course of action, or the other.

Among all the works of Jeremy Taylor, that to which he undoubtedly devoted the most toil and his learning was his *Ductor Dubitantium,* or the Rule of Conscience. He engaged in it when he was in the ripeness of his powers, when he had leisure to gather up the treasures of his thought and reading; all that he had learnt from Jewish Rabbis, from Greek Tragedians, Comedians, Historians and Philosophers, from Roman Orators and Jurists, from the Fathers, from the Schoolmen of the middle ages, from the Jesuits and from those who had opposed the Jesuits in his own

LECT. V.

His catholicity.

His love of goodness.

The Ductor Dubitantium.

day. He had the strongest sense of the mischiefs which mankind had suffered from the foreign Casuists who had obtained the greatest popularity as deciders of moral questions. · "Though by violence and force," he exclaims, "they have constrained their Churches "into a union of faith, like beasts into a pound, yet "they have made their cases of Conscience and the "actions of their lives unstable as the face of the "waters, and immeasurable as the dimensions of the

"moon." He was anxious to provide the Reformed Churches "with a semination and culture which were "much wanted in them; for our labours," he says, "have hitherto been unemployed in the description "of the rules of Conscience and of casuistical Theo-"logy." He knew, he says, "that all practical truths "were to be found out without much contradiction and "dispute, but that what God had made plain men had "intricated, and the easy commandment was wrapped "up in uneasy learning."

The sincerity of Taylor's intention to provide a real aid to his countrymen in their daily practice, and an escape from the sophistries by which they had been turned into disputers, is evident from every page of his work as well as from the tenour of his life. Cir-

cumstances seemed to conspire with his design. He had composed his book in what he considered a period of trouble and desolation; his preface is dated 'from 'my study in Portmore in Kilultagh' the year before

the Restoration. But he was able to dedicate his labours, To the Most Sacred Majesty of Charles II. King of Great Britain, France and Ireland, Defender of the Faith. "We have been," he could say, "sorely "smitten and for a long time......But now our duty

"stands on the sunny side, it is our work to rejoice in
"God and in God's Anointed, and to be glad and
"worthily to accept of our prosperity is all our busi-
"ness......It was impossible to live without our King, *The joy of*
"but as slaves live, such as are civilly dead, and per- *the loyal.*
"sons condemned to the metals; we lived to the lusts
"and insolvency of others, not at all to ourselves, to
"our own civil and religious comforts. But now our joys
"are mere and unmixed; for that we may do our
"duty and have our reward at once, God hath sent
"your Majesty amongst us that we may feel the plea-
"sures of obedience, and reap the fruits of that govern-
"ment which God loves and uses." Then having
modestly asked His Majesty to accept his two mites
as a signification of his joy; he adds this reason for
his choice of a gift, "For your Majesty being by God *Prospects*
"appointed *Custos utriusque tabulæ*, since like Moses *of the new*
"you are descended to us with the two tables of the *reign.*
"law in your hand, and that you will best govern by
"the arguments and compulsory of Conscience, and
"this alone is the greatest firmament of obedience,
"whatsoever be the measure of Conscience *res est fisci*,
"is part of your own propriety and enters into your
"exchequer."

The work which this Dedication introduces is *Plan of the*
divided into four Books. The first treats of Con- *book.*
science, the kinds of it and the general Rules of
conducting them. Under this head we hear of the
Right or Sure Conscience, of the Confident or Erro-
neous Conscience, of the Probable or Thinking Conscience, of the Doubtful Conscience, of the Simple
Conscience. The two following are on Laws natural, *Division*
human and divine; the fourth is on the Nature and *of Con-*
sciences.

Causes of Good and Evil, their limits and circumstances, their aggravations and diminutions. The dedication and the division will shew you how seriously Taylor engaged in his task; what pains he bestowed upon it. I hope to derive valuable lessons from both. But I am afraid one of the lessons will be, that Rules of the Conscience, even when they are unfolded with the greatest ability by a thoroughly good earnest practical man, are unfavourable to goodness and earnestness, and are not helpful in practice. I do not think Taylor's labour was wasted if it demonstrated this point; if it shewed where we *cannot* turn for aid in our straits. Such a man however will not leave us to a merely negative conclusion. There are hints scattered throughout his book which, if we use them aright, may tell us what we do want, though all the most skilfully framed rules should fail us.

Definition of the Conscience.

I. As Taylor proposes to treat of the Conscience and its different kinds he begins with a definition of the Conscience. It is this. *Conscience is the mind of a man governed by a Rule and measured by the proportions of Good and Evil, in order to Practice,* viz. *to conduct all our Relations, and all our intercourse between God, our neighbours, and ourselves; that is, in all moral actions.* A most difficult passage surely to construe; a definition which requires a

The definition examined.

number of definitions to make it intelligible. Without striving to devise such definitions let us consider how it will meet the wants of a man in any perplexity about that which he ought or ought not to do.

Supposed dialogue with a man seeking help.

'*Conscience is the mind of a man.*' But cries the man, 'I have two minds. I am drawn two ways. I 'want to know which mind I should be of, which way

'I should take. That is the very doubt which has
'brought me to your book.' The answer would be,
'Do not you perceive what I am telling you? Con-
'science is the mind of a man *governed by a rule.*'
'Just so,' would be the rejoinder, 'it is the Rule that
'I have come to seek for. I want a rule to tell me
'which of my two minds is the proper mind.' 'We
'shall come to that presently. I am going to furnish
'you with a set of Rules for all different cases.' 'Ex-
'cellent! I shall rejoice to hear them. But just now
'I am occupied with *this* case. How am I to decide
'that?' '*It must be measured by the proportions of*
'*good and evil.*' 'I am sure it must, and you will
'teach me to apply the measures; you will shew me
'what the proportions are.' 'All in due time. To-
'wards the end of my treatise you will have rules
'about the nature and causes of good and evil.' 'Yes,
'but I have something which I must do, or leave
'undone, now.' 'That is most desirable. All these
'measures and rules and proportions are *in order to*
'*Practice.*' 'Must I defer my action then till I have
'made myself master of them all?' 'If I tell you
'how *to conduct all your relations towards God, your*
'*neighbour, and yourself, that is, all moral actions,* you
'will surely be able to find out the propriety or im-
'propriety of this particular action.' Taylor, however,
would not leave his poor client or patient in the utter
despair which such an announcement must produce.
He would tell him of various cases through which *A*,
and *B*, and *C* and *D* had passed. He would tell him
that *A* had a confident Conscience, *B* a doubtful Conscience, *C* a probable or thinking Conscience, *D* a
scrupulous Conscience. 'And mine, which is it of all

The result.

'these?' 'Oh, you shall have rules which may enable 'you to discover that point.' 'And then I shall want 'more rules to know how to use the rules that fitted 'the case of *A* or *B* or *C* or *D*.'

The scrupulous Conscience.

Let us take one instance, that of the scrupulous Conscience, to see how this will work. Under rule I. we read this: "A scruple is a great trouble of mind "proceeding from a little motive, and a great indis-"position, by which the Conscience though sufficiently "determined by proper arguments dares not proceed "to action, or if it do it cannot rest." An admirable description; who is not able to verify it in his own experience? It is further illustrated by these lively remarks. "Very often it hath no reason at all for "its inducement; but proceeds from indisposition of "body, pusillanimity, melancholy, a troubled head, "sleepless nights, the society of the timorous, from "solitariness, ignorance, or unseasoned imprudent no-"tices of things, indigested learning, strong fancy or "weak judgment, from anything that may abuse the

Felicitous description of it.

"reason into irresolution and restlessness. It is in-"deed a direct walking in the dark where we see "nothing to affright us, but we fancy many things, "and the fantasms produced in the lower regions of "fancy, and nursed by folly, and borne upon the arms "of fear do trouble us. But if reason be its parent, "then it is born in the twilight, and the mother is so "little that the daughter is a fly with a short head "and a long sting, enough to trouble a wise man, "but not enough to satisfy the appetite of a little "bird. The reason of a scruple is ever as obscure as "the light of a glowworm, not fit to govern any action, "and yet is sufficient to stand in the midst of all "its enemies, and like the flies of Egypt, vex and "trouble a whole army." You see how charmingly Taylor writes when he forgets his rules and gives himself to painting pictures which was his proper occupation. There is not a page of his book which will not furnish you with some exquisite gem of this kind sometimes taken from an older writer and made far better by its setting, sometimes derived from the stores of his own imagination, good for use if we will search for it, as well as for ornament. But when we return from such flights to those rules which are in order to practice, the solutions are so puzzling that the author is driven to say—"God hath ap- "pointed spiritual persons guides of souls whose office "is to direct and comfort, to refresh the weary and "to strengthen the weak, to confirm the strong and "to instruct the doubtful, and therefore to use their "advice is the proper remedy which God hath ap- "pointed." That may be so; but were not these rules of Conscience drawn up expressly because these guides of souls had "made the cases of conscience and the "actions of men's lives as unstable as the water and "immeasurable as the dimensions of the moon"? Can it be the ultimate resource to fall back upon them, to confess that the rules are impotent without them, and that the final appeal must be to their wisdom? And yet if the comparison is between rules and the very lowest kind of human sympathy, the man who is in any difficulty will choose the latter. If he is not able to find the amount of illumination which he craves for, he will suppose that there must be some one in whom it dwells and to whose guidance he can fully trust himself. Whatever delusion there is in that

Margin notes:
LECT. V.

Works, *Vol.* XII. *p.* 174.

Lame and impotent conclusion, *p.* 180.

Men will always prefer a man to a rule.

Rules tested by the first class of Cases— those concerning Pleasure.

opinion, Taylor has not shewn us the way out of it; he has done much to strengthen it.

If what I have said to you before about the Conscience is true, the failure of such rules was inevitable. Try them by any of the cases of which I spoke in my last lecture. A man is disposed to indulge in certain pleasures, say of the appetite. He doubts whether he ought to indulge them, whether they will not interfere with his health or his work. The physician may give him some hints about the first; about the second he knows better himself than any one can tell him. General rules will only lead him to that comparison of his own case with others which issued, as I observed, in so many bewilderments, in such in-

The Result; perpetual vacilla.ion.

sincerity of practice. The rules prescribe for a multitude; what he wants is a prescription for himself. He will therefore do as Taylor bids him. He will ask the spiritual guide to interpret the rules, to apply them to his circumstances. And then he may be involved in all that system of alternate severities and indulgences, the perils of which induced Taylor to undertake his treatise. The passage from sound Asceticism to the Asceticism which glorifies pain for its own sake, to the Asceticism which reckons how much pleasure or exemption from pain can be secured by the relinquishment of pleasure or the endurance of pain, will be promoted not hindered by the formal rule as well as by the special expounders of it.

Cases of obedience or disobedience to social maxims.

So in those cases which regard Society. Taylor proposed to lay down rules which may help us to conduct all our relations. I said that a man often finds himself in circumstances which lead him to ask, 'Ought 'I to do what the Corporation of which I am a mem-

'ber commands? Can I fulfil my relations to this 'man or that set of men if I do?' Of all the abuses to which the Casuistry of spiritual doctors had led, and which Taylor desired to correct, there were none so great and scandalous as those which concerned this subject. The ecclesiastical Corporation of Christendom had taught with pertinacity the lesson which had a Jewish origin. "*If a man shall say to his father and mother, It is Corban, that is to say, a gift,* (to some ecclesiastical treasury) *he need no more do ought for his father and mother.*" The maxim of the Society had been used to disparage the relation in which the man found himself at his birth. So again the maxim that no faith is to be kept with heretics, is just as legitimate a deduction from the principle that the heretic stands in no relation to those who have excommunicated him, as the doctrine that there can be no contract with a slave is from the principle that the slave is a chattel. But could any *rules* about men's relations counteract, even in the smallest degree, theories of this kind or the acts and habits which were justified by them? The relations must be closer to the man than the rules can ever be; if he makes them dependent upon rules he renounces them. He will ask what acts or gifts will compensate the neglect of care for the father or mother; pecuniary compensations will occur to him as the most natural, since the money scales will be those in which he has learned to weigh all affections. And the Society which he has been taught to regard as that which adjusts compensations and as more sacred than all others will be the one to receive the offerings. The rules will be found inoperative, the man with the doubtful conscience will go to the

The ecclesiastical Corban.

Rules will not counteract it.

7—2

LECT. V.

guide of souls to interpret them, and that will be the result.

Third case; commands pretending to be divine.

So again in those more tremendous cases, of which the sacrifice of Iphigenia furnished us with an instance, no one knew better than Taylor how little directors of the Conscience were to be trusted; no one would have tried more zealously to find some rules which might avert the tragedies they had caused. But it is just in these very cases that the force of rules is scattered to the winds. How can they be alleged against a claim which is said to have proceeded from a superhuman authority? That must override all rules devised by men; it comes forth with the boast that it can. It is to a power which owns no rules that the father surrenders his daughter.

In what circumstances rules may be profitable.

Why then do men who strive to be practical, as Taylor strove in the best sense of the word—why do men who claim to be practical in a much lower sense than his—agree in liking rules which, on this shewing, are not practical, but the reverse of practical? The explanation is this. Rules have a use of their own which it would be absurd and ungrateful to deny.

Difference between maxims of behaviour and principles of life.

There are many points in a man's demeanour towards his fellow-men which without any evil intention on his part, nay, when his intentions are full of kindness, may irritate and wound them. There are many influences which he may receive from them, through the very frankness and openness of his disposition, which may do him harm. The maxims and rules of experience are directed most beneficially to these particulars of conduct. They are often effectual when we meet with them in books applied to persons, real or imaginary, whose blemishes and awkwardnesses remind us of our own. They are more likely to be effectual when they come from the lips of some parent or judicious friend; then they bear upon us with the momentum of affection and prudence combined; the Conscience recognises them in recognising the voice which utters them. But the parent or friend if he is wise as well as prudent,—if he is not a stranger to inward struggles,—will not apply such admonitions to any of those great debates of the man with himself which give the force and interpretation to the word Conscience. He will understand that these affect the resolution to act, not the mode or shape which the action shall take when it has been resolved on.

I would illustrate this difference from the play of *Polonius the man of maxims.* Hamlet. Old Polonius is a man of great experience, within certain limits he is a man of prudence. He is moreover kind-hearted, a good father, full of affection for his son and daughter, though inclined to be fussy with them as with everybody. He is taking leave of Laertes, who is on his way to France. What lessons *Where the maxims have force.* can be more sensible, more likely to impress themselves on the memory of a dutiful son, exaggerating, as it became him to do, his father's knowledge of the world, than these rules? They are familiar to you of course; still I will read them.

> And these few precepts in thy memory
> See thou character. Give thy thoughts no tongue,
> Nor any unproportion'd thought his act.
> Be thou familiar, but by no means vulgar.
> The friends thou hast, and their adoption tried,
> Grapple them to thy soul with hoops of steel;
> But do not dull thy palm with entertainment
> Of each new-hatch'd, unfledg'd comrade. Beware
> Of entrance to a quarrel: but, being in,

Bear't that the opposed may beware of thee.
Give every man thine ear, but few thy voice :
Take each man's censure, but reserve thy judgment.
Costly thy habit as thy purse can buy,
But not express'd in fancy; rich, not gaudy:
For the apparel oft proclaims the man ;
And they in France of the best rank and station
Are of a most select and generous chief in that.
Neither a borrower, nor a lender be :
For loan oft loses both itself and friend ;
And borrowing dulls the edge of husbandry.
This above all,—To thine ownself be true;
And it must follow, as the night the day,
Thou canst not then be false to any man.
Farewell; my blessing season this in thee !

Where they become contemptible.

But this same Polonius tries to penetrate the secret of a man whose Conscience is engaged in a fearful struggle, with whom 'To be or not to be' is the question. What becomes of his rules and maxims then? Hamlet calls him a prating meddlesome fool and we ratify his opinion. The sagacious counsellor, the well-trained diplomatist, has ventured into a region of which he knows nothing. He has tried his ordinary rules and

They may lead to outrages on the Conscience.

plummets, and they fail ludicrously. He has no resource but in the vulgarest cunning,—in expedients which must have struck the better man that was in him as grovelling and which seem to us as foolish as they were mean.

The two Tables.

II. From these instances of the use of rules I might pass very easily to the two books of Taylor on Laws, natural, human and divine. But I should only bewilder you if I drew you into these distinctions before I led you to reflect on Law itself, and its relation to the Conscience. Another lecture must be devoted to that subject. I will not however leave the one in which we have been engaged without giving you a hint or two chiefly drawn from the experience of Taylor's LECT. V. time, partly illustrated by our own, which may help you to perceive the enormous difference between Rules and Laws. Charles the Second, Taylor tells us, descended like Moses with the two Tables of the Law in his hand. Like Moses he broke both those Tables; only not through horror of the idolatry and the revelries to which he saw his people inclined, rather because the Tables inconveniently forbad the idolatry and the revelries. Rules of the Conscience, with all the exceptions and indulgencies which rules involve, he could approve; rules he would enforce upon the Consciences of his subjects. It was only the Law which bound subjects and monarch both that he cast aside. Some of you may have looked this summer at Mr Frith's picture of the scene in Whitehall the night before Charles' last illness of which Evelyn was witness; most of you will have read Lord Macaulay's description of that scene. Compare that with Taylor's dedication, and you will have some notion of that government by 'the arguments and compulsory of the Conscience' which the year 1660 was to inaugurate.

Mr Frith's elaborate design recalls to me one by another artist, which I like better to think of and which, if as sad in itself, contains a more hopeful moral. I do not know how many of you may have seen Mr Holman Hunt's picture of the Awakened Conscience. Those who have seen will not I fancy have forgotten it. There is not the crowd of figures which distract us in the Whitehall group. There are only two, a man and a woman sitting in a somewhat gaudily furnished room beside a piano. His fingers are on the instrument. His face, which is reflected in a mirror, is handsome

Marginal notes:
Charles II. no enemy of Rules,

but a hater of Law.

The Awakened Conscience.

and vacant, evidently that of a man about town who supposes the brightest part of creation is intended to minister to his amusement. A music-book on the floor is open at the words, 'Oft in the stilly night.' That tune has struck some chord in his companion's heart. Her face of horror says what no language could say, 'That tune has told me of other days when I was not as I am now.' The tune has done what the best rules that ever were devised could not do. It has brought a message from a father's house.

This excellent artist has drawn me away for a moment from the age of Charles II., reminding me that events which were passing in that time are repeated in ours—that the laws of both times are the same. I return from his picture to a series which represents *The Windsor beauties.* most truly the same period as Mr Frith's. They are those which hang round the state apartments in Windsor Castle. They commemorate the beauties who once shone in the Court of the Restoration. Those portraits sometimes exhibit a life like that which Lord Byron describes as still lingering over the faces of the dead ; sometimes only the blankness and dreariness of death. But taken in connection with Mr Hunt's sketch I cannot help dreaming that some one of these may have listened to Taylor's brilliant and terrible eloquence, may have even practised not a few of his rules,—yet continuing in the same bondage as before:—and then may in some note of other days, some snatch of forgotten music, have heard a mightier voice saying, " Loose her, and let her go."

Degrees of Good and Evil. III. If that is but a dream, at least it is one which forbids me to speak of Taylor's book about Good and Evil, their nature and causes, their limits and circumstances, their aggravations and diminutions. For the poor woman with an awakened Conscience will have said, 'Talk not to me of limits and circumstances, of 'aggravations and diminutions. These are two powers, 'to one of which I must yield up my soul and body.' I am sure Taylor would have said in his inmost heart as a man, whatever he may have written as a *Ductor Dubitantium*, 'By one of these I will hold for ever, 'against the other I will fight for ever.'

LECTURE VI.

LIBERTY OF CONSCIENCE.

LECT. VI.

Are there two Consciences?

WE are very familiar with the phrase 'Liberty of Conscience.' We hear it from panegyrists of England who boast that we have more of it than other nations, from Sects which complain that they are deprived of it. Is the Conscience of which these panegyrists and these complainers speak the one with which Casuistry is occupied? In Butler's Discourses on Human Nature, the Conscience is largely discussed. Are there any sentences in these discourses that suggest the thought which this phrase suggests to those who repeat it?

As I have especially desired to shew you that the Conscience has no technical signification which is distinct from its signification in every-day life, I must be anxious to relieve your minds from a doubt of this

Evil of the notion that there are.

kind. The study of Casuistry must be mischievous if it leads us to the use of words in double senses, if it establishes a school nomenclature which is composed out of the words that are current in the world, and

The doc-trine that the Con-science must al-ways be in

which puts on them an entirely different stamp. It may be very useful if it brings ordinary words to some test, if it redeems them from the service of clubs and platforms where they acquire a sense just as artificial, just as misleading as any which a College Lecturer

could impose on them. Be sure that Liberty of Conscience is a sacred expression, however much it may
have been profaned. But is it not a political expression? Does it not point to the policy of statesmen,
and of the nations which they direct? It may have
much to do with their policy. *What* it has to do
with that I believe we shall not understand unless
we first understand what it has to do with you and me.
I have treated the Conscience, its cases and its rules, in
reference to each of us, distinctly. Unless each of us
called himself an I, the Conscience I have said would
signify nothing. Only by remembering that position
have I been able to get any glimpse of light respecting
the Liberty of Conscience.

But if I adhere strictly to my method, I must begin
by changing this form of speech; by inverting it. I
have never allowed myself to lose sight of the origin of
the word Conscience. Though I have distinguished it
from Consciousness, and shewn you how utterly unlike
the Self-conscious man is to the Conscientious man, I
have always treated them as kindred words. In examining Taylor's definition of the Conscience, it became
evident that we should fall into inextricable confusion
if we let the plain etymology escape, and translated the
Conscience into 'a mind governed by a rule.' The
Conscience of Liberty is therefore for me a more intelligible phrase than Liberty of Conscience. I would not
part with that. We cannot safely part with any form
of speech which has been accepted as a veritable utterance of their thoughts by our ancestors and our contemporaries. I shall hope to enter more thoroughly
into their meaning if you allow me for a little while
to pursue my own course.

LECT. VI.

*each man
not to be
departed
from.*

*The phrase
Conscience
of Liberty*

*not intend-
ed to dis-
place the
other.*

The advantage which I gain by the change is this. I do not wish to assume that the Conscience is something good in itself. Taylor talks, as I told you, of a scrupulous Conscience, a doubtful Conscience, a confident Conscience. Most men have talked of an Evil Conscience. Horace says:

Hic murus aheneus esto
Nil conscire sibi, nullâ pallescere culpâ.

He deems it a protection for a man to be free from the conscience of faults which make him turn pale. Those who dwell on the misery of an accusing Conscience endorse his opinion. We cannot neglect any of these hints. They all betoken some actual experience; they have all their worth in practice. The words 'Liberty of Conscience,' taken by themselves, still more when taken with their ordinary associations, seem to intimate that the Conscience left to itself is always grand and glorious, incapable of debasement or degradation. No such impression is conveyed by the words Conscience of Liberty. They do not import that there may not be also a Conscience of Slavery. The very first remark which I shall have to make in considering them is, that there *always* will be a Conscience of Slavery where there is a Conscience of Liberty.

(1) Mr Bentham has taught us to despise the Stoics, calling them Ascetics, and saying that they preferred Pain to Pleasure. I have admitted that there were Stoics who deserved his censures, who did learn to regard Pain with a certain complacency, as if it were a good in and for itself; who glorified themselves on the endurance of it. I did *not* admit that either Asceticism or Stoicism necessarily involved this honour to

pain, or this vanity in the choice of it. I did not think the essence of the doctrine or of the practice lay in the abuse of it. For ourselves I maintained that those were in the greatest danger of sliding into the least profitable kinds of Stoical Asceticism who had accepted the doctrine that Pleasure and Pain are our Sovereigns most cordially, and had acted upon it most habitually. In revenge for the injuries to health and for the imbecility which had been the fruits of indulgence, they were apt to plunge headlong into a scorn of enjoyment, an entertainment of penances and tortures.

If I had gone further into the question historically, I might have told you that the vulgarest Stoics were to be found among some of the Greek Professors of the theory, who merely maintained it as a theory against Epicureans or other opposers, and that there were among their Roman disciples men who were not professors but practisers, who did not care for the theory except as it helped them to do what they believed they were appointed to do, to suffer what they were appointed to suffer. In such men I have thought, as most students have thought, that there was along with some error and weakness great nobleness. After listening to the denunciations of Mr Bentham against all who dare to hold that opinion, I think so still.

I am going to speak to you of one of these men. He belongs to the period of the Roman Empire. He cannot be called a Greek though he spoke and wrote in Greek. He cannot be called a Roman, for he was a slave, the slave of a freedman of Nero. You are familiar with the name of Epictetus. His Enchiridion, or that collection of his sayings which is abridged from the reports of him by Arrian, may almost I suppose be called a school-book. I remember reading it as a boy without much profit. If I had recurred to it as a young man I think it might have done me some service, at least might have made me ashamed of what I was, and of what a heathen slave was able to be.

The slave pitying the Emperor. Unquestionably he had all the Conscience of Slavery which a man in his condition could have. He was born in that condition. Could he rise out of it? What a chasm separated him even from his master Epaphroditus! who could measure that which separated him from the Emperor of whom that master was the freedman? Shall he . fill the world with his groans that he cannot bē like Nero; that an irresistible fate has made one the king over all kings, and the other not even a citizen? Epictetus has sent down to us not his groans but his thanksgivings, that he was not bound to be a slave such as he perceived Nero was; that, being Epictetus, he might enjoy freedom if he did not cast it away. For this he said was slavery, to be the victim of the representations made to the senses,—of the impressions which we receive from *The source of Slavery.* without. To this ignominious state of bondage Nero was reduced. Able to command all pleasures, able to decline all pains, the poor man was the passive victim of the things about him; he was sinking lower and lower under their dominion; he was less and less *No man forced to be a slave.* able to assert himself. If Epictetus was a slave, submission to these impressions, not the power of a master to send him to the metals or to inflict chastisement on him, was the cause of his slavery. If he did not fasten the chains upon himself, no one else could put them on him; he had the key of the prison-doors.

That is the Stoicism of Epictetus. It is the Stoicism

of a man with an intense conscience of slavery, with an intense conscience of freedom. Mere opinions, call them Stoical or any other, he would have dismissed as bewildering like the impressions on his senses, if they did not shew him his way to the freedom—for which he felt that he was intended—which was implied in his being a man, though all his circumstances were ever so much conspiring to enslave him. And do not suppose that there was in him that arrogant notion of his own power to defy his circumstances and his nature which we commonly ascribe to the Stoic. The question with him was too real a one—it too intimately and directly concerned him—to allow of his deluding himself with any vain pretensions. If one moment he maintained that the key of his prison was in his own keeping—in other words, that he could not be a slave unless he yielded to the impressions which made him one—he asserted as strongly the next that he must turn for deliverance to a god who was near him, and watching over him. If he could not trust his impres- sions, he could not trust himself. He must have a helper, who was higher than himself, who cared more for him than he cared for himself, who knew him better than he knew himself. Epictetus the Heathen did not worship Pain or Pleasure or Nature or any modi- fication of these, however he might be confused by the notions which he had been taught respecting Gods of Pleasure and Pain, or Gods that were merely Powers of Nature. He confessed amidst all perplexities a God over himself, who would set him free from the tyranny of Pain and Pleasure. I wish that all of us who are called Christians had as strong a faith in such a God as he had. Here is an instance of the

Conscience of Liberty existing beside the Conscience of Slavery; an instance which encourages us to believe that the most outwardly unpropitious circumstances may be the means of leading a man to know what his state is and to claim it. Mr Hunt's picture, of which I spoke in the last Lecture, extended that observation to a woman who had fallen into the most ignominious servitude,—servitude to her own passions, and to one in greater bondage than herself. The recollection of liberty, the hope of liberty, may come to any, as Epictetus said, who find that there is a stronger force within than the likings and impressions which fasten them to outward things. The Conscience is bidding each of us seek for that liberty; we cannot be content till we have found it.

The Conscience of Social Slavery and of a deliverance from it.

(2) It is exceedingly difficult in practice, as both these examples may shew, to separate the tyranny of Pleasure from the tyranny of Society. They weave together silken chains, which mere strength will never rend asunder. It may be as hard for the Roman slave or the English slave to defy the fashion and the contempt of the Society in which he dwells, as to overcome his own inclinations. I hinted when I was speaking of Cases of Conscience, that the Conscience of Obligation, which is only another word for the Conscience of Relations, was the great antagonist power to this Social oppression. The victim feels, ' I cannot be a ' member of Society unless I set at nought the maxims

Marcus Aurelius.

' and decrees of Society.' A very remarkable example of this rebellion is afforded by a man, not far removed in time from Epictetus, sharing many of his habits of thought, in a position more unfavourable, as Epictetus deemed, to freedom than his own; for instead of being the slave of an Emperor's freedman, he was himself an Emperor.

I speak of Marcus Aurelius Antoninus. He wrote in Greek; he dwelt in all the effeminacy of a Court. But he desired above all things, he says, to be a male and a Roman. What he meant by that we can understand from his acts, and also from his thoughts; for he is one of those who has let us look into the secrets of his life; who has told us what he was striving to be, and what helps and hindrances he met with in his strivings. He had evidently taken account of the causes which had made the Roman a ruler of the world. He had seen that self-restraint had been one main secret of his power; that reverence for the relations in which he found himself had been another. Out of both had come the habit of obedience; that obedience was involved in the oath of the soldier; that obedience was the only security for the fidelity of the citizen. The Roman had been inferior to the Greek, Marcus saw, in the quickness of his perceptions, in his power of interpreting nature. He appreciated the words of Anchises.

The desire to be a male and a Roman.

What it meant.

The secret of Roman power and degradation.

Excudent alii spirantia mollius æra
Credo equidem, vivos ducent de marmore vultus
Orabunt causas melius, cælique meatus
Describent radio et surgentia sidera dicent.
Tu regere imperio populos Romane memento
Hæ tibi erunt artes.

But what had become of the Arts which had led to this supremacy? Where was the reverence for fathers, the sacredness of the hearth, the devotion of the wife? Where was the security that the soldier would not feel that his weapons were much mightier than his oath;

The habits of Society under the Empire.

that the citizen would not feel that every other citizen stood in his way ? Civil wars had rent the Commonwealth in pieces. An Empire had succeeded it. The rulers of the world had felt that they were its gods, and that the business of gods was to draw all the amusement they could out of it, to inflict all the misery they might upon it. Such habits and opinions had become traditional. The atmosphere of the Empire was impregnated with them. To resist them was to resist that education by which, as Mr Bain says, Society brings its pupils into consent with its opinions and its tone.

Struggle against them.

Marcus Aurelius did resist this Education. His whole life, at home and abroad, was one continuous effort against it. He aimed at freedom through self-government, through that triumph over external influences and over his own tendencies which Mr Bentham would have called Asceticism, though no one deprecated more than Marcus any useless or

Gratitude to helpers in the struggle.

affected Asceticism. Specially he aimed at it by the cultivation of reverence for all those to whom he was united by ties of blood, or ties of service. Under that last name he included those who had served him and those whom he was appointed to serve. Nothing that I know is more touching than his enumeration of the debts which he owed to his mother, to his predecessor who had adopted him, to his instructors in every department, to the friends who had preserved him from any flattery, who had given him hints for the fulfilment

The Emperor's conception of Duty.

of any duty. For Duty meant to him exactly the reverse of that which it means in the philosophy of Mr Bain. It was literally that which, under no dread of punishment but with great thankfulness, he con-

fessed to be *due* from him. He was aware of the
temptation to neglect it; that was the slavish impulse;
freedom to perform it was what he sought with all
earnestness. To aid his purpose of being a Roman he
would avail himself of the helps which Greek professors of philosophy could afford him, admiring those
who frequented his court far more than they deserved,
humbly using the books which they or their predecessors had compiled, always shunning the display for
which so many of them were eager, not caring to
decide between the claims of their different schools,
but ready to learn from any of them if they warned
him of any insincerity into which he was likely to
fall, or showed him a better way than he knew of
improving his character and shaping his actions. Philosophy was never an excuse to him for avoiding
troublesome business; he denounces in words that
make many of us quiver the disposition which private
men, as much as Emperors, feel not to answer letters,
or to keep suitors waiting. He had a conscience of
the bondage into which we bring ourselves by the
neglect of little things; he would have accepted those
grand words of our poet in his ode to Duty, which
recognise all freedom and all joy as springing from
submission to its commands.

And of Marcus Aurelius it is as true as of Epictetus,
that he did not depend upon himself for protection
against the slavery of which he was conscious, or for
attainment of the freedom of which he was conscious.
He spoke as Epictetus had spoken, of a God near him,
a God within him, who was watching over him, and to
whom he must have recourse if he wished to live a
true life. He might sometimes call the true life, a life

LECT. VI.

*The philo-
sophers of
his court.*

*His care
for little
things.*

*His sub-
mission to
divine
rule.*

The Roman faith in it vanishing.

His dread of any who might enfeeble it further.

according to Nature, as Butler does, but it was this Lord and teacher of himself, not some external power, in whom he trusted to make such a life possible for him. Marcus, however, it must be remembered, was not merely the ruler of himself. He was the ruler of a people in whom faith and reverence were fast disappearing, on whom the traditions of their land were losing their hold, whom he saw no way of imbuing with his higher convictions. What should he do to keep the people straight, to prevent them from sinking lower? How could he sustain that which was perishing in them? Must he not use the powers which had been committed to him to punish any who induced them to distrust their old divinity? These reflections led Marcus to acts of which I may speak presently, acts in which he has had many imitators among those who have not generally taken him as a model.

Slavery to unseen powers.

(3) There is another kind of slavery to which men are liable, besides that to Pleasure or to Society, one which may be combined with either or both of these. They may dread the caprice and cruelty of unseen powers which demand such sacrifices as those of Iphigenia. The Conscience of liberty which comes from trust in a Being who is not capricious and cruel, who is emphatically a Deliverer, was that which gave

The martyr's defiance of them.

all the emphasis to the 'I ought' and the 'I ought not' of the Christian witness under the Roman Empire. 'I ought not to bow before this demon. I ought not 'to sacrifice to the image of the Divus Imperator'—that was his formula. The formula became real for him, it issued in martyrdom, when he could say, 'I do 'not reject a faith, but an unbelief. I do not set up 'a God for myself. I cling to the God who is the

'Deliverer of my race.' When the Christian's profession was merely the assertion of an opinion—formed after weighing the probabilities for or against it—there was no strength in him for any martyrdom. What did ignorant men and weak women understand about probabilities? Wiser men could overthrow any probabilities with their scorn or their stakes. But if there had come to the Conscience the certainty of an actual Deliverer, then the threefold cord of immediate punishment, of loathing by Society, of threatened vengeance hereafter, could be rent in pieces by the feeblest. If you read Opinion for Conscience, you change the history of that age and of all subsequent ages.

At this point I may pass without effort, from the inverted phrase which I have adopted, to the old phrase Liberty of Conscience, which I said I should be most sorry to lose. What I hope you will have learnt is, that this last phrase *cannot* bear some senses which loose thinkers attach to it. (1) Liberty of Conscience cannot mean liberty to *do* what I like. That we have seen, in the judgment of the wisest men, of those who speak most from experience, is bondage. It is from my likings that I must be emancipated if I would be a freeman. (2) It cannot mean liberty to *think* what I choose. Such men as Marcus Aurelius discovered the slavery which came from thinking what they chose, the necessity of bringing their thoughts under government lest they should become their oppressors. Every teacher of physical Science, here or elsewhere, repeats the same lesson. The scientific man bids us seek the thing as it is. He tells us that we are always in danger of putting our

LECT. VI.

He did not die for a probability.

What Liberty of Conscience cannot be.

No right to do or think as we like.

thoughts or conceptions of the thing between us and that which is. He gives us a discipline for our thoughts that they may not pervert the facts which we are examining. From not heeding this discipline men assumed that the Sun must travel round the Earth, because it appeared the most natural thing to them that it should, the most strange thing that it should not. If Galileo (according to the old tradition) said, 'And yet the earth does move,' he said, 'Neither 'my thoughts nor the thoughts of all the doctors and 'priests that live now or ever have lived can the least 'alter facts. You have no right, I have no right, to 'determine what is. All our determinations must fall 'before the truth when that is discovered to us.' (3) So again Liberty of Conscience cannot be a gift which men are to ask of Senates or Sanhedrims or Assemblies of the People. They have it not to bestow; if they had, no one could receive it from them. Those who groan because any of these bodies withhold it from them have not yet learnt what it is. The slave Epictetus would shew them that it could not be kept by mere external force from any one.

But when we have got rid of these confused notions which have fastened themselves to the cry for Liberty of Conscience, there remains a most wholesome and indispensable protest in it to which no Statesmen or Churchmen or Philosophers can be indifferent, except at their great peril. The opinion has prevailed among all three, that the Conscience is a troublesome disturber of the peace, which it may be necessary to endure but which it would be very desirable to silence. So long as that doctrine prevails, so long as any fragment or shred of it remains in our minds, we may talk

Galileo a protestant against his own judgment as well as the Pope's.

Liberty of Conscience not obtained by votes in Parliament.

What it is.

Jealousy of the Conscience amongst Statesmen and Churchmen.

about persecution as much as we please; we may boast of our age for having discovered the inutility of persecution; but we shall, under one pretext or other, persecute. The most ingenious political, ecclesiastical, philosophical excuses will always be ready to prove that the particular persecution we are practising deserves another name and belongs to a class of acts altogether different from that which we denounce in other countries, or in former days. What satisfactory demonstrations there will be that we are really vindicating toleration when we are most intolerant, that we are not interfering with a man's belief, but only with his desire to crush ours! Therefore I deem it needful to proclaim that in every instance to which we can point, a Society which has succeeded in choking or weakening the Conscience of any of its members has undermined its own existence, and that the defeat of such experiments has been the preservation and security of the Society that has attempted them. The banishment of the Moors from Spain helped to turn a chivalrous and Christian nation into an ambitious, gold-worshipping, tyrannical nation. Philip II. resolved that the consciences of his Protestant subjects in Spain and in Holland should be crushed. He succeeded in the first case, and the greatest nation in Europe sunk to a third-rate power. He was defeated in the other, and Holland, from an insignificant province, became a people. Louis XIV. was cursed with success in his dealings with Jansenists and Protestants during the next century. He enfeebled and impoverished his land, and prepared a revolution for his successors. His disciples, the Stuarts, sought to extinguish the Puritans and Covenanters in England and Scotland; we owe any

The philosophical recognition of it very precarious.

Punishment of Rulers who have succeeded in coercing the Conscience.

vigour which there is in Great Britain to their failure. These are the commonplaces of history. Often as they have been repeated, we have need to consider them again, and to lay them to heart; they contain lessons which are never obsolete for one set of men or another. Each Sect and School in the day of its adversity bears

Punishment of Sects. a grand witness on behalf of the Conscience. Each Sect and School in the day of its prosperity glorifies its own thoughts and opinions, and instead of appealing to the Conscience in its members tries to silence it. They are punished by an increase of the strifes and divisions which they hope to extinguish; they lose their convictions in the vehemence with which they talk of them.

War against Science. So again in respect to Science. It is no doubt true that a man who follows his own notions and vagaries may be as far from the laws of the universe as the man who accepts all the traditions of other days.

Why it is a war against Conscience. But those who, under pretence of hindering notions and vagaries, try in any degree to forbid or discourage the exercise of men's thoughts in reference to these laws, are labouring that they may be always hidden. The laws may reveal themselves to any seeker if he be ever so blundering a one. They will not reveal themselves to any one who is content with his own opinions, and does not wish to change them for truth. It is a reasonable assertion that any man who interferes with these investigations, is an enemy of the Liberty of Conscience. He wishes that men should affirm something which the Conscience in them says that they ought not to affirm or to deny something which the Conscience in them says they ought not to deny.

Mill on Liberty. A philosophical protest on behalf of Liberty has appeared in our days from Mr Mill. Some of you will have read it; those who have must have appreciated its power and its earnestness. I hold it to be a valuable testimony against certain opinions which are prevalent among philosophers; especially among those who worship Society as the supreme Divinity. It is no less important as a warning against a tendency which exists among those who are not philosophers to make uniformity in practice or in opinion the great object of their ambition. I do not doubt with Mr Mill that *Value of* diversities, even eccentricities, are much better than *this Trea-* the dead level from which all inequalities are removed, *tise.* than the desert which some would create under pretence of making peace. But I would warn you that *Liberty* the Liberty we have been speaking of to-day, the *not to be* liberty which Epictetus and Marcus Aurelius sought, is *ed with* far remote from eccentricity. They did not care to be *Eccentri-* different in their ways from other men; they would *city.* rather be like their fellows. They refused to be the slaves of the fashions and habits of their time, or of any time; but since there must be fashions and habits they would rather take what they found than change them for others which in themselves were equally unimportant. A man may make himself a slave by adopting the modes of some other time and country, or by devising new modes of his own, as well as by copying all that he sees about him. And so as to acts. The supporters of some faction may fancy they are asserting their liberty by claiming their right to bite their thumbs because their opponents defy them to do it. The man who under- *Tempta-* stands what Liberty of Conscience is will tell himself *tion to* that he has no right to bite his thumb; that he is *them.* yielding to one of his own whims and fancies in such biting; and that whims and fancies are mischievous tyrants. I do not believe that Mr Mill meant to confound Liberty with the right to be peculiar. I am sure he has a sense of its grandeur which would make such a definition of it quite intolerable to him. But there are passages in the Essay which are open to that interpretation. And since some who do not love Liberty may be glad that it should be so represented, and some may be even ready to accept this poor and withered shadow of it in place of the substance; I have desired that the slander should not even seem to have the countenance of so high an authority.

Marcus Aurelius an invader of the Liberty of Conscience.

Mill on Liberty, p. 50.

I had another reason for referring to this remarkable Essay. In the course of it Mr Mill alludes to the Emperor Marcus, and confirms, in much better language, the opinion which I have expressed about him. But he fills up a blank which I had left. "Marcus Aure-"lius, the gentlest and most amiable of philosophers "and rulers, under a solemn sense of duty, authorised "the persecution of Christians. To my mind," adds Mr Mill, "this is one of the most tragical facts in all history. "It is a bitter thought how different the Christianity of "the world might have been if it had been adopted as "the religion of the Empire, under the auspices of "Marcus Aurelius, instead of those of Constantine." To the lamentation and the wish contained in these last sentences I do not in the least subscribe. I believe that Christianity would not have been the least better for being taken under the patronage of this good Prince.

Would Christians have been better for his patronage?

I believe it proved its vital strength much more by evoking his hostility. I do not imagine that its professors would have been free from any of the sins into which they fell, or would have been more faithful to their

principles, if they had passed through the trial of
alliance with a doomed Empire—a far greater trial than
any persecution—in his days rather than in the days of
Constantine. But the other part of the paragraph
belongs to facts and not to speculation. There is no
doubt that the gentlest of philosophers and rulers
authorised the persecution of Christians, and authorised
it from a solemn sense of duty. He believed that he
was doing his duty as a ruler by keeping alive the reverence of his subjects. He believed he was doing his
duty as a philosopher by putting down men who, as he
thought, mimicked the endurance of pain which belonged to philosophy without entering into its principles. And when Mr Mill goes on to press the moral
upon Christians that they cannot be sure they are
doing right in persecuting any form of infidelity, if
they hold Marcus to have been utterly wrong in persecuting that which he deemed infidelity, I should only
complain of the charge for its inadequacy and feebleness. I am not the judge either of him or of the
Christians who have followed in his steps. But there
were excuses for him which it would be impossible to
plead for them. If we believe that the Redeemer of
the Conscience has come, what is any attempt to corrupt it or stifle it but an act of direct treason against
Him ?

LECT. VI.

*His mo-
tives for
persecu-
tion*

*far better
than any
which we
can allege:*

LECTURE VII.

THE SUPREMACY OF CONSCIENCE.

LECT. VII.

The claim of Butler for the Conscience.

I HAVE spoken to you about the Liberty of Conscience. Butler appears to demand for it much more than Liberty. He claims for it Supremacy.

The phrase is not used carelessly. It occurs frequently in the Discourses on Human Nature. What value the writer of them attached to it you may guess from these sentences. 'You cannot form a notion of 'the faculty Conscience, without taking in judgment, 'direction, superintendency. This is a constituent part 'of the idea; that is of the faculty itself; and to pre- 'side and govern, from the very economy and constitu- 'tion of man, belongs to it. Had it strength as it has 'right; had it power as it has manifest authority, it 'would absolutely govern the world.'

Second Sermon on Human Nature.

This strong language proceeds from a man who had an instinctive dislike of rhetorical exaggerations; who was cautious, even to excess. If he had found any more moderate words which would have expressed his meaning, we may be sure he would have preferred them. Nevertheless Dr Whewell, when he was sending forth the Discourses as a text-book for our use, showed an impatience of this language. He quoted other

Dr Whewell's demurrer.

passages from Butler, which might be taken as modifying it; according to him we have no need to construe it literally.

LECT. VII.

It may be true that Butler did not frequently speak of the conscience as having a 'right to govern the 'world.' He could scarcely sustain his speech on such a level; his voice must often have fallen into a lower key. But I cannot believe that he would ever have consented to soften words which were uttered with such solemnity and deliberation; what he said was implied in the very idea of the Conscience he must have ascribed to it habitually; otherwise he would have retracted not a few sentences, but his whole treatise.

Butler would not have admitted it.

So far as Dr Whewell attempted to empty Butler's doctrine of its *force,* I think he failed: but he may help us to perceive wherein it is *weak;* what there is in it which is inconsistent with the idea of the Conscience; what there is in it which prevents us from recognising the highest function of the Conscience. The education of Dr Whewell was altogether different from that of Butler; it may have enabled him to recognise some of our necessities to which his predecessor was less alive.

Can we?

Any one who reads Dr Whewell's Moral Treatises will be aware of the importance which he attached to Laws; to laws in their simplest sense as enforced by particular nations on their own subjects. Bringing to the study of the 'microcosm, the little world of man,' the habits which he had acquired while studying 'the macrocosm, the great world of Nature,' he must have sought for all signs and vestiges of an order in human existence. He might have imagined a possible savage, or tried to discover the condition of an actual savage. But the facts which lay before him—those which di-

The searcher for Laws in Nature recognises Laws among men.

rectly concerned his own life and the life of his neighbours—surely deserved his first attention. Amongst
these none was more obvious, none was more wonderful
than this, that men obey laws, laws which they did
not create, laws which they speak of as having come
down to them from ancestors, laws which they associate
with the existence of the body whereof they are mem-
Are Laws bers. With these Laws, Dr Whewell perceived that the
the ground
of Right words Right and Wrong become inseparably blended;
and they assume to be the preservers of Right, the pro-
Wrong? tectors against Wrong. So earnestly did he dwell upon
this observation, that he was accused of making morality
dependent upon positive Laws though they are subject
to continual changes. He repelled the charge indig-
nantly. The Laws, he said, pointed to a Right which
they did not make, to a Wrong which it was not in their
Or the wit- power to put down. It was the business of the Moralist
nesses of
Right and to search for the radical meaning of the distinction which
Wrong? they indicated. While some discovered in the varieties
of local laws an evidence that there is no fixed standard
of Right and Wrong, Dr Whewell looked upon their
varieties and imperfections as witnesses that there must
be such a standard.

Butler had always been occupied ·with the microcosm. He only contemplated the macrocosm in
reference to that. The arrangements of the outward
world were profoundly interesting to him, but interesting as instruments for the discipline and education of
Dr Whe- men. That he should have recognised an Order in this
well's sym-
pathy with sphere as real as that which men of Science had per-
Butler. ceived in the other, was a bond between him and Dr
Whewell. Butler could be hailed as a witness for fixed
Laws. But when he began to talk of a tribunal within

a man which might,—so he seemed to affirm,—reverse *LECT. VII.*
any decrees that had not issued from it, we cannot
wonder that his admirer should have felt considerable
alarm. Could the Conscience claim an authority above *Revulsion*
and against laws? Would not such a pretension, be- *from him.*
sides interfering with their dominion, interfere with
the fixed standard of Right which was implied in
them? Might not the Conscience boast that it was
itself the creator of the Right?

These were not fantastic dangers; language had been
used, acts had been done, which evidently assumed for
the Conscience a supremacy as complete, as irresponsible
as this. I apprehend Dr Whewell did good service in
warning us of the peril; I am not equally sure that he
discovered the way of avoiding it. That way I would *Object of*
now endeavour to seek, not trusting at all to my *this Lec-*
own wisdom, but profiting as much as possible by the *ture.*
lights which both these teachers afford for our guidance.

You may remember that in my last Lecture I proposed a change in a customary form of speech. For
'Liberty of Conscience,' I read 'Conscience of Liberty.'
I explained my reasons for the inversion. I did not
wish to deprive the phrase of its old force, but rather to
recover that force by stripping it of some confused
notions which had attached themselves to it. Above *Conscience*
all, I wished to give the word *Conscience* its original *of Supre-*
import, to restore that link between it and conscious- *macy.*
ness, which is almost inevitably severed when it is
treated as a faculty of Human Nature. If I make the
same experiment on the term which we are now considering, I shall not be doing violence to one which has
acquired a traditional and popular sacredness; I shall

be dealing with the phrase of a particular writer, whose courage and independence of thought teach us that we shall often honour him most when we depart from his rubric. In this case I am less scrupulous, because I am convinced that the change of expression may not only be the means of reconciling him with the most eminent of his Commentators, but of justifying what sounds inflated and outrageous in his own statement.

Reason for such an expression. 'The Conscience of Supremacy' may seem to be no substitute for the 'Supremacy of Conscience,' but the very opposite of it. Nevertheless it may show us *what* 'judgment, direction, superintendency is involved in the 'very idea of the conscience,' in *what* sense 'it may have a right to govern the world.'

Conscience and Law, their relation to each other. When I spoke to you of the discipline which was suggested by a distinguished writer of our day for implanting 'the sentiment of the forbidden' in children, that they might as men become the dutiful servants of a majority, I urged that such a scheme, if it were successful (and there were too many instances of its success to warrant us in speaking lightly of it) would destroy a Conscience, supposing it be that which has borne the name among men hitherto, that which has sustained any great cause or defied any oppression. I added, that the sentiment of which Mr Bain speaks, often leads to a transgression of the general *laws* of the land. I instanced the case of Contracts respecting Property. The Laws enforce these. It is admitted that they are for the interest of Society. But there are not only temptations in men to break them for the sake of their own immediate advantage ; there is a social opinion,— it may dwell in a union of workmen, of tradesmen, or of Nobles,—which is more mighty than any distant terrors, such as the legislation of the country may have devised to sustain its own decrees. LECT. VII.

The instances to which I alluded are notorious; they belong to a high stage of civilization—to a country where a philosophy like that of Mr Bain is much esteemed and reckoned a faithful summary of admitted popular maxims. They lead us to ask ourselves these questions. May not this Conscience, which has been regarded with so much suspicion by Lawgivers, be in truth the great bulwark of Law? Need its strength be abated that the strength of the Law may be increased? Will not the strength of one be greatest when the strength of the other is greatest? Do not Laws call forth the Conscience; when that has acquired the utmost superiority which can be claimed for it, is there not the greatest, the only, security that Law will be reverenced? *Reference to a former Lecture.*

It is this doctrine which I desire to enforce upon you. If you fully receive it, you will not wish to cripple Butler's language by qualifications and evasions, yet you will pay the fullest and most grateful respect to the protest of Dr Whewell.

1. I would appeal first to your own experience. Schoolmasters, says an old poet, deliver us to Laws. In the nursery we are acquiring among other sentiments 'the sentiment of the forbidden,' either according to Mr Bain's plan, by trembling at the rod which will descend on us if we do what we are told not to do, and so contracting a dread of the person who wields the rod; or, as I have maintained, by discovering that the forbidder is wiser than we are and cares to save us from the injuries that we should do to ourselves by following our own likings. Of course there are irregularities and *When Law begins to assert itself.*

Not in the family.

M. C.   9

caprices in all mortal discipline. The two maxims may be often mixed together. He who most tries to act on the one may drop through passion into the other. But I believe many a man can say, 'Whatever true sentiment of the forbidden I have, whatever in me is not crouching but manly and erect, was nurtured by this fatherly treatment. God be thanked for that.' Still this was not Law. The apprehension of *that* arises when we are introduced into a Society consisting of boys each with a desire for independence, each with a sense of bodily energies corresponding to this desire, each with tendencies which may lead to mere savagery ; yet each capable of understanding that he has relations to his fellows, each capable of saying, I ought to do *Office of the School-master.* this, I ought not to do that. To bring forth this conviction in its full force is the function of the School-master. Many in our day have clearly understood that it is their function. The difference between them and some of their predecessors is, not that they enforce laws less strictly, not that they tolerate the breaking of them under any circumstances, but that they appeal to something in the boy which recognises the worth of laws ; to that in him which confesses punishment to be directed against acts of his which are wrong. The *The School-master of the last age acted on the maxims of modern wisdom.* Schoolmaster of this age owes his nobleness not to his invention of new Canons, but to his vindication of those old simple maxims which had been exchanged in the practice of the last generation for the more refined principles of conduct that Mr Bain has so ably illustrated and defended.

2. All School discipline points in the same direction. We learn the rules of grammar. They are learnt out of a book. There is a list of exceptions to them.

But they remind us of laws to which speech must conform itself, laws that must somehow account for the
exceptions. They say to each of us, Thou, if thou
speakest, and wouldest make thyself intelligible, must
speak according to a Law. And we are taught this
lesson not that we may be hindered from uttering ourselves freely, distinctly, each saying what he has to say,
but that we may do this. We are shewn by exercises
in writing how the words must follow each other to
make sense. If we do not care to speak or write, the
laws will never explain themselves to us. It is always
the same. The Law demands individual energy to
fulfil it. The more the individual energy is awakened,
the more it recognises its need of a Law.

3. In general we get this instruction respecting
the laws of speech and of writing mainly from two
languages which we do not speak and write commonly; which we do not use to express our ordinary
wants. So we are reminded, first, that there is a
variety in the laws of speech; that Greeks had forms of
speech which Latins had not; that both had forms of
speech which we have not; secondly, that there are
laws of speech to which Greek, Latin, and English must
all conform themselves; thirdly, that these laws do not
affect the things which are spoken of, but govern those
who speak. We are recalled, as I said before, all study
of language must recall us, to the I. The more general
the laws are, the more they suggest the individual.

4. So we are prepared for the study of the most
obvious and striking facts in the history of the peoples
whose languages have occupied us. Why should you
read about Greeks or Romans more than about any
barbarous tribes? Find distinct men among the bar-

9—2

LECT. VII.

*The teach-
ing of
grammati-
cal Laws.*

*Use of the
old lan-
guages.*

*History;
why civi-
lized men
are more
interesting
than bar-
barians.*

barous tribes, men who can express themselves, and they become as interesting to us as any of their conquerors. A Caractacus or a Galgacus is more dear to us than a Suetonius Paullinus, perhaps than an Agricola. But we must get a Tacitus to tell us of a Caractacus or a Galgacus. They stand out clear and brilliant figures before us, because the Roman historian has recognised them as such. And how does he differ from the countrymen of Caractacus or Galgacus? He has learnt the worth of Laws, he belongs to a law-governed people. The Savages form a horde, out of which a living form, an actual I, starts up ever and anon to remind us what the horde consists of, what each element in it ought to *Reverence for national life implies reverence for Laws.* be. But of nations which recognise Laws, it is the characteristic that they are composed of I's; that is to say, the Laws have awakened the Conscience, and the Conscience being awakened owns the majesty of Laws. So we are reconciled to the triumph of Romans over Britons. We do not give up our reverence for national life; we do not worship the force of arms. But we perceive that a true national life could only be called forth, could only be sustained, by Laws; we are sure that when it has been called forth, the Laws will be respected more than the force which has been the instrument of establishing them.

5. Greek history tells you the same lesson, and *Sparta and Athens.* also another which much concerns our subject. You find, among the Greek tribes, the greatest esteem for Legislators; all the greatest men they have dreamt of in the ages which are not historical or known in those that are belong to this class. That they feel to be one of their distinctions from the barbarians. Their freedom is the other. The Savage, they say, is not a

free man, not a citizen. But there is the greatest difference in the characters of the different States. The
predominant thought in Sparta is subjection to the
Laws. It is the glory of Leonidas, and those who fall
with him, that they die in obedience to the laws. The
predominant thought in Athens is personal liberty.
The Spartan welcomes that which he finds, that which
he has inherited, that which is laid down for him. The
Athenian always likes to think that he has a share in
making the laws which bind him. Each State is in
continual danger of perishing, through rigid formality
or through restlessness. But neither does perish till
the reverence for Law is lost, or almost lost, in a dread
of power of some kind or other; when that becomes
supreme, the *nation* ceases to exist. Thus we come to
understand that there are distinct laws which influence
the conduct as there are distinct laws which direct the
speech of different races; but that there is a homage to
Law, as such, lying beneath the respect for particular
laws, springing out of that which is in all races. That
is what I have called the Conscience. It must have a
Law. It recognises the appropriateness of different
laws in different places; the Spartan's 'I ought' may
not be the Athenian's 'I ought.' But there is an 'I
ought' for the Spartan and the Athenian also; if that
is not confessed there will be no subjection to any laws,
local or general—only anarchy, and with anarchy the
extinction of that sense of individual existence which
seems to have produced it.

6. Hence we are led to notice a fact which is
brought out in your home and your school experience;
one which no observer of the modern world can overlook.
Along with those laws of Lacedæmon, Athens, and Rome,

which form so conspicuous a subject in our classical studies, there come before us the ten Commandments which were given to the Jews. These, like the others, belong to a peculiar nation; they are the groundwork of Statutes which we believe to have been abrogated *Its power* for us. How have these survived? Why do parents *over the* in the furthest west, in the most cultivated times, *Western* teach them to their children? How have they estab- *Nations.* lished themselves among nations each having a code of its own? They prohibit acts to which the inhabitants of those nations were and are addicted. They were handed down by a people whom these nations hated, whom they were taught by their priests to hate. Their *Opposition* priests would fain have persuaded them that their own *to it from* authority was higher than the authority of these laws, *Priests* that they could set aside some, dispense with others. *and Philo-* It is clear that no arguments about the authenticity of *sophers.* documents can have had the slightest weight with the tribes which accepted this Code, can never have been the least intelligible to them. How then can we ac- count for their general diffusion, for their general adoption, in spite of the influence of religious teachers who would have much preferred to substitute their own numerous rules, in spite of the contempt of sages, scandalized that an ignorant people in Palestine should have become lawgivers to the world? I shall say nothing here about the history of this Code or the sanction of it. But it belongs to our present subject to remark that the command, 'Thou shalt not,' would have been uttered in vain, if there had not been called forth an 'I ought not' in the hearer; that when these two meet together the decrees or indulgences of Sove- reigns or of Priests prove feeble against them. And

this too must be noticed, that the claim of the Conscience to Liberty is recognised in the very first words
of this Code; that every article of it is associated with
deliverance from bondage. The Conscience of men has,
I believe, testified to this union, has owned that Slavery
is inevitable for me while I am under the yoke of my
own appetites and inclinations, that the Law which
forbids me to serve these points to the highest freedom
if it cannot confer the freedom; points to a 'direction,
superintendency, judgment,' in which lies the very secret
both of obedience and freedom.

7. I alluded to this subject before when I com-
mented on some remarkable words of Taylor respecting Charles II. *Custos utriusque Tabulæ* was the
title which he bestowed on that monarch in addition to
his authority over England, France, and Ireland, and
his claim to be defender of the Faith. I was obliged to
observe that he broke both the Tables of which he was
the guardian, and taught his subjects to do the same.
And yet no one sanctioned so many acts which tended
to bind the Consciences of his subjects. His own indo-
lent disposition assuredly would not have prompted
such acts; he desired indulgence from others and would
have granted it to others. But indulgence and tyranny
are linked closely together; reverence for law is the
only protection of reverence for Conscience. Charles
could not reverence the last in himself or in his subjects because he did not reverence the first. I do not
say the same of those ecclesiastics who urged him to
enforce restraints upon the Puritans of England or the
Covenanters of Scotland. They had a confused notion
that they paid honour to the fixedness and uniformity
of Laws by not suffering diversities of Opinion. Their

mistake was that terrible one of which I spoke in my last Lecture, the identification of Conscience with Opinion. But this mistake was as fatal to the claims of Law upon obedience as it was to the dignity of the Conscience itself. If the Conscience is one with Opinion, the moment our opinion runs contrary to any law,— the moment we think it may be advantageously altered —we shall set it at nought. Whereas the Conscience having a profound reverence for Law as Law, turning to it for a protection against mere opinion, will rather incur any punishment than trifle with its authority. Law carries with it for the Conscience a witness of divinity even when those who administer it have become devilish. Those lawgivers therefore who would weaken the Conscience cut away from under them the ground on which security for Law must rest, just as the ecclesiastics who would crush it deliberately destroy the greatest witness for the direction, superintendency, judgment of a righteous God. I accept the testimony of Butler to the supremacy of the Conscience, notwithstanding what I take to be the imperfection of his language, as a grand recantation and repudiation, from an illustrious divine of the English Church who was to become one of its Bishops, of all those apologies for restraints upon the Conscience which members of his Communion had put forward in former days; a protest against all similar apologies which should be devised in the times to come. His language about the Conscience is as different from Taylor's as can be. One would fence it with rules; the other appears to assert for it a strange independence of rules. But Taylor had partially anticipated Butler's claim in his Liberty of Prophesying, had even drawn conclusions from it to which

Conscience the defence of Law against Opinion.

Butler a true Protestant against the oppressors of Conscience.

The Liberty of Prophesying.

Butler might have demurred. And they like Butler and Dr Whewell need not be at issue if we exchange Rules for Laws, and if we suppose the Conscience of Laws to involve the Conscience of Supremacy in an essentially righteous Lawgiver.

Do not suppose that by the Conscience of such a supremacy I mean the general recognition of a Supreme Power existing somewhere to whom the world is subject, and therefore to whom I as one of its inhabitants am subject. The Conscience has nothing to do with such vague and distant propositions. It is emphatically the witness of a supremacy over me directly, not over me as one of the atoms of which the world is composed. I do not proceed from the world to myself; but from myself to the world; I know of its governor only so far as I know of mine. Nor do I begin from the acknowledgment of a Power who *as a Power* governs me. In Butler's bold language I own only one who has a *Right* to govern. The Conscience takes no account of Power except as it is joined to Right, except as it has its ground in Right. The very business and function of the Conscience is to disclaim and repudiate any other, to say that it will serve no other. Here is the vindication of Dr Whewell's demand for a fixed unchangeable standard of Right. He does not approach nearer to it by supposing that the Right exists somewhere else, and that the Conscience has a certain qualified or subordinate authority in affirming what it is. *Then* we may ask, as Mr Bain asks, *What* Conscience has this authority, and how much has it? But if we hold that in every man there is a Conscience of judgment, direction, superintendency, and that in every man the Conscience, so far as it testifies of this, testifies

The Conscience speaks of my Ruler.

The Conscience speaks of subjection to Right never to mere Power.

'truly—we avoid any such difficulties; the Conscience in itself has no authority; its authority begins when it goes out of itself, its supremacy consists in its abdication of supremacy.

The paradox of the Conscience.

9. That you will say is a paradox. I told you that when we begin to speak of the Conscience, we find ourselves amidst paradoxes; it is impossible to escape them except by denying the very existence of that which we are investigating. It was Butler's reluctance to face this paradox which brought him into collision with his commentator and I think into contradiction with himself. If the conscience is a *property* of mine, and if it implies judgment, superintendence, direction, I must be my own judge, superintendent, director. Then *jura nego mihi nata.* They are created by me, not for me. But if there is that in me which is higher than anything I call my own; if there is that in me which carries me beyond myself—if the Conscience is this,—then I may indeed speak loftily of it; for it testifies of every man in whom it dwells, that

The peril of regarding Conscience as my possession.

Its true glory.

> Igneus est illi vigor et cœlestis origo.

He may have a clothing of earth, he may have wrapped himself closely in it. But there is in him a fire which the earth did not kindle, there are the signs of a parentage which must be divine.

Its liability to debasement.

10. And yet it is here that one finds a justification for the very hardest epithets that have ever been bestowed on the Conscience. Butler, as I hinted before, appears not to recognise the truth of these epithets; he would scarcely have liked to speak of a corrupt or evil Conscience. But no theory of his or of any man can undo the facts to which these adjectives point; the truth

which any theory contains will be disbelieved and will be inoperative, if justice is not done to them. Once admit that the Conscience is that in a man which points to what is above him, which declares the supremacy of a right that he did not mould and cannot alter, and the meaning of these expressions becomes frightfully evident. Disavowing this supremacy, I become what is so pathetically expressed in a line of Byron's *Lara:*

> Lord of myself, that heritage of woe.

The more there is of Conscience in me—the more I *Heights* confess a higher law—the greater will be my degrada- *and* tion and the sense of it. And as the depth of this *Depths.* degradation is measured by the elevation of which I have the Conscience, so all those pettier and more ignominious forms of self-consciousness to which I adverted in my first lecture,—all the tricks of vanity which may make us laugh or weep when we recollect them in ourselves or others,—are accounted for in the same way. This self-consciousness attests the grandeur of which the man is capable, it shews that he cannot be satisfied with looking at mere things which are out- side of him. But it verifies the two assertions of the *Self Con-* poet, which often sound contradictory, that the man *ceit and* who is occupied with himself is occupied with the *spect.* meanest of all objects in creation and yet that he is wise

> Who still suspects and still reveres himself
> In lowliness of heart.

11. I have touched upon the subject of the Laws of Nations solely as it bears upon the question of the Supremacy of the Conscience. Any direct treatment of that subject must be reserved for Lectures on

*The Con-
science of
a Nation.*

*Does it in-
terfere
with the
individual
Consci-
ence ?*

*True and
false Pro-
phets.*

*What each
may do.*

Social Morality. But I cannot omit to notice a phrase which you will often hear from the wisest men and find in the best books; 'The Conscience of a Nation.' Can I accept that form of speech after taking so much pains to connect the Conscience with each man, with the word I? Most heartily do I accept it; I should regard the loss of it as an unspeakable calamity. It reminds us that the Nation is composed of I's; that therein consists its preciousness; that a Society such as Mr Bentham describes, which is 'a fictitious body composed of the individual persons who are considered as constituting, as it were, its members,' is not a Nation at all. Men are not wont to live and die for an 'as it were.' The Nation for which men are content to live and die must have a Conscience; a Conscience to which each of its citizens feels that an appeal can be made, a Conscience which makes it capable of evil acts; a Conscience which gives it a permanence from age to age. Leave fictions to the philosophers who care for them; let every one of us claim his place as the citizen of a real Nation, real because it has a Conscience. And let me conjure every one of you who may hereafter have the opportunity of speaking to men as a divine, an advocate or a legislator, every one who possesses any gift or faculty of addressing multitudes, to beware how he uses this opportunity and that faculty. It is no trifle to speak to the Conscience of any body of men. You may raise it or you may corrupt it. You may turn your countrymen—any of them, rich or poor—into a base mob, you may exalt them into citizens. Think of the great men who have set the last object before them. The curse of God is upon those who pursue the other.

12. In this union of the Nation with the Individual one of the deep mysteries of the Conscience is involved. The might of Law is that it speaks to a whole body; that it addresses each member of that body as a Thou. The might of Law and also the terror of Law is there. Many a man would be glad to escape from 'the sentiment of the forbidden' which it creates, to that sentiment of the forbidden which is merely a shrinking from the lash. The Israelites were faithful specimens of our race when they longed to exchange the dreariness of a wilderness with subjection to a Law, for the flesh-pots of Egypt with its task-masters. That change is not possible for any one who is a citizen or is to become a citizen. He is brought face to face with a Law; his acts are tried by a Law; if it condemns any acts in a neighbour it condemns the same in him. As he approaches the inner sanctuary in which his thoughts and purposes dwell, he is startled by finding that there is a Law over them also; nay, is it not the highest Law, is it not that which speaks directly of wrong, which says, Thou art wrong? Here is the penalty of having a Conscience, of being under a Law, of not being a brute. A penalty which is far more terrible than all which the Legislature can inflict for the violation of the Law; who might not be glad to commute the Conscience of wrong and guilt for the worst of these?

But the Conscience of Wrong implies a Conscience of Right. The Law must have come from one who is Right, from one who must be the enemy of Wrong. Is not the enemy of Wrong the Deliverer from Wrong? The Law looked at as a mere code of letters, fixed and irrevocable, is a chain upon a man which he would give worlds to break but which winds itself ever more closely about him because he has a Conscience. The Law contemplated as expressing the righteous mind of the Lawgiver, speaks to the Conscience of the liberty which it craves. It recognises Law and Liberty as essentially united. Its freedom consists in its obedience—not to Decrees or Statutes, not to a Society, but—to a Being who is right and seeks to make it right.

Thus Right and Wrong become ultimate distinctions which can be resolved into no others. There is a deep truth in the claim of Supremacy for the Conscience. There is a deep truth in the protest on behalf of Law against any supremacy in a man which interferes with its supremacy. Both together lead us to the question, 'Good or Evil, which of them 'is supreme, which of them is at last to govern me and 'the world?'

LECTURE VIII.

THE EDUCATION OF THE CONSCIENCE.

I HAVE given some hints in several of my Lectures, especially in the last, about the influence which the Education of the Nursery and of the School may have in crushing or in awakening the Conscience. Two questions I think must have occurred to you in reference to this subject. Both concern you and me greatly. The first is *Quis custodit ipsos custodes?* Is there any Guide for the Parent and the Schoolmaster who may teach them not to destroy that which it is their function to cultivate and preserve? Philosophers it seems may furnish them with ingenious receipts for stifling the Conscience. Divines and Casuists have written long tomes which, if we may believe so fair a witness as Jeremy Taylor, utterly bewilder it. Supposing these are the ultimate rulers of the Conscience, what chance is there that it will retain any freedom,—any mastery over the inclinations which rise up against it? The second question is this— 'Under what guidance do we fall when we are loose from the control of parents and schoolmasters?' Can the discipline of what Mr Bain calls 'Society' be trusted then? Will that take care of the Con-

Who teaches Teachers?

Who takes the command of us when we are left to choose for ourselves?

science with which you have said it is so often called to do battle?

These are questions which men have been compelled to ask themselves in all times. It appears to me that those have been the wisest and truest who have asked them most earnestly, who have been most resolute not to go without an answer. I spoke in my first Lecture of Socrates. I regarded him as the philosopher who had least cared to invent a System in which he could himself repose, or which he could transmit to disciples; who had most cared to pursue the enquiry 'What am I?' who had most stimulated disciples to enter upon that enquiry. In pursuing our studies respecting the Conscience I have been drawn away from him to teachers of our own country who have undertaken to illustrate its operations and its history. I come back to him because I think he has something to tell us which they have not told us; nay, which their very eagerness to glorify the Conscience and assign it independent powers had prevented them from telling us. To explain what I mean I must turn from later interpreters of Socrates, whether they have admired or disparaged him, to the testimonies of those who experienced the effects of his lessons upon themselves, who knew best what had inspired his enemies with their dislike to him, and given them an excuse for condemning him. Upon these subjects the evidence of Xenophon is most explicit. He speaks with the affection of a friend, with the frankness of a soldier.

Recurrence to Socrates.

Testimony of Xenophon.

I shall not require you to dive far into his *Memorabilia,* or to accept any opinions of mine as to the force of his words. Open the first pages of his book; read them as simply as they are written. They refer to the Dæmon who, as Socrates declared, was the Guide of his thoughts and his acts. Xenophon had every temptation to avoid this topic. He might have explained away the language of his master, as many have done subsequently. He might have said that it did not affect his judgment on other questions, that he was a great practical moralist in spite of what he dreamed about an invisible director. He takes no such course. He introduces the Dæmon to us at once. He does not pretend to account for any part of the doctrine or life of Socrates without it. He had heard him continually speak of such a Guide and Reprover, who checked him when he was choosing any crooked path, who gave him hints and intimations of the road which he ought to choose. Xenophon had never known him tell a lie. He must have been a confirmed liar if he uttered these words, so deliberately, so habitually, without meaning them. His pupil had not found him yielding to fancies; Socrates affirmed that he was hindered from yielding to them by these admonitions. Xenophon must give up all faith in him if he counted him a deceiver or a victim of self-deception in such professions.

You will say that Xenophon, as well as Socrates, accepted the traditional belief of his countrymen, and that this was but an article of their traditional belief. Look at the passage to which I am referring before you adopt that interpretation of it. You will find that the author of the *Memorabilia* treats the acknowledgment of the Dæmon as the main offence which had led to the charge against Socrates; the charge of *outraging* the traditional opinions of his

Or a defiance of it ?

The ground of the sentence upon Socrates.

Learned quibbles; 'Consciousness of a Conscience.'

countrymen. He had brought in new Dæmons. Xenophon assumes, with obvious reasonableness — even if we are not bound to admit so well-informed a contemporary as able to speak positively—that his accusers meant *this* Dæmon; and that the Judges condemned him because his allusions to one who was always near him were so notorious. Undoubtedly there was added to this count of the indictment the other, that he was corrupting the minds of the youth. But what was the corruption except that he tempted them also to confess this Teacher, and so withdrew them from the objects of customary Athenian homage? He might be really more devout than most of the Athenians in the performance of the ordinary rites,— he might desire a cock to be given to Æsculapius on his death-bed; but the instinct of his judges was assuredly right. The service of such a guide as he described the Dæmon to be did interfere most dangerously with the service of the gods of nature, the gods of power and not of right, whom the rulers of Athens desired that its young men should revere.

Some have fancied that they should relieve Socrates of a stigma, and bring him more into harmony with modern opinions, if they called this Dæmon the Conscience. I trust you know enough by this time of the force which I give to the word Conscience not to suspect me of such an evasion. If Socrates had been without a Conscience he would never have acknowledged a divine Guide, as if he had been born deaf he would never have known anything of the sweetest voice; but he could no more identify the Conscience with the Guide than he could identify his hearing with the voice. He was *conscious* of one superior to himself who, he said, was directing him and superintending him; it would be the very outrage upon his veracity against which Xenophon protested, to suppose that he only intended to signify that he *had* a Conscience. That is a notable instance of the subterfuges by which the plain words of a great man are explained away, to the immense injury, I conceive, of the little men who invent the explanation.

Socrates wrote no books; he lived and discoursed. But the disciple who took him for the chief speaker in his Dialogues was just as much obliged as Xenophon to recognise the Dæmon as his teacher. Plato knew that he must leave out Socrates, if he left out this conviction of his. In it lay a chief part of the influence which the great questioner had exerted over him and over the young men of Athens. And Plato could not say what he had to say except through Socrates. Putting himself for his master he would have lost that mighty power which Cicero and Augustine felt not less than the Greeks who could taste the honey as it fell from his lips. The life, the humour, the actual Plato would have gone, and nothing would have been left but the dry bones of a System called Platonism, which no mortal could believe or care for; which never had any existence but in the digest of Brucker or Tennemann.

Plato.

The Dæmon in the Dialogues.

It is quite true that we hear little of the Dæmon when we leave the contemporaries of Socrates, those who put him to death, and those who embalmed his memory. Aristotle talked much of the Soul, but he supposed that he might leave the enquiry 'What am I?' as one that did not require further elucidation; his vocation was to arrange studies in their relation

Banished to a great extent from the later schools.

10—2

Aristotle.

Ridiculous to all makers of Systems.

Chrysippus and Cleanthes.

to each other, not to pursue this study as the central one of all. The need therefore of such a Guide may not have come very distinctly before him. Yet Aristotle, with all his love of System, was an essentially practical man; one who preserved a healthy acquaintance with the living creatures that walk the Earth, with their doings and with their needs. He must therefore have reverenced Socrates; we know that he did. He must have learned much from him. Whether he could understand what was said about the Dæmon or not, he will have respected it. Those who framed schemes of the Universe, introducing into them in place of men what could be managed much more conveniently, abstract notions—those who, if the facts did not fit conveniently into their systems, said bravely with the Abbé Raynal, 'So much the worse for them'—these have always despised Socrates as one who never could manipulate notions, and was a reckless disturber of Systems.

There is a man among the Greek Stoics whose name is chiefly familiar to us by those lines in Horace wherein he says that Homer

> ...quid sit pulchrum quid turpe quid utile quid non
> Plenius et melius Chrysippo et Crantore dicit.

Chrysippus was one of those grand System builders whom his contemporaries regarded with the profoundest admiration. They contrasted him with another of the same school, whom they described as a very lout in philosophy, an ass under panniers. His name was Cleanthes. But this despised man, instead of being commemorated in two lines, has left behind him a hymn to Jupiter. He had discovered that he needed something else than a System of which he could boast that it had a place for everything, and that everything was in its place; that he needed one who actually knew him, and could direct him. I can never read this hymn without wonder and shame, especially these concluding lines of it.

'But, O Jove, giver of all gifts, dark in thy clouds, 'ruler of the Lightning, Be pleased to deliver men from 'miserable ignorance. Scatter that, O Father, from 'the soul, grant us to inherit that understanding in the 'confidence whereof thou with right dost govern all 'things. So being honoured ourselves, we shall return 'honour to thee, Praising thy works continually as it 'becomes a mortal; seeing that there is no greater 'reward to mortals or to God than ever righteously to 'celebrate that Law which is common to both.' Think of the poor ass between panniers, finding out that his great necessity was to be delivered from his ignorance, to dwell in light instead of darkness; and that there was somewhere, whether he could name his name or not, one who could hear his cry for deliverance and for light; one whom it was the blessing of all creatures to praise and magnify, because Right dwelt in Him, because He ruled by right!

The man who makes all things fit and the man who prays for light.

As we come down lower in the history, and encounter those grand figures of the Slave and the Emperor, concerning whom I spoke to you two weeks ago, we become more and more aware of the difference between the man who puts together a set of opinions which satisfies him, and which is to satisfy his disciples, and the man who is seeking a living guide for himself and so is able to point out one to them. I have told you already how impossible Epic-

The Slave

The battle for life raises him above his school.

What he thought of Divination.

The Diviner who guesses and the Diviner who knows.

tetus found it to obtain the freedom which he deemed the great necessity for man, unless he could look up to a God, not at a distance from him, but a judge and superintendent of him, of his thoughts as well as his acts. You will scarcely realize the truth of this remark if you merely turn to the *Enchiridion*, where his doctrines are digested into short sayings, and look as if they were delivered ex cathedrâ. In the conversations which are reported by Arrian you see more into the actual struggle of the man for life, his struggle even with the opinions of the school to which he belonged when they interfered with practice. For instance. The Stoics, as you may learn from Cicero, were champions of Divination. They had their own way of explaining it. They could compel the superstitions of their people to accord with their philosophy. But they were superstitious nevertheless. Hear how Epictetus speaks on this subject. I will take Mrs Carter's version, which was made in the last century, and is apt to weaken rather than strengthen the force of the author's words on subjects of this kind. "From an "unreasonable regard to Divination we omit many "duties. For what can the Diviner see besides Death "or Dangers or Sickness or such things? When it "is necessary then to expose one's self to danger for "a Friend, or a duty to die for him, what occasion "have I for Divination? Have I not a Diviner within "who has told me the essence of Good and Evil, "and who explains to me the indications of both? "What further need have I of the entrails of Victims "or the flight of Birds? Can I bear with the other "diviner when he says, 'This is for your interest'? "For doth *he* know what is for my interest? Doth he

"know what good is? Hath he learned the indica-
"tions of good and evil as he hath those of the Vic-
"tims? If so, he knows the indications likewise of
"fair and base, Just and Unjust. Do you tell me, Sir,
"what is indicated to me, Life or Death, Riches or
"Poverty? But whether those things are for my inter-
"est or not I shall not enquire of you. * * * * * What
"is it that leads so often to Divination? Cowardice;
"the dread of Events. Hence we flatter the Diviner,
"'Pray, Sir, shall I inherit my father's estate?' 'Let
"us see, let us sacrifice upon the occasion.' 'Nay, Sir,
"just as fortune pleases.' Then if he says, 'You shall
"inherit it,' we give him thanks as if we received
"the inheritance from *him*. The Consequence of this
"is that they play upon us. What then is to be done?
"We should come without previous desire or aversion;
"as a Traveller enquires the road of a Person whom
"he meets, without any desire for that which turns
"to the right hand more than to the left; for he
"wishes for neither of them; but that only which
"leads him properly. Thus we should come to God
"as a Guide. Just as we make use of other guides;
"not persuading them to show us one object rather
"than another, but receiving such as they present to
"us. But now we hold the bird with fear and trem-
"bling, and in our invocation to God entreat him—
"'Have mercy upon us; suffer me to come off safe.'
"You wretch, would you have anything then but what
"is best? And what is best but what pleases God?
"Why do you, as far as in you lies, corrupt your Judge
"and seduce your Adviser?"

We may take this memorable passage as explaining the meaning of all the discourses of Epictetus,

The wish to be deceived.

Should we pray for good luck or for guidance into Truth?

Passage into the new world.

and the relation between his discourses and his life. It has an historical value which is greater than its biographical. It illustrates the passage from the old world into the new; it explains the demands of men which some Revelation of God must answer. If there was such a Diviner over men, as Epictetus affirmed there was, could He not show in some way to other men besides Epictetus what He was and how they might find Him?

The Emperor conversing with himself.

The evidence in the case of Marcus Aurelius is no less remarkable. His books are addressed to himself. It is with himself he carries on his Dialogues; it is himself that he warns of continual temptations to laziness, indulgence, cowardice; it is himself that he stimulates to energy and manliness. He recalls himself from speculations about the thoughts, schemes, devices of other men to take cognisance of that which is passing within him. He refers continually to a

The Dæmon of Marcus Aurelius.

governing part in his soul, to a God or a Dæmon close to him who is able to preserve him from the influences of external things and the phantasies of his own mind. I grant you that you will often have to question yourselves whether this ruling part of the soul was to keep Marcus from falling into what was corrupt and base, or whether he was to keep it. Do not avoid that doubt; do not try to settle it by any peremptory decision. The difficulty was in the writer of the *Meditations;* the difficulty is in you. To face

Does he rule it, or is he ruled by it?

it is the way to be delivered from it. You will find also much in Marcus Aurelius about the 'whole' of which we form a portion; many lessons drawn from the relations which the parts bear to the 'whole.' All such passages throw light upon his character and upon

his efforts to act as the Ruler of a mighty Empire
ought to act. He felt the danger of forgetting his
people, whilst he was thinking of himself, as well as
the danger of losing himself in the multitude of things
and men that were continually passing before him.
The struggle to reconcile these two claims was one *The man and the Statesman.*
of the great struggles of his life; is it not in our little
sphere your struggle and mine? The perplexities of
this kind which an honest and serious man discovers
to us, are worth far more than the most elaborate
devices for concealing them, or for adjusting them.
But beware of listening to any commentators or translators who try to account for them by certain tenets
of the Stoics which Marcus Aurelius had embraced.
You cannot read him and believe that. His tenets
were webs which had spun themselves more or less
closely about him. They gave him hints of certain
principles which he needed for action; before he could
act he had to break through them. Thus, for instance,
the 27th Aphorism of his 5th Book is to this effect.
" To live with the Gods is our calling. He lives *Living with the Gods.*
" with the Gods who continually exhibits to them his
" own soul, pleased with the things which are ap-
" pointed for him, ready to do whatsoever that Dæmon
" desires whom Jupiter hath given to each as a guide
" and governor over him; which Dæmon is indeed an
" offshoot from Him. And this is the Mind or Reason
" of each man." It may be—as a learned Scotchman *Not dwell-ing among particles of Ether.*
informs me who published a translation of the *Medi-*
tations some 100 years ago, which Mr Long's must
have made obsolete, if it ever had any circulation—
that the Stoics conceived the divine substance to be
an infinitely diffused and all-pervading Ether, and that

souls were particles of this Ether, and so on. Well! I dare to say they may have had that conception and many others equally sagacious. But Marcus Aurelius was not talking about Ether; he was enquiring after a Ruler for himself. And the slightest glimpses of light which he gained about that question are worth something in this day to us, to whom his theories about Ether are worth nothing.

Plutarch on the Socratic Dæmon.

These distinguished men, Cleanthes, Epictetus, Marcus Aurelius, do not speak to us of the Socratic Dæmon; each speaks of a Guide or Teacher of whom he had need for himself. There was an earlier Philosopher (in the reign of Trajan) whose vocation was especially to revive the images of the past; who has revived them for English men and English children, as well as for the Greeks and Romans among whom he dwelt and whose ancestors he compared. Plutarch of Chæronea was a faithful student of the lives and acts of Philosophers, as well as of the lives and acts of Statesmen. He has a curious and characteristic dialogue on the subject of the Dæmon. I have not leisure to give you a full account of it. But I must allude to a passage which evidently expresses the judgment of the writer. Various explanations of the Dæmon have been given, some resolving it, as a modern sage might, into one of the forms of ancient superstition, some accounting for it in a purely material way, some by sheer self-deception. Then it occurs to one of the speakers as rather strange that birds, dogs, serpents should be counted more sacred to the Gods and more able to express their minds than men. And he suggests that as one who is fond of horses does not devote himself to the whole class but picks out some one of special

Possibly the divinity cares for men as much as for lower animals.

promise and beauty, and devotes all his diligence to the training of that, so it may be that the Gods select a man like Socrates and educate him for higher apprehensions and greater work than the rest of his kind, and that as some horses need continual curbs or whips, while others are attentive to the least sound of the master's voice and obey that, so it may have been with the human disciple; that the divine voice speaking in his mind may have been more effectual in deterring him from wrong and guiding him to right than any force from without could have been.

I was anxious to quote these words of Plutarch because they bear directly upon the Education of the Conscience—the subject of which I undertook to speak this morning—and because they raise a most important doubt. Plutarch seems to treat it as a singular felicity or privilege of Socrates due to his difference from other men, to some rare natural gifts, that he had these internal monitions. The suggestion sounds most plausible; I know not how any thinkers of the old world could have thoroughly rejected it. And yet if it were so, whence came the influence of Socrates over his contemporaries, his influence over subsequent generations? If he could not say to all who heard him, 'My guide is also your guide, you can hear 'his voice as I do,' what right had he to converse with them, what understanding could. there be between them? In that case his declaration that he only drew forth from his disciples what was in them, had no meaning or truth; he carried that in him with which they had nothing to do.

The name Philosopher was, to one who used it faithfully, a renunciation of this boast. The Wisdom was sought, pursued, longed for. It was always near the seeker, but it never could become a possession or property which he could hold against adverse claimants. He who tried to do that was a Sophist. That word, as Mr Grote the historian has shown, did not necessarily involve the notion of trickery or imposture. It did involve the assumption that the man held Wisdom in fee simple; that he had it to give or to sell in different portions to those who came asking for it. Socrates might think rightly or wrongly that such a profession led in a majority of cases to quackery in the vendor of the article, to much delusion and disappointment in the purchaser of the article. But apart from all such suspicions, it was the profession itself that he contended against; the lesson he taught was that the youth who wanted wisdom could not beg it, steal it, or buy it of any second-hand retailer; that there was an inexhaustible well of it, and that to this he must find his way and drink for himself. Hard though it may be not to contemplate Socrates as above his contemporaries because he was a Philosopher, the name itself and all that he said was indicated by it must perish if we give him that credit.

Before the days of Epictetus, Plutarch and Marcus Aurelius, there had appeared in Alexandria a Jew who had earnestly meditated on this puzzle and who thought he saw the solution of it. He had been formed by the study of the Law and the Prophets of his own race. He had mixed with the Greeks who brought to the city of the Ptolemies different philosophical wares. Philo was a man of much subtlety, given to indulge his fancy in conceits and allegories,—which was the Jewish disease in his day and many other days,—with some vanity, but on the whole with an earnest purpose, a real desire for Truth. He found that in his Scriptures Wisdom was represented as coming to men—to simple men—as illuminating them concerning their own condition and the condition of their land; as teaching them of the past, and the present, and the future. Here it seemed to him was that which answered to the philosophy or search for Wisdom among the Heathens. Must not the same Wisdom who awakened the beliefs and hopes of those who had been honoured as prophets in his land have also been the source of all the strivings and aspirations of other men? These thoughts of his were mixed, as I said, with many conceits and with a strange self-exaltation (alternating with real humility), both on the ground of his Jewish descent, and of those sympathies with Gentile learning which Jews dreaded. Evidently something was wanting in his interpretation of the Sphinx riddle, if it was the human riddle; he had not seen how common life, and the wants of common men, could be connected with that lore which the great men had spoken of and had wished to impart. But he had given a hint which could not be forgotten. It made a deep impression upon certain men in the next generation who had accepted a belief which he, if he heard of it, had rejected.

These were the teachers in the Christian School of Alexandria, men who had exposed themselves more than the members of almost any Church to the contempt and indignation of Jews and of philosophers, of proconsuls and Emperors, by receiving the message that a crucified man was the Lord of the World—and

LECT. VIII.

His strength and his weakness.

The Christians of Alexandria.

who more than the members of almost any Church
had laboured to diffuse that message. That which
was peculiar in their teaching arose from the exceed-
ing strength of their conviction that He whom they
reverenced was that Wisdom or Word who had been
in all ages imparting light to the consciences of men,
and who had been manifested in the latter days as
the Guide of human beings. This idea is especially
developed in the Παιδαγωγὸς of Clemens. He had
already addressed the Gentiles in what he called a
Λόγος προτρεπτικός, an argument designed to shew
them how all their superstitions had been withdrawing
them from an unseen and divine Teacher, and how
many testimonies there were in their Poets, their
Philosophers, in their very legends, to the existence of
such a Teacher. In the more expanded work which
I have mentioned he traced the course of discipline
by which this Teacher (to whom he applies that name
which Plutarch opposed to the lover of birds, *the lover
of men*) withdrew them from the service of pleasure
and of the lower appetites, to the consciousness of Him
and submission to His guidance. The habit which
Philo had cultivated in his readers, and which was
promoted by the circumstances of men without homely
or national experiences—the habit of fantastic alle-

gorizing—had descended upon Clemens. His indulgence in it makes the practical tendency of his treatises, as a whole, more conspicuous, though it has
deservedly weakened his influence in later times.

*His at-
tempt to
connect
Heathen
wisdom
with Jew-*
From want of confidence in his own leading principle, he was often tempted to imagine a communion
between the sages of the other nations and the Jewish
prophets for which there is no historical justification.

Later criticism by confuting these hypotheses has added force to the truth which they overshadowed. There are in Clemens many indications how the Asceticism which, as I said in a former lecture, every philosopher of every school, nay, every man with work to do, has found needful, may pass into the frivolous Asceticism which is linked to superstition. These faults, if we observe them in an honest not a captious spirit, may be as useful to us as those merits which made Clemens one of the most remarkable of the early Greek fathers. I notice him as the first among Christian writers who distinctly and formally dealt with that question which I said was forced upon us, Whether there is any one who is in the highest and truest sense a Teacher of men, who therefore suggests what is good, controls what is mischievous, in the subordinate Teachers.

LECT. VIII.

*ish tradi-
tions a
desertion
of his
principle.*

Every step in the after history of the Church shewed how great was the temptation of those who ruled in it and taught in it to keep that question out of sight. While they asserted for themselves divine powers to superintend and judge the Conscience, they were continually denying, in practice if not in words, that there was any one who superintended and judged them. It was not that Philosophy was banished from the Church. After a vigorous effort to proscribe Aristotle the ecclesiastical doctors submitted to him. His dogmas not only mingled with theirs but determined what form theirs should take. Philosophy was profoundly honoured as a System of Wisdom, only it ceased to be a search after Wisdom. Therefore the belief of a Wisdom which was searching for men and educating them was inevitably obscured though it could

*The doc-
trine of
the Pæda-
gogue, why
offensive to
the later
Church.*

*Not be-
cause they
dreaded
the mix-
ture of
philosophi-
cal System
with reve-
lation.*

not be banished. Ever and anon some of the greatest Systematisers, like that Boethius of whom I spoke in my inaugural Lecture, in hours of sorrow and persecution discovered their need of an actual Teacher and Consoler; and their words, spoken in the solitude of some prison, were accepted by rulers and statesmen as giving them what no systems could give. An unknown monk, whose very name is disputed, though he is called Thomas à Kempis, writing in uncouth Latin and expressing more than an indifference to the scholasticism of his time, has had an influence deeper and more widely spread than that of the most learned men, only because he spoke of an unseen Teacher who conversed with the Consciences of men and to whom they might turn in their troubles and their ignorance.

The lessons of this monk did not cease to be recognised when another monk of firmer and clearer purpose spoke to the Consciences of his contemporaries of one who could deliver them from their own evils as well as from the burthens which doctors and Systematisers had

laid upon them. The Reformation which Luther inaugurated was an emphatic declaration that there is a Conscience in a man which must have a personal helper and deliverer. But Luther found this assertion made so strongly in the Bible, so much denied elsewhere, that he dwelt upon its claims to man's faith and trust till his followers began to exalt it into the place of the living Guide for whose sake the Reformer loved it.

I am approaching topics which belong more to Moral Theology. But I cannot omit to notice here that the belief of such a living Teacher as Socrates dreamed of and the Christian fathers affirmed to exist

for all men, removes that difficulty about direction,
superintendence, and supremacy, which we found had
led to a strife between Butler and Dr Whewell. Nei- *Butler.*
ther of them had the least sympathy with the tenets
of the Alexandrian teachers, both had a healthy dis-
taste—derived either from a logical or mathematical
training, still more from the practical occupations of
England—for the fancies in which they indulged. But
they might, I think, have discovered the best correction of these as well as a solution of the great problem
of the Conscience which they have set before us in
different aspects, if they had been less afraid of ven-
turing on dangerous ground or of incurring unjust
suspicion. Butler braved that peril when he accepted *He ac-*
as the text of his *Analogy* a passage from Origen, the *cepted an*
Alexan-
most fantastical of all the Alexandrian school ; Clemens *drian*
might have helped him quite as usefully in his *Ser-* *teacher*
in his
mons on Human Nature. *Analogy.*

Our days are different in many respects from But- *The zeal*
ler's. Amongst us, more than amongst our fathers of *for educa-*
tion in our
the last century, the questions are debated, How are *day.*
we to educate ourselves, how are we to educate men
and women and children of different classes, from the
highest to the lowest? Till we determine what we
are, what there is in these men and women and children which can be educated, till we settle whether we
are to be treated and are to treat others as atoms
of a mass, or whether each of us is a distinct I, and
must be taught to believe that he is so and to act
as if he were, I cannot conceive that we shall make
much advance in the science of Education; though
we may be overwhelmed with statistics that bear upon
it, with new theories and mechanical arrangements

which might be profitable, if we knew for what purposes they were to be used. But if education means not the dwarfing as much as possible every individual boy and man, but the awakening him to a consciousness of what he is, to a conscience of what he ought to do, then we must press the demands which I made at the beginning of this Lecture, 'Who directs those 'who undertake to educate, who educates us when 'they leave us or their power over us is exhausted?' Those who try to evade that great controversy really settle it in their own way, which is, it seems to me, an utterly mournful way, a way that leads to despair. I cannot but hold that there is a solution of it which encourages the best hopes, which justifies the most steady and vigorous efforts, in the education of others and of ourselves.

How it drives us to the old question.

LECTURE IX.

THE OFFICE OF THE CASUIST IN THE MODERN WORLD.

I HAVE been now lecturing for some weeks on Casuistry. I began by saying that I accepted that old word which Dr Whewell had thrown aside because he believed it not adapted to our times. I told you that if I agreed with him in his premises I should at once adopt his conclusion. It is a duty to the memory of a founder not to follow the letter of his instructions if by departing from it we can better fulfil the spirit of them. We cannot fulfil the spirit of any founder's instructions if we speak of that which does not concern our own age, however much it may have concerned his. I have adhered in this instance to language of the 17th century because I consider it the best language for the 19th century, because I think Casuistry is even more wanted for the England of our days than for the England of any previous day.

Am I then using the word Casuistry in some unwonted sense? There is an excuse for the suspicion, since I have told you that I entirely disclaim an office which many Casuists have deemed their principal one. I do not undertake to lay down any rules

11—2

for the Conscience. I have tried to show you why I think no rules can be of use to the Conscience. If you say, 'Then you are deluding us by the use of 'an ancient phrase; you still call your instrument the 'same knife though it has a new blade and a new 'handle;' my answer is, 'No! I adhere strictly to 'the original sense of the word. It always meant 'the study of Cases of Conscience. That is what I 'mean by it.' The reason I gave for not liking rules of Conscience, even when they are recommended by such eloquence as Taylor's, was that they do not settle the Cases of Conscience which they undertake to settle; that they leave those cases more unsettled than ever. Cases of Conscience want, I think, a different treatment. The Conscience asks for Laws, not rules; for freedom, not chains; for Education, not suppression. It is the Casuist's business to give it aid in seeking for these blessings. What special calls there are for his occupation in this present time it is proper that I should tell you before I conclude my Course. Then you will perhaps see more clearly why I refuse to confound his work with that of the Moral Philosopher, properly so called, why I suppose Casuistry is the right introduction to Moral Philosophy.

Analysis of character and motives.

First, then, I do not think there is any kind of writing in our day which is so popular as what is called 'the Analysis of human feelings and motives.' I am not speaking of philosophical books. I may allude to them by-and-bye. I am thinking of newspapers, magazines, novels. The greatest talent, so far as I know, which is to be found in any of these, is exhibited not in the invention of plots, not in that which is properly the dramatist's art, the shewing forth persons in action, but in the careful dissection of their acts, and of the influences which contributed to the formation of their acts. When such a craft is much pursued, there will of course be a number of bunglers in it; operators who give themselves credit for the skilful and delicate use of the knife when they have really no skill at all and are never likely to acquire any, though they may inflict considerable pain and do some permanent mischief whilst they are trying to acquire it. But if there are many of these, there are *The skill* also many, both men and women, who display a degree *of our* *times.* of cleverness in these processes which would have caused our ancestors great admiration. Though there is much delicacy of observation in all the more eminent Essayists of the last century, in the best of them a calmness which I am afraid we have almost lost— though a novelist like Fielding had a very remarkable insight into many of the deceptions which men·practise on themselves, as well as into some of their better impulses—yet in the peculiar kind of observations and criticisms to which I am referring, I doubt if they could bear comparison with several of our contemporaries who in mere artistical gifts may be far inferior to them. Criticism is that of which our age boasts, and in which no doubt it excels. We are nothing if not critical. Much of this faculty may be directed towards books; but the books are treated as indexes to the character of the person who has composed them. He is brought out of his hiding-place, even if the critic prefers to remain within his own. I do not regret that it is so. We ought to look upon books *Books* not as a collection of written letters, but as the utter- *treated as* *exhibitions* ances of living men; if they are not, they are nothing. *of the men*

LECT. IX.

from whom they proceed.

There may be much cruelty, often much baseness, in the exposures which are made of the ways and habits of authors who have not been the least anxious to obtrude them upon the world, who have only wished to say something which they thought they had to say. But on the whole it is good that a man should be recognised as a being, and not merely as a speaker; as having spoken out something of his own very self. At all events, for good or for evil it has come to pass that our discourses of every kind tend to assume a personal character. Our statesmen, soldiers, preachers, must either be photographed, or sketched by an artist who thinks he understands their features better than the sun does.

How we may see clearly to take motes out of our neighbour's eye.

To complain of that which one finds so much the habit of our time as this is useless and not very wise. We are a part of our time; its ways are our ways; in finding fault with them we are sure to be unconsciously finding fault with ourselves. That is just the account to which I would turn these remarks. I think a critical age wants to be reminded that it is criticising itself; and critical men that they are criticising themselves. We are apt to forget that there is a critic within us, a sterner, fairer judge than we are, who is taking account of what we do and speak and think; who is now and then saying to me when I am pouring out my righteous indignation against the robber of the ewe lamb—much more distinctly than any prophet could say it—'Thou art the man.' The Casuist is called to remind us of this fact. He must say to the critic, " Yes, this analysis of other " men's acts and motives is wonderfully clever and " acute. It may do those much good whom you desire

" to improve. But then am not I, are not you—con-
" scious of something which is nearer than that man's
" acts and motives? You pronounce what he ought
" to have done and ought not to have done. Is not
" that 'ought' and 'ought not' derived from a Con-
" science to which thou canst appeal in him because
" it is in thee?" I do not mean of course that such
language should be addressed to any particular critic
in the flush of his triumph. It would be merely tormenting to him, very little likely to get a hearing.
But when the critical temper is diffused through a
land so that it affects all classes, all ages, both sexes,
when it receives so much nourishment from all that we
read and all that we hear, it does seem well that this
branch of our education should not be cast aside
as if it had lost its meaning. No general Philosophy
can supply the place of a personal Philosophy in an
age which loves Personality so much as ours loves it.

I used to feel a little irritated when I read Mr *Mr Thack-*
Thackeray's novels, by his frequent interpellations of *eray's Ca-*
suistry.
'Well Sir, or Well Madam, do you treat your servants,
' or your neighbours, any better than these gentlemen
' or ladies, whom I am describing, treated theirs?'
The repetition seemed to savour of mannerism; the
writer appeared to be excusing offences which deserved condemnation. I do not think so now. I believe Mr Thackeray was aware of the temptation which
there was in himself to forget the command, 'Judge
' not that ye be not judged;' and felt that he should
be doing his readers harm if he suffered them to forget
it. He was trying honestly to correct a tendency
which our age cherishes, and which the most deservedly popular talent may foster. I make that re-

*The Ca-
suist and
the Clergy-
man.*

mark specially for this reason. It may be said that the function I am claiming for the Casuist is rather that of the preacher. Mr Thackeray used to talk of week-day preachers, and to demand a place among them for himself. As a Sunday preacher I am inwardly and painfully convinced that no persons more require the kind of monition which he supplied than those whose regular business obliges them to tell other men of their wrong doings and temptations. Their function cannot therefore, I apprehend, supersede that of the Casuist. Clergymen may learn from him when they are preparing for their after work some of the perils to which it will expose them.

*He cannot
supply pre-
scriptions
for differ-
ent ail-
ments.*

I might easily induce some of this class to engage in the study of Casuistry, if I could hold out a promise that they would obtain from it a set of ready-made prescriptions for various diseases of conscience, or even accurate diagnoses of those diseases. I can offer no such promise. The good which Casuistry can do us is, I conceive, of precisely the opposite kind. It warns us against the quackery of these prescriptions; it shews us why we cannot obtain any diagnosis of other men's symptoms, except by acquaintance with our own. But it is not therefore profitless to those who encounter many troublesome diseases, and are beset with demands for prompt methods of curing them. That habit of looking for other men's faults to which I have alluded is often signally punished. A man who has yielded to it may begin to accuse himself as vehemently as he has ever accused any of his fellows. He may become the most laborious analyst of his own motives; he may turn his thoughts outwards, and may pronounce them all selfish and base. That kind of self-criticism will lead to no result or to very unwhole- some results. It will be pursued for a while, and then the self-tormentor will beg for some anodyne or for some counter-irritant from an external penance; in time he will probably be weary of all such experi- ments, or will practise them only as formalities, and will determine that it is best to drift along wherever the currents of fashion and opinion may carry him. The Casuist would say to him, 'Neither this course, ' my friend, nor that will avail you. Suppose you have ' all these various or contradictory or bad motives that ' you speak of determining your acts, who determines ' the motives? What are you? The mere victim of ' motives? Not at all. Thou usest the word 'I'; the ' conscience in thee says, These motives have no right ' over me; I ought not to be their slave; they did ' not make me. Is there any one who did? If there ' is, perhaps he will help me not to be their slave.' To that issue the Casuist would lead this curious en- quirer into the different forces which are driving him to the right or to the left. He may allow him to entertain himself with Taylor's descriptions of the scrupulous conscience, and the doubtful conscience, and the confident conscience; if he has leisure for such a selection, he may range himself in one class or the other. But after all he must be reminded that the Conscience in him is the man in him; he cannot divide himself from it; he cannot measure or weigh the fetters which bind it, but must above all things seek to be delivered from the fetters.

And the Casuist may help him in some degree towards this emancipation by one suggestion. He is not dealing honestly with himself when he says that there is nothing in him but what is mean and selfish. He may think that he is exhibiting a praiseworthy humility in saying so. It is not humility at all, nor is it the least praiseworthy. On the contrary, he is often secretly crediting himself with being better than he gives himself out to be, often thinking that he may make a little capital out of his self-depreciation. He will not be humble till he owns that there is a good always present with him, a good which he inwardly desires, a good which he ought to pursue. Then he will begin in very deed to feel the evil which is adverse to the good; he will understand that it ought in some way or other to be cast off. There is no work of the Casuist more important than this, or more needful in our days. Numbers presume that wrong is the law of their being, that right is only the exception to wrong. So far as they hold that opinion they never think that anything which they do is really wrong, however they may pretend to think so; they have no standard with which to compare it. Wrong for them is right. The Conscience protests continually against this horrible inversion. The conscience of a right which I cannot let go holds me up when I am most wrong. And the same Conscience says that the wrong into which I have fallen never can be anything but wrong; anything but a contradiction of the law under which I exist.

Systems based upon the Examination of motives.

II. These are practical topics concerning every man, the most ignorant as well as the wisest. It is with such that the Casuist is occupied. He is to be testifying in season and out of season, that the subject which he speaks of is a subject for books only because it is a subject for men and women, and that it would

remain the same if all the books that ever have been
written were burnt to ashes. But for this very reason
he must mingle in the battle of the books; he cannot
overlook the systems which philosophers are constructing, and sending forth into the world. That is the
second topic of which I meant to speak. We have
heard in these Lectures that there are Systems, very
popular in our day, which present men as the slaves of
certain motives, which use the analyses of these motives to determine what men will be, must be, and
therefore ought to be. We have heard again that as
the necessary corollary from these maxims, they do not
allow Right and Wrong to be ultimate distinctions.
Such teachers may have done good in telling us what
motives are likely to influence us in different circumstances; they may have done great good by correcting
certain false impressions about these motives which
have been made the basis of legislation or of individual
actions. Of all this good the Casuist may gladly avail
himself. But he is bound to struggle to the death
against their primary assumption; that simply destroys what he maintains to be the root of a man's
existence. If the System which starts from this denial
were only a System, only for philosophical men, he
might leave it to itself. But it embodies and justifies
all those tendencies which I have just spoken of; those
which take a religious form in some, a form of worldly
Cynicism in others. They conspire with the popular
taste for detecting and exposing other men's motives,
with the more dangerous habit of detecting and exposing our own. Though they seem to treat all motives
as inevitable and therefore as harmless, they do not
involve the least tolerance or tenderness to those who

*The de-
niers of
Right and
Wrong not
specially
tolerant.*

commit what are to be called not sins or evils but only 'acts inconsistent with the interests of the Community.' A man against whom, under that title, Mr Bentham hurls his anathemas, might, except for the honour of the thing, as soon be called a bad man according to the manner of the ancients. The Conscience of the philosopher slips in the obsolete phrases which he ridicules with the indignation which appertains to them. The Casuist who maintains the language of the Conscience to be the true language relieves the Benthamic curses of many troublesome circumlocutions; he may lead the curser to hesitate a little before he deals them out.

Similar remarks apply to that philosophy which would make our acts depend in a great measure upon our emotions and upon certain conditions of our physical organization. Whatever any *psychologist* may tell us about these emotions,—even if he succeeds in analyzing the feeling of a mother to her child mainly into certain feelings connected with the roundness and smoothness of its cheeks—let us receive thankfully, in the last instance with the wonder which some of old deemed the first step to knowledge. Whatever wisdom the teacher has obtained at second hand from great *physiologists* about the brain and the nervous system, let us accept, so far as we can enter into it, with even more fervent gratitude. But the Casuist having done all homage to these lessons, will torment his instructor with these rude and troublesome notes and queries— 'Yes! that is very remarkable indeed. And do these 'emotions then and this nervous system make me? 'Did not you say I had them? You might not perhaps 'think it worth while to give me the additional infor-

The Emotional Nature and the Nervous System.

'mation who *I* am?' No! that is not in the bond. And therefore there is a function for the Casuist, who asserts that it is not only in his bond to consider that question, but that it is precisely the one which he has to consider. In this case also it is not the System which he is at all anxious to confute. But if there is a disposition in our days to make our emotions, our nervous system, or anything else, an excuse for not doing what we ought to do, or being what we are created to be—if that disposition as well as the faculty which I have claimed for our age are both flattered by the assurance that the highest philosophy is occupied in the analysis of these emotions, tracing the processes by which the nervous system becomes our supreme ruler; he must repel the negations of the system that he may maintain his own position.

So it is also with that doctrine about Society of which we have heard so much in these Lectures. Society has been used as a bugbear to frighten us; the Conscience must do what it bids or cease to be. If that is Society there are no terms to be kept with it. The Casuist's business is in the name of the Conscience to mock it and defy it. He must be more fierce in his mockery and defiance than he might have thought it necessary to be in any former age. For this theory is put forth as the last result of modern wisdom. It must spread wherever luxury abounds; wherever the passion for liberty is changed for an easy profession of liberality; wherever Opinion under one pretext or other is confounded with Truth. The worshippers of Society may soon tear each other in pieces when they have to settle how its votes shall be taken, who is to be the returning officer. But all lazy people will agree

The prevalence and popularity of the doctrine that Society is to make the Conscience.

that somehow the strongest or the most numerous ought to decide what they shall do or leave undone. If the Casuist merged his work in that of the Moral Philosopher he could scarcely, I conceive, hold his ground in this conflict. He would then be always harassed with the doubt, ' Am I to find the individual man somewhere outside of Society? Or am I to trace his doings in Society?' The satisfaction of that doubt seems to me this. You cannot contemplate the individual man out of Society: you will scarcely find him among savages if you look diligently for him. But you must vindicate his position in order that you may shew what Society is; of what it consists. If it does not consist of I's, of Persons, the Moralist has no concern with it. If it does consist of I's, of Persons, begin with asserting that character for it, then go on to investigate the relations in which the members of it stand to each other. That means, as I conceive, when translated into the book speech, ' Begin with Casuistry; go ' on to Moral Philosophy. First make it clear what you ' mean by a Person; that you will do when you make ' it clear what you mean by a Conscience; then treat ' these Persons as if they did form real bodies, and tell ' us out of history, not out of your own fancy, what ' these bodies are.'

Hereafter then, in any Course I may deliver upon Ethics, I shall be in the strictest sense occupied with Society; but with Society, as consisting of Persons; with Society, as implying the existence of a Conscience; strong in proportion as that is strong, weak as that is weak. We ought not to overlook any theory about Society which has had considerable influence on any considerable number of men. But no theory ought to occupy us except so far as it is an interpretation of facts. The facts must come first; we should collect them as carefully as we can, in as natural an order as we can; if the theories are adequate to account for them, let us erect any trophies to the authors of them that we think will honour them most.

For this reason I rejoice greatly that I belong to a country which is so little interested in Mental Philosophy merely as such, so much interested in Politics, as England is. I believe the soundest Moral Science will be that which is demanded by the necessities of Practical Politics; that out of such a Science a living and Practical not a technical and artificial Mental Philosophy may in time be developed. The Moralist never maintains his own position so well as when he asserts the highest dignity for the Politician. The separation between them has been an intolerable mischief; there will be Pæans in earth and heaven to celebrate their reconciliation.

CAMBRIDGE: PRINTED BY C. J. CLAY, M.A. AT THE UNIVERSITY PRESS.

September 1871.

A Catalogue of Theological Books, with a Short Account of their Character and Aim,

Published by

MACMILLAN AND CO.

Bedford Street, Covent Garden, London.

Abbott (Rev. E. A.)—BIBLE LESSONS. By the Rev. E. A. ABBOTT, M.A., Head Master of the City of London School. Second Edition. Crown 8vo. 4*s.* 6*d.*

Among the subjects treated in this volume are:—"The Times of Christ," "The Life of Christ," "Christ's Miracles," "Christ's Sacrifice," "Love," "Forgiveness," "Faith," and "Prayer." The book is written in the form of dialogues carried on between a teacher and pupil, and its main object is to make the scholar think for himself. The great bulk of the dialogues represents in the spirit, and often in the words, the religious instruction which the author has been in the habit of giving to the Fifth and Sixth Forms of the City of London School. "Wise, suggestive, and really profound initiation into religious thought."—Guardian. The Bishop of St. David's, in his speech at the Education Conference at Abergwilly, says he thinks "nobody could read them without being the better for them himself, and being also able to see how this difficult duty of imparting a sound religious education may be effected."

1

Ainger (Rev. Alfred).—SERMONS PREACHED IN THE TEMPLE CHURCH. By the Rev. ALFRED AINGER, M.A. of Trinity Hall, Cambridge, Reader at the Temple Church. Extra fcap. 8vo. 6s.

> *This volume contains twenty-four Sermons preached at various times during the last few years in the Temple Church, and are characterised by such qualities as are likely to make them acceptable to cultivated and thoughtful readers. They are free from conventionality in subject and treatment, while they are at the same time, earnest and impressive in manner. The following are a few of the topics treated of:—"Boldness;" "Murder, Ancient and Modern;" "The Atonement;" "The Resurrection;" "The Fear of Death;" "The Forgiveness of Sins, the Remission of a Debt" (2 Sermons); "Anger, Noble and Ignoble;" "Culture and Temptation;" "The Religious Aspect of Wit and Humour;" "The Life of the Ascended Christ." "It is," the* British Quarterly *says, "the fresh unconventional talk of a clear independent thinker, addressed to a congregation of thinkers . . . . Thoughtful men will be greatly charmed by this little volume."*

Barry, Alfred, D.D.—The ATONEMENT of CHRIST. Six Lectures delivered in Hereford Cathedral during Holy Week, 1871. By ALFRED BARRY, D.D., D.C.L., Principal of King's College, London. Fcap. 8vo. 2s. 6d.

> *In writing these Sermons, it has been the object of Dr. Barry to set forth the deep practical importance of the doctrinal truths of the Atonement. "The one truth," we quote from the Preface, "which, beyond all others, I desire that these may suggest, is the inseparable unity which must exist between Christian doctrine, even in its more mysterious forms, and Christian morality or devotion. They are a slight contribution to the plea of that connection of Religion and Theology, which in our own time is so frequently and, as it seems to me, so unreasonably denied." The* Guardian *calls them "striking and eloquent lectures."*

Binney.—SERMONS PREACHED IN THE KING'S WEIGH HOUSE CHAPEL, 1829—69. By THOMAS BINNEY, D.D. New and Cheaper Edition. Extra fcap. 8vo. 4*s.* 6*d.*

> *In the earnestness and vigour which characterize the sermons in this volume the reader will find a clue to the vast influence exerted by Mr. Binney for forty years over a wide circle, particularly young men. In the concluding sermon, preached after the publication of the first edition, he reviews the period of his ministry as a whole, dwelling especially on its religious aspects. "Full of robust intelligence, of reverent but independent thinking on the most profound and holy themes, and of earnest practical purpose."*—London Quarterly Review.

Burgon.—A TREATISE on the PASTORAL OFFICE. Addressed chiefly to Candidates for Holy Orders, or to those who have recently undertaken the cure of souls. By the Rev. JOHN W. BURGON, M.A., Oxford. 8vo. 12*s.*

> *The object of this work is to expound the great ends to be accomplished by the Pastoral office, and to investigate the various means by which these ends may best be gained. The earlier chapters treat of Pastoral study. Full directions are given as to preaching and sermon-writing, pastoral visiting in times both of sickness and health, village education and catechising, and confirmation. Under the heading of "Pastoral Method" two chapters are devoted to shewing how each of the occasional offices of the Church may be most properly conducted, as well as how a clergyman's ordinary public ministrations may be performed with the greatest success. The best methods of parochial management are examined, and an effort is made to exhibit the various elements of the true pastoral spirit. "The spirit in which it approaches and solves practical questions is at once full of common sense and at the same time marked by a deep reverential piety and a largeness of charity which are truly admirable."*—Spectator.

Butler (G.)—Works by the Rev. GEORGE BUTLER, M.A., Principal of Liverpool College :

FAMILY PRAYERS. Crown 8vo. 5*s*.

The prayers in this volume are all based on passages of Scripture—the morning prayers on Select Psalms, those for the evening on portions of the New Testament.

SERMONS PREACHED in CHELTENHAM COLLEGE CHAPEL. Crown 8vo. 7*s*. 6*d*.

These Sermons, twenty-nine in number, were delivered at intervals from the opening of Cheltenham College Chapel in 1858, *to the last Sunday of the year* 1861, *and contain occasional references to the important events which occurred during that period—the Indian mutiny, the French campaign in Italy, the liberation of Sicily and Naples, the establishment of the kingdom of Italy, the American Civil War, and the deaths of many eminent men. They embrace a great variety of subjects of practical interest to all Christians. "These sermons are plain, practical, and well adapted to the auditors. . . . . We cordially recommend the volume as a model of pulpit style, and for individual and family reading."*—Weekly Review.

Butler (Rev. H. M.)—SERMONS PREACHED in the CHAPEL OF HARROW SCHOOL. By H. MONTAGU BUTLER, Head Master. Crown 8vo. 7*s*. 6*d*.

Whilst these Sermons were prepared to meet the wants of a special class, there is a constant reference in them to the great principles which underlie all Christian thought and action. They deal with such subjects as " Temptation," " Courage," " Duty without regard to consequences," " Success," " Devout Impulses," and " The Soul's need of God." " These sermons are adapted for every household. There is nothing more striking than the excellent good sense with which they are imbued."—Spectator.

A SECOND SERIES. Crown 8vo. 7*s*. 6*d*.

"Excellent specimens of what sermons should be,—plain, direct, practical, pervaded by the true spirit of the Gospel, and holding up lofty aims before the minds of the young."—Athenæum.

Butler (Rev. W. Archer).—Works by the Rev. WILLIAM ARCHER BUTLER, M.A., late Professor of Moral Philosophy in the University of Dublin :—

SERMONS, DOCTRINAL AND PRACTICAL. Edited, with a Memoir of the Author's Life, by THOMAS WOODWARD, Dean of Down. With Portrait. Eighth and Cheaper Edition, 8vo. 8*s.*

This volume contains twenty-six Sermons by one of the most earnest, thoughtful, and eloquent preachers of his time. Almost every point of evangelical doctrine and Christian practice is treated of in a clear, rich, and not unfrequently original and even poetical style. The following selections from the titles of the sermons will give a fair idea of the contents of the volume :—" The Mystery of the Holy Incarnation;" " The Daily Self-Denial of Christ;" " The Power of the Resurrection;" "Self-Delusion as to our Real State before God;" " The Faith of Man and the Faithfulness of God;" " The Wedding-Garment;" "Human Affections Raised, not Destroyed by the Gospel;" " The Rest of the People of God;" "The Divinity of our Priest, Prophet, and King;" " Church Education in Ireland" (two Sermons). The Introductory Memoir narrates in considerable detail and with much interest, the events of Butler's brief life; and contains a few specimens of his sweet and tender poetry, and a few extracts from his thoughtful addresses and essays, including a long and eloquent passage on the Province and Duty of the Preacher.

A SECOND SERIES OF SERMONS. Edited by J. A. JEREMIE, D.D., Dean of Lincoln. Sixth and Cheaper Edition. 8vo. 7*s.*

In this volume are contained other twenty-six of the late Mr. Butler's Sermons, embracing a wide range of Christian topics, as will be seen by the following selection from the titles :—" Christ the Source of all Blessings;" " The Hope of Glory and the Charities of Life;" " The Holy Trinity;" " The Sorrow that Exalts and Sanctifies;" " The Growth of the Divine Life;" " The Folly of Moral Cowardice;" "Strength and Mission of the Church;" " The Blessedness

Butler (Rev. W. Archer.)—*continued.*

*of Submission;" "Eternal Punishment."—"These Sermons,"
says the editor, "are marked by the same originality and vigour of
expression, the same richness of imagery and illustration, the same
large views and Catholic spirit, and the same depth and fervour of
devotional feeling, which so remarkably distinguished the preceding
Series, and which rendered it a most valuable accession to our
theological literature."* The North British Review *says, "Few
sermons in our language exhibit the same rare combination of ex-
cellencies; imagery almost as rich as Taylor's; oratory as vigorous
often as South's; judgment as sound as Barrow's; a style as
attractive but more copious, original, and forcible than Atterbury's;
piety as elevated as Howe's, and a fervour as intense at times as
Baxter's. Mr. Butler's are the sermons of a true poet."*

LETTERS ON ROMANISM, in reply to Dr. Newman's
Essay on Development. Edited by the Dean of Down. Second
Edition, revised by Archdeacon HARDWICK. 8vo. 10s. 6d.

*These Letters contain an exhaustive criticism, written in the author's
most vigorous and polished style, of Dr. Newman's famous " Essay
on the Development of Christian Doctrine." An attempt is made
to shew that the theory is opposed to the received doctrine of the
Romish Church; that it is based on purely imaginary grounds,
and necessarily carries with it consequences in the highest degree
dangerous both to Christianity and to general truth. Whilst the
work is mainly polemical in its character, it contains the exposition
of many principles of far more than mere temporary interest.
"A work which ought to be in the Library of every student of
Divinity."*—BP. ST. DAVID'S.

LECTURES ON ANCIENT PHILOSOPHY. *See* PHILO-
SOPHICAL CATALOGUE.

Cambridge Lent Sermons. — SERMONS preached during Lent, 1864, in Great St. Mary's Church, Cambridge. By the BISHOP OF OXFORD, Revs. H. P. LIDDON, T. L. CLAUGHTON, J. R. WOODFORD, Dr. GOULBURN, J. W. BURGON, T. T. CARTER, Dr. PUSEY, Dean HOOK, W. J. BUTLER, Dean GOOD-WIN. Crown 8vo. 7s. 6d.

The names of the preachers of these Sermons are a guarantee that they are worth reading. They were preached on the Wednesdays and Fridays during Lent 1864, and treat of the following among other subjects:—"God in His Perfections the Measure of the Sinfulness of Sin in the Creature," by the Bishop of Oxford; "Adam hiding himself from the Presence of the Lord," by the Rev. H. P. Liddon; "God the Hope and Joy of the Penitent," by the Rev. T. T. Carter; "David in his Sin and his Penitence," by the Rev. Dr. Pusey: "God the Consolation of the Afflicted," by the Very Rev. Dean Hook; "God the Reward of the Faithful," by the Rev. W. J. Butler.

Campbell. — Works by JOHN M'LEOD CAMPBELL :—

THE NATURE OF THE ATONEMENT AND ITS RELATION TO REMISSION OF SINS AND ETERNAL LIFE. Third Edition, with an Introduction and Notes. 8vo. 10s. 6d.

Three chapters of this work are devoted to the teaching of Luther on the subject of the Atonement, and to Calvinism, as taught by Dr. Owen and President Edwards, and as recently modified. The remainder is occupied with the different aspects of the Atonement as conceived by the author himself, the object being partly to meet the objections of honest inquirers, but mainly so to reveal the subject in its own light as to render self-evident its adaptation to the spiritual wants of man. The book has been found richly suggestive by many of the profoundest minds in the Church. Professor Rolleston, in quoting from this book in his address to the Biological Section of the British Association (Liverpool, September, 1870), speaks of it as "the great work of one of the first of living theologians." "Among the first theological treatises of this generation." — Guardian.

Campbell (J. M'Leod.)—*continued.*

CHRIST THE BREAD OF LIFE. An Attempt to give a profitable direction to the present occupation of Thought with Romanism. Second Edition, greatly enlarged. Crown 8vo. 4*s.* 6*d.*

In this volume the Doctrines of the Infallibility of the Church and Transubstantiation are regarded as addressed to real inward needs of humanity, and an effort is made to disengage them from the truths whose place they usurp, and to exhibit these truths as adequate to meet human cravings. The aim is, first, to offer help to those who feel the attractions to Romanism too strong to be overcome by direct arguments addressed to sense and reason; and, second, to quicken interest in the Truth itself. "Deserves the most attentive study by all who interest themselves in the predominant religious controversy of the day."—Spectator.

Cheyne.—Works by T. K. CHEYNE, M.A., Fellow of Balliol College, Oxford :—

THE BOOK OF ISAIAH CHRONOLOGICALLY AR-RANGED. An Amended Version, with Historical and Critical Introductions and Explanatory Notes. Crown 8vo. 7*s.* 6*d.*

The object of this edition is to restore the probable meaning of Isaiah, so far as can be expressed in appropriate English. The basis of the version is the revised translation of 1611, *but alterations have been introduced wherever the true sense of the prophecies appeared to require it. The* Westminster Review *speaks of it as "a piece of scholarly work, very carefully and considerately done." The* Academy *calls it "a successful attempt to extend a right understanding of this important Old Testament writing."*

NOTES AND CRITICISMS on the HEBREW TEXT OF ISAIAH. Crown 8vo. 2*s.* 6*d.*

This work is offered as a slight contribution to a more scientific study of the Old Testament Scriptures. The author aims at completeness, independence, and originality, and constantly endeavours to keep philology distinct from exegesis, to explain the form without pro-

nouncing on the matter. He has endeavoured to sift the materials already collected before presenting his own conclusions. Saad Yah's Arabic Version in the Bodleian has been referred to, while Walton and Buxtorf have been carefully consulted. The philological works of German critics, especially Ewald and Delitsch, have been anxiously and repeatedly studied. The student will find here much valuable aid to the critical study of the Book of Isaiah. The Academy *calls the work "a valuable contribution to the more scientific study of the Old Testament."*

Choice Notes on the Four Gospels, drawn from

Old and New Sources. Crown 8vo. 4s. 6d. each Vol. (St. Matthew and St. Mark in one Vol. price 9s.).

These Notes are selected from the Rev. Prebendary Ford's Illustrations of the Four Gospels, the choice being chiefly confined to those of a more simple and practical character. The plan followed is to go over the Gospels verse by verse, and introduce the remarks, mostly meditative and practical, of one or more noted divines, commentators, and other religious writers, on the verses selected for illustration. The names of the writers from whom the remarks are taken are invariably appended to the extracts, and amongst others to be met with, are the following:—J. Ford, Bonaventura, William Law, Pascal, Austin, Dr. Donne, Bonnell, Flavel, Bishop Hall, Dr. John Scott, Thomas Scott, R. Cecil, St. Ambrose, Bengel, Bishop Reynolds, J. H. Newman, George Herbert, Bishop Jewel, Jeremy Taylor, Cardinal Bellarmine, Quarles, St. Augustine, Archbishop Trench, Archbishop Leighton, Lord Bacon, Dr. Pusey, St. Chrysostom, Dr. Arnold, Thomas Fuller. Thus, it will be seen, the selection is made in a catholic spirit, and the reader will find it a safe and useful companion in his meditations on 'the word.'

Church.—SERMONS PREACHED BEFORE the UNI-

VERSITY OF OXFORD. By R. W. Church, M.A., Dean of St. Paul's. Second Edition. Crown 8vo. 4s. 6d.

Sermons on the relations between Christianity and the ideas and facts of modern civilized society. The subjects of the various discourses are:—" The Gifts of Civilization," " Christ's Words and Christian Society," " Christ's Example," and " Civilization and Religion." " Thoughtful and masterly . . . We regard these sermons as a landmark in religious thought. They help us to understand the latent strength of a Christianity that is assailed on all sides."— Spectator.

Clay.—THE POWER OF THE KEYS. Sermons preached in Coventry. By the Rev. W. L. CLAY, M.A. Fcap. 8vo. 3s. 6d.

In this work an attempt is made to shew in what sense, and to what extent, the power of the Keys can be exercised by the layman, the Church, and the priest respectively. The Church Review *says the sermons are " in many respects of unusual merit."*

Clergyman's Self-Examination concerning the APOSTLES' CREED. Extra fcap. 8vo. 1s. 6d.

The Author thus explains the object of this publication:—" These Confessions have been written by a clergyman for his own use. They speak of his own unbelief. Possibly they may help some of his brethren, who wish to judge themselves that they may not be ashamed before the Judge of all the earth." He takes each clause of the Creed and examines it candidly and in the light of common sense, in order to obtain its real meaning; searching at the same time his own heart to discover to what extent he really believes the statements so frequently uttered by him. Not only is it calculated to afford material aid to a proper understanding of the Creed, but from the reverential manner in which the Examination is conducted, will also be found extremely useful as a manual of devotion.

Collects of the Church of England. With a beautifully Coloured Floral Design to each Collect, and Illuminated Cover. Crown 8vo. 12s. Also kept in various styles of morocco.

In this richly embellished edition of the Church Collects, the paper is thick and handsome, and the type large and beautiful, each Collect, with a few exceptions, being printed on a separate page. The distinctive characteristic of this edition is the floral design which ac-

companies each Collect, and which is generally emblematical of the character of the day or saint to which it is assigned; the flowers which have been selected are such as are likely to be in bloom on the day to which the Collect belongs. Each flower is richly but tastefully and naturally printed in colours, and from the variety of plants selected and the faithfulness of the illustrations to nature, the volume should form an instructive and interesting companion to all devout Christians, who are likely to find their devotions assisted and guided by having thus brought before them the flowers in their seasons, God's beautiful and never-failing gifts to men. The Preface explains the allusion in the case of all those illustrations which are intended to be emblematical of the days to which they belong, and the table of contents forms a complete botanical index, giving both the popular and scientific name of each plant. There are at least one hundred separate plants figured. " This is beyond question," the Art Journal *says, " the most beautiful book of the season." "Carefully, indeed livingly drawn and daintily coloured," says the* Pall Mall Gazette. *The* Guardian *thinks it " a successful attempt to associate in a natural and unforced manner the flowers of our fields and gardens with the course of the Christian year."*

Cotton.—Works by the late GEORGE EDWARD LYNCH COTTON, D.D., Bishop of Calcutta :—

SERMONS PREACHED TO ENGLISH CONGREGA-TIONS IN INDIA. Crown 8vo. 7s. 6d.

> *These Sermons are selected from those which were preached between the years* 1863 *and* 1866 *to English congregations under the varied circumstances of place and season which an Indian Bishop encounters. " The sermons are models of what sermons should be, not only on account of their practical teachings, but also with regard to the singular felicity with which they are adapted to times, places, and circumstances."*—Spectator.

EXPOSITORY SERMONS ON THE EPISTLES FOR THE SUNDAYS OF THE CHRISTIAN YEAR. Two Vols. Crown 8vo. 15s.

> *These two volumes contain in all fifty-seven Sermons, being one for*

every Sunday of the year, and for Christmas, Good Friday, and a few other Church holidays. They were all preached at various stations throughout India, and from the nature of the circumstances which called them forth, the varied subjects of which they treat are dealt with in such a manner as is likely to prove acceptable to Christians in general. Each sermon, according to the Preface, is intended to furnish some account of the context and general scope of the epistle for the day, with a careful paraphrase of it, and with an explanation of any important difficulties occurring in it; and in conclusion, to draw out the main truths or precepts of the epistle. The Preface gives an account of the origin of the Book, and contains some sensible remarks on "Complaints against Modern Sermons," "Expository Preaching," "Plan of the Sermon," and other topics.

Cure.—THE SEVEN WORDS OF CHRIST ON THE CROSS. Sermons preached at St. George's, Bloomsbury. By the Rev. E. CAPEL CURE, M.A. Fcap. 8vo. 3s. 6d.

These seven Sermons were preached at St. George's, Bloomsbury, during the season of Lent, each having for its text one of the seven last sayings of Christ while He hung on the Cross, as they are recorded in the following places:—(1) Luke xxiii. 34; (2) Luke xxiii. 43; (3) John xix. 26; (4) Matthew xxvii. 46; (5) John xix. 28; (6) John xix. 30; (7) Luke xxiii. 46. Of these Sermons the John Bull says, "They are earnest and practical;" the Nonconformist, "The Sermons are beautiful, tender, and instructive;" and the Spectator calls them "A set of really good Sermons."

Davies.—Works by the Rev. J. LLEWELYN DAVIES, M.A., Rector of Christ Church, St. Marylebone, etc. :—

THE WORK OF CHRIST ; or, the World Reconciled to God. With a Preface on the Atonement Controversy. Fcap. 8vo. 6s.

The reader will here find, amongst others, sermons on " The forgiveness of sins," " Christ dying for men," " Sacrifice," " The Example of Christ," " The Baptism of Christ," " The Temptation of Christ," "Love, Divine and Human," " Creation by the Word,"

Davies (Rev. J. Llewelyn)—*continued.*

"Holy Seasons," and " The Coming of the Son of Man." The Preface is devoted to shewing that certain popular theories of the Atonement are opposed to the moral sense of mankind, and are not imposed on Christians by statements either in the Old or New Testaments.

SERMONS on the MANIFESTATION OF THE SON OF GOD. With a Preface addressed to Laymen on the present Position of the Clergy of the Church of England ; and an Appendix on the Testimony of Scripture and the Church as to the possibility of Pardon in the Future State. Fcap. 8vo. 6s. 6d.

The Preface to this work is mainly occupied with the distinction between the essential and non-essential elements of the Christian faith, proving that the central religious controversy of the day relates, not, as many suppose, to such questions as the Inspiration of Scripture, but to the profounder question, whether the Son of God actually has been manifested in the person of Jesus of Nazareth. The grounds on which the Christian bases his faith are also examined. In the Appendix the testimony of the Bible and the Anglican formularies as to the possibility of pardon in the future state is investigated. The sermons, of which the body of the work is composed, treat of the great principles revealed in the words and acts of Jesus. " This volume, both in its substance, prefix, and suffix, represents the noblest type of theology now preached in the English Church."—Spectator.

BAPTISM, CONFIRMATION, AND THE LORD'S SUPPER, as Interpreted by their Outward Signs. Three Expository Addresses for Parochial use. Fcap. 8vo., limp cloth. 1s. 6d.

The method adapted in these addresses is to set forth the natural and historical meaning of the signs of the two Sacraments and of Confirmation, and thus to arrive at the spiritual realities which they symbolize. The work touches on all the principal elements of a Christian man's faith.

Davies (Rev. J. Llewelyn)—*continued.*

THE EPISTLES of ST. PAUL TO THE EPHESIANS,
THE COLOSSIANS, and PHILEMON. With Introductions
and Notes, and an Essay on the Traces of Foreign Elements in
the Theology of these Epistles. 8vo. 7s. 6d.

> *The Author believes the Epistles to the Ephesians and Colossians to*
> *be specially adapted to the wants of the present age. The chief aim,*
> *therefore, of the translations and notes in the present volume is*
> *simply to bring out as accurately as possible the apostle's meaning.*
> *The text adopted is that of Tischendorf. The volume opens with*
> *a General Introduction, treating mainly of the time and circum-*
> *stances in which Paul is believed to have written these Epistles.*
> *To each Epistle there is a special introduction, dealing with the*
> *questions of genuineness and authenticity, and presenting in their*
> *order the leading ideas of the writer. The Essay " On the Traces*
> *of Foreign elements in the Doctrine of these Epistles" discusses the*
> *question how far the ideas in the Epistles which resemble gnostical*
> *systems are to be found in books and traditions to which St. Paul*
> *and his contemporaries had access—that is, in the Apocrypha, in*
> *Philo, and in the Zend-Avesta. "A valuable contribution to the*
> *literature of the Pauline Epistles."*—Freeman.

MORALITY ACCORDING TO THE SACRAMENT
OF THE LORD'S SUPPER. Crown 8vo. 3s. 6d.

> *These discourses were preached before the University of Cambridge.*
> *They form a continuous exposition, and are directed mainly against*
> *the two-fold danger which at present threatens the Church—the*
> *tendency, on the one hand, to regard Morality as independent of*
> *Religion, and, on the other, to ignore the fact that Religion finds*
> *its proper sphere and criterion in the moral life.*

THE GOSPEL and MODERN LIFE. Sermons on some
of the Difficulties of the Present Day, with a Preface on a Recent
Phase of Deism. Extra fcap. 8vo. 6s.

> *The " recent phase of Deism" examined in the preface to this volume*
> *is that professed by the "Pall Mall Gazette"—that in the sphere of*

Davies (Rev. J. Llewelyn)—*continued.*

*Religion there are one or two "probable suppositions," but nothing more. The writer starts with an assumption that mankind are under a Divine discipline, and in the light of this conviction passes under review the leading religious problems which perplex thoughtful minds of the present day. Amongst other subjects examined are—"Christ and Modern Knowledge," "Humanity and the Trinity," "Nature," "Religion," "Conscience," "Human Corruption," and "Human Holiness." "There is probably no writer in the Church fairer or more thoroughly worth listening to than Mr. Llewellyn Davies, and this book will do more than sustain his already high reputation."—*Globe.*

De Teissier.—Works by G. F. DE TEISSIER, B.D.:—

VILLAGE SERMONS, FIRST SERIES. Crown 8vo. 9s.

This volume contains fifty-four short Sermons, preached by the author in the ordinary course of his duty as a village clergyman, and embracing many subjects of practical importance to all Christians. The Guardian says they are "a little too scholarlike in style for a country village, but sound and practical." The following are a few of the titles of the Sermons :—"Death of the Prince Consort;" "Particular Providence;" "The Suffering Christ;" "Charity the Crown of Christianity;" "On Self-Deceit;" "On Hypocrisy;" "Christ Risen;" "The Comfort of Religion;" "Good Neighbourhood;" "The Return of Spring;" "A Harvest Sermon;" "Heart-Religion."

VILLAGE SERMONS, SECOND SERIES. Crown 8vo. 8s. 6d.

"This second volume of Parochial Sermons, written and delivered after the same manner as the first, is given to the public in the humble hope that it may afford many seasonable thoughts for such as are Mourners in Zion." There are in all fifty-two Sermons embracing a wide variety of subjects connected with Christian faith and practice.

De Teissier (G. F.)—*continued.*

THE HOUSE OF PRAYER; or, a Practical Exposition of the Order for Morning and Evening Prayer in the Church of England. 18mo. extra cloth. 4*s.* 6*d.*

> "*There is in these addresses to the Christian reader,*" *says the Introduction,* "*which were once delivered in the form of sermons, an attempt to set forth the* devotional *spirit of our Church in her daily forms of Morning and Evening Prayer, by shewing how all the parts of them may have a just bearing upon Christian practice, and so may have a deep influence upon the conduct of all our honest worshippers, under every possible relation and circumstance of life.*" *The* Literary Churchman *says of this book:—*"*For a certain devout tenderness of feeling and religious earnestness of purpose, this little book of Mr. De Teissier's is really noteworthy; and it is a book which grows upon you very much when you read it.*"

Ecce Homo. A SURVEY OF THE LIFE AND WORK OF JESUS CHRIST. 23rd Thousand. Crown 8vo. 6*s.*

> *It is needless to say anything in recommendation of a book so widely known, and whose striking merit has been recognised by men and periodicals of all varieties of opinion. The following are a few selections from the very favourable notices with which the press has received it.* "*A very original and remarkable book, full of striking thought and delicate perception; a book which has realised with wonderful vigour and freshness the historical magnitude of Christ's work, and which here and there gives us readings of the finest kind of the probable motive of His individual words and actions.*"— Spectator. " *The magnificent argument which 'Ecce Homo'* . . . *has brought before us* . . . *The author of 'Ecce Homo' sees Him as the introducer of an altogether novel force into the world of human motive. He bates not a jot of Christ's pretensions* . . . *Miracles he insists upon as* . . . . *an integral part of the history.* . . . *With a generous-minded sceptic* . . . *this book may lead him on to give earnest and persistent attention to Christianity.* . . . *The best and most established believer will find it adding some fresh buttresses to his faith. Finally* . . . *it traces the working of the great principles of*

Christian charity through all the ramifications of character and action."—Literary Churchman. "*The Divine nature is never left out of sight for a moment.*"—Reader. "*This is a dangerous book to review. The critic of it, if he is prudent, will feel that it is, more than most books, a touchstone of his own capacity, and that, in giving his judgment upon it, he cannot help giving his own measure, and betraying what he is himself worth. If we have not misunderstood him, we have before us a writer who has a right to claim deference from those who think deepest and know most.*"— Guardian.

Farrar.—Works by the Rev. F. W. FARRAR, M.A., F.R.S., Head Master of Marlborough College, and Hon. Chaplain to the Queen :—

THE FALL OF MAN, AND OTHER SERMONS. Second and Cheaper Edition. Extra fcap. 8vo. 4s. 6d.

This volume contains twenty Sermons, three of which—"The Fall of Man," "The Law of Death, and the Means of Deliverance," and "The Path of Christ,"—were delivered before the University of Cambridge, the others at various places and for various purposes. Among the latter are sermons on "The Resurrection from the Dead," "Ascension with Christ," "Righteousness the Strength of Nations," "A Sermon to Volunteers," "The Animal and the Spiritual," "The Blessed Trinity," etc. No attempt is made in these sermons to develope a system of doctrine. In each discourse some one aspect of truth is taken up, the chief object being to point out its bearings on practical religious life. The Nonconformist *says of these Sermons,—"There is beauty in every page, almost in every line of them. Mr. Farrar's Sermons are almost perfect specimens of one type of Sermons, which we may concisely call beautiful. The style of expression is beautiful—there is beauty in the thoughts, the illustrations, the allusions—they are expressive of genuinely beautiful perceptions and feelings." The* British Quarterly *says,—"Ability, eloquence, scholarship, and practical usefulness, are in these Sermons combined in a very unusual degree."*

2

Farrar (F. W.)—*continued.*

THE WITNESS OF HISTORY TO CHRIST. Being the Hulsean Lectures for 1870. Crown 8vo. 5*s.*

In these Lectures, Mr. Farrar endeavours to grapple with the most recent manifestations of infidelity, and endeavours to prove the divinity of Christ and the supernatural origin of Christianity on rational grounds, and by an appeal to the origin and progress of the Christian Religion itself. In the copious notes which illustrate the text, many references are given to more elaborate works by authors of all shades of opinion, which will be found of great use to the enquiring student. The following are the subjects of the Five Lectures:—I. " The Antecedent Credibility of the Miraculous." II. "The Adequacy of the Gospel Records." III. "The Victories of Christianity." IV. "Christianity and the Individual." V. "Christianity and the Race." The subjects of the four Appendices are:—A. " The Diversity of Christian Evidences." B. "Confucius." C. "Buddha." D. "Comte." "Here," the Standard *says, "we have eloquence combined with abundant information on all points of importance, both as regards theology and classical accuracy. This renders the book one of lasting value."*

SEEKERS AFTER GOD. The Lives of Seneca, Epictetus, and Marcus Aurelius. *See* SUNDAY LIBRARY at end of Catalogue.

Fellowship : LETTERS ADDRESSED TO MY SISTER MOURNERS. Fcap. 8vo. cloth gilt. 3*s.* 6*d.*

The Seven Letters contained in this little volume are written by one who has herself been shrouded in the darkest shadow of affliction consequent on being bereaved of one in whom her whole life was built up. In these Letters she tells her own sorrowful tale in unaffected, tender, touching words, which cannot but appeal to all who are placed in a similar comfortless position. She does not attempt to preach or to aggravate the sorrow and sense of loss of mourners by administering advice which they cannot take, or quoting texts and sentiments calculated only to irritate and insult. She speaks of her loss and consequent grief in such a way as only a genuine mourner can; of the well-meant but aggravating comfort and useless advice admininistered her by her many comforters, and shews her fellow-mourners by what means, in course of soothing time, she got consolation and arrived at calmness and resignation. "A beautiful little volume, written with genuine feeling, good taste, and a right appreciation of the teaching of Scripture relative to sorrow and suffering."—Nonconformist. *"A very touching, and at the same time a very sensible book. It breathes throughout the truest Christian spirit."*—Contemporary Review. *"Tender and unobtrusive, and the author thoroughly realises the sorrow of those she addresses; it may soothe mourning readers, and can by no means aggravate or jar upon their feelings."*—Athenæum.

Forbes.—THE VOICE OF GOD IN THE PSALMS. By GRANVILLE FORBES, Rector of Broughton. Cr. 8vo. 6s. 6d.

This volume contains a connected series of twenty Sermons, divided into three parts, the two first parts being Introductory. Part I. treats of the "Ground of Faith," and consists of four Sermons on "Faith in God," "God's Voice within us," "Faith in God the Ground of Faith in the Bible," and "God's Voice in the Bible." Part II. treats of "The Voice of God in the Law and the Prophets," on which there are four Sermons; and Part III., occupying the greater part of the volume, deals with "The Voice of God in the Psalms," and consists of twelve Sermons. The last Sermon is on "The Voice of God in History." The Literary Churchman *says these Sermons are "characterized throughout by a strong realisation of the Providence and Fatherhood of God, and by their vivid apprehension of the Voice of God within man as answering to and accepting the Revelation of God to Man."*

Gifford.—THE GLORY OF GOD IN MAN. By E. H. GIFFORD, D.D. Fcap. 8vo., cloth. 3s. 6d.

This is a connected sequence of four Sermons which treat of "The Unrighteousness of Man," "The Righteousness of God," "Life in Christ," and "The Love of the Spirit." Notes are appended in which the sentiments of various authors on the statements made are quoted or referred to. "The sermons are short, thoughtful, and earnest discussions of the weighty matter involved in the subjects of them."—Journal of Sacred Literature.

Golden Treasury Psalter.—THE STUDENT'S EDITION. Being an Edition with briefer Notes of "The Psalms Chronologically Arranged by Four Friends." 18mo. 3*s.* 6*d.*

In making this abridgment of "The Psalms Chronologically Arranged," the Editors have endeavoured to meet the requirements of readers of a different class from those for whom the larger edition was intended. This volume will be found to meet the requirements of those who wish for a smaller edition of the larger work, at a lower price for family use, and for the use of younger pupils in Public Schools. In amending the text, while the results of critical research have been incorporated, the least possible alteration has been made in words familiar to every Englishmen. The short notes which are appended to the volume will, it is hoped, suffice to make the meaning intelligible throughout. The aim of this edition is simply to put the reader as far as possible in possession of the plain meaning of the writer. As in the larger book, the Psalms have been arranged chronologically according to the principle adopted by Ewald. "It is a gem," the Nonconformist *says.*

Hardwick.—Works by the Ven. ARCHDEACON HARDWICK :

CHRIST AND OTHER MASTERS. A Historical Inquiry into some of the Chief Parallelisms and Contrasts between Christianity and the Religious Systems of the Ancient World. New Edition, revised, and a Prefatory Memoir by the Rev. FRANCIS PROCTER, M.A . Two vols. crown 8vo. 15*s.*

After several introductory chapters dealing with the religious tendencies of the present age, the unity of the human race, and the characteristics of Religion under the Old Testament, the Author proceeds to consider the, Religions of India, China, America, Oceanica, Egypt, and Medo-Persia. The history and characteristics of these Religions are examined, and an effort is made to bring out the points of difference and affinity between them and Christianity. The object is to establish the perfect adaptation of the latter faith to human nature in all its phases and at all times. "The plan of the work is boldly and almost nobly conceived. . . We commend the work to the perusal of all those who take interest in the study of ancient mythology, without losing their reverence for the supreme authority of the oracles of the living God."—Christian Observer.

A HISTORY OF THE CHRISTIAN CHURCH. *See*
HISTORICAL and EDUCATIONAL CATALOGUES.

Hervey.—THE GENEALOGIES OF OUR LORD AND
SAVIOUR JESUS CHRIST, as contained in the Gospels of
St. Matthew and St. Luke, reconciled with each other, and shown
to be in harmony with the true Chronology of the Times. By Lord
ARTHUR HERVEY, Bishop of Bath and Wells. 8vo. 10s. 6d.

> *The difficulties and importance of the subject are first stated, the three
> main points of inquiry being clearly brought out. The Author
> then proceeds to shew that the genealogies of St. Matthew's and
> St. Luke's Gospels are both genealogies of Joseph, and examines
> the principle on which they are framed. In the following chapters
> the remaining aspects of the subject are exhaustively investigated.*

Hymni Ecclesiæ.—Fcap. 8vo. 7s. 6d.

> *A selection of Latin Hymns of the Mediæval Church, containing
> selections from the Paris Breviary, and the Breviaries of Rome,
> Salisbury, and York. The selection is confined to such holy days
> and seasons as are recognised by the Church of England, and to
> special events or things recorded in Scripture. This collection was
> edited by Dr. Newman while he lived at Oxford.*

Kempis, Thos. A. — DE IMITATIONE CHRISTI.
LIBRI IV. Borders in the Ancient Style, after Holbein, Durer,
and other Old Masters, containing Dances of Death, Acts of
Mercy, Emblems, and a variety of curious ornamentations. In
white cloth, extra gilt. 7s. 6d.

> *The original Latin text has been here faithfully reproduced. The*
> Spectator *says of this edition, it "has many solid merits, and is
> perfect in its way." While the* Athenæum *says, "The whole word
> is admirable; some of the figure compositions have extraordinary
> merit."*

Kingsley.—Works by the Rev. CHARLES KINGSLEY, M.A., Rector of Eversley, and Canon of Chester. (For other Works by the same author, *see* HISTORICAL and BELLES LETTRES CATALOGUES).

The high merits of Mr. Kingsley's Sermons are acknowledged. They are meant and calculated to influence the every-day "walk and conversation" of those to whom they are addressed, free from all abstruse and useless discussions. Whether preached to the rustic audience of a village Church or to the princely congregation of the Chapel Royal, these Sermons are invariably characterized by intense earnestness and manly magnanimity, combined with genuine charity and winning tenderness; the style is always clear, simple, and unaffectedly natural, abounding in beautiful illustration, the fruit of a rich poetic fancy and a cultivated taste. No matter what a man's creed, or social position, or education may be, if he be still capable of pure, simple, natural joy, the reading of these Sermons must gladden his heart and stimulate him to strive at least to lead a noble, manly, Christ-like life.

THE WATER OF LIFE, AND OTHER SERMONS. Fcap. 8vo. 6*s.*

This volume contains twenty-one Sermons preached at various places —Westminster Abbey, Chapel Royal, before the Queen at Windsor, etc. The following are a few of the titles:—"The Water of Life;" "The Wages of Sin;" "The Battle of Life;" "Ruth;" "Friendship, or David and Jonathan;" "Progress;" "Faith;" "The Meteor Shower" (1866); "Cholera" (1866); "The God of Nature."

VILLAGE SERMONS. Seventh Edition. Fcap. 8vo. 2*s.* 6*d.*

The following are a few of the titles of these Sermons:—"God's World;" "Religion not Godliness;" "Self-Destruction;" "Hell on Earth;" "Noah's Justice;" "Our Father in Heaven;" "The Transfiguration;" "The Crucifixion;" "The Resurrection;" "Improvement;" "On Books;" "The Courage of the Saviour."

Kingsley (Rev. C.)—*continued.*

THE GOSPEL OF THE PENTATEUCH. Second Edition. Fcap. 8vo. 4*s.* 6*d.*

> *This volume consists of eighteen Sermons on passages taken from the Pentateuch. They are dedicated to Dean Stanley out of gratitude for his* Lectures on the Jewish Church, *under the influence and in the spirit of which they were written. "With your book in my hand," Mr. Kingsley says in his Preface, "I have tried to write a few plain Sermons, telling plain people what they will find in the Pentateuch. I have told them that they will find in the Bible, and in no other ancient book, that living working God, whom their reason and conscience demand; and that they will find that He is none other than Jesus Christ our Lord."*

GOOD NEWS OF GOD. Fourth Edition. Fcap. 8vo. 4*s.* 6*d.*

> *This volume contains thirty-nine short Sermons, preached in the ordinary course of the author's parochial ministrations. A few of the titles are—" The Beatific Vision;" " The Life of God;" "The Song of the Three Children;" "Worship;" "De Profundis;" " The Race of Life;" "Heroes and Heroines;" "Music;" "Christ's Boyhood;" "Human Nature;" " True Prudence;" " The Temper of Christ;" "Our Deserts;" " The Loftiness of God."*

SERMONS FOR THE TIMES. Third Edition. Fcap. 8vo. 3*s.* 6*d.*

> *Here are twenty-two Sermons, all bearing more or less on the every-day life of the present day, including such subjects as these:— "Fathers and Children;" "A Good Conscience;" "Names;" "Sponsorship;" "Duty and Superstition;" "England's Strength;" " The Lord's Prayer;" "Shame;" "Forgiveness;" " The True Gentleman;" "Public Spirit."*

Kingsley (Rev. C.)—*continued.*

TOWN AND COUNTRY SERMONS. Second Edition. Extra fcap. 8vo. 6*s.*

> *Some of these Sermons were preached before the Queen, and some in the performance of the writer's ordinary parochial duty. There are thirty-nine in all, under such titles as the following :—"How to keep Passion-Week;" "A Soldier's Training;" "Turning-points;" "Work;" "The Rock of Ages;" "The Loftiness of Humility;" "The Central Sun;" "Εν Τουτω Νικα ;" "The Eternal Manhood;" "Hypocrisy;" "The Wrath of Love." Of these Sermons the* Nonconformist *says, "They are warm with the fervour of the preacher's own heart, and strong from the force of his own convictions. There is nowhere an attempt at display, and the clearness and simplicity of the style make them suitable for the youngest or most unintelligent of his hearers."*

SERMONS on NATIONAL SUBJECTS. First Series. Second Edition. Fcap. 8vo. 5*s.* Second Series. Second Edition. Fcap. 8vo. 5*s.*

> *The following extract from the Preface to the 2nd Series will explain the preacher's aim in these Sermons :—"I have tried......to proclaim the Lord Jesus Christ, as the Scriptures, both in their strictest letter and in their general method, from Genesis to Revelation, seem to me to proclaim Him; not merely as the Saviour of a few elect souls, but as the light and life of every human being who enters into the world; as the source of all reason, strength, and virtue in heathen or in Christian; as the King and Ruler of the whole universe, and of every nation, family, and man on earth; as the Redeemer of the whole earth and the whole human race...... His death, as a full, perfect, and sufficient sacrifice, oblation, and satisfaction for the sins of the whole world, by which God is reconciled to the whole human race. Therefore I have called these National Sermons." The 1st Series contains twenty-three, and the 2nd Series twenty-five Sermons.*

Kingsley (Rev. C.)—*continued.*

DISCIPLINE, AND OTHER SERMONS. Fcap. 8vo. 6s.

Herein are twenty-four Sermons preached on various occasions, some of them of a public nature—at the Volunteer Camp, Wimbledon, before the Prince of Wales at Sandringham, at Wellington College, etc. A few of the titles are—"Discipline" (to Volunteers); "Prayer and Science;" "False Civilization;" "The End of Religion;" "The Humanity of God;" "God's World;" "Self-Help;" "Toleration;" "The Likeness of God." Of this volume the Nonconformist says,—"Eminently practical and appropriate ...... Earnest stirring words." The Guardian says,—"Of this we can speak with much admiration. There is much thought, tenderness, and devoutness of spirit in these Sermons, and some of them are models both in matter and expression."

DAVID. Four Sermons: David's Weakness—David's Strength—David's Anger—David's Deserts. Fcap. 8vo. 2s. 6d.

As the title declares, these four Sermons were preached before the University of Cambridge, and are specially addressed to young men. Their titles are,—"David's Weakness;" "David's Strength;" "David's Anger;" "David's Deserts." The Freeman says of them,—"Every paragraph glows with manly energy, delivers straightforward practical truths, in a vigorous, sometimes even passionate way, and exhibits an intense sympathy with everything honest, pure, and noble."

Lightfoot.—Works by J. B. Lightfoot, D.D., Hulsean Professor of Divinity in the University of Cambridge.

ST. PAUL'S EPISTLE TO THE GALATIANS. A Revised Text, with Introduction, Notes, and Dissertations. Third Edition, revised. 8vo. cloth. 12s.

The subjects treated in the Introduction are—the Galatian people, the Churches of Galatia, the date and genuineness of the Epistle, and its character and contents. The dissertations discuss the question whether the Galatians were Celts or Tartars, and the whole subject

Lightfoot (Dr. J. B.)—*continued.*

*of " The Brethren of the Lord," and " St. Paul and the Three."
While the Author's object has been to make this commentary
generally complete, he has paid special attention to everything re-
lating to St. Paul's personal history and his intercourse with the
Apostles and Church of the Circumcision, as it is this feature in
the Epistle to the Galatians which has given it an overwhelming
interest in recent theological controversy.* The Journal of Sacred
Literature *characterizes the work as "interesting and scholarlike;"*
the Reader *calls it "an emphatic gain to English scholarship;"*
while the Spectator *says "there is no commentator at once of
sounder judgment and more liberal than Dr. Lightfoot."*

ST. PAUL'S EPISTLE TO THE PHILIPPIANS. A
Revised Text, with Introduction, Notes, and Dissertations. Second
Edition. 8vo. 12s.

*The plan of this volume is the same as that on " The Epistle to the
Galatians." The Introduction deals with the following subjects :
—" St. Paul in Rome," " Order of the Epistles of the Captivity,"
" The Church of Philippi," "Character and Contents of the Epistle,"
and its genuineness. The Dissertations are on " The Christian
Ministry," " St. Paul and Seneca," and " The Letters of Paul
and Seneca." "No commentary in the English language can be
compared with it in regard to fulness of information, exact
scholarship, and laboured attempts to settle everything about the
epistle on a solid foundation."*—Athenæum. *" Its author blends
large and varied learning with a style as bright and easy, as telling
and artistic, as that of our most accomplished essayists."*—Nonconformist.

ST. CLEMENT OF ROME, THE TWO EPISTLES TO
THE CORINTHIANS. A Revised Text, with Introduction
and Notes. 8vo. 8s. 6d.

*This volume is the first part of a complete edition of the Apostolic
Fathers. The Introductions deal with the questions of the genuineness and authenticity of the Epistles, discuss their date and character,*

Lightfoot (Dr. J. B.)—*continued.*

and analyse their contents. An account is also given of all the different epistles which bear the name of Clement of Rome. "By far the most copiously annotated edition of St. Clement which we yet possess, and the most convenient in every way for the English reader."—Guardian.

ON A FRESH REVISION OF THE ENGLISH NEW TESTAMENT. Crown 8vo. 6*s.*

*The present volume is the expansion of a paper originally read by Canon Lightfoot to the members of a clerical meeting. The Author begins with a few words on S. Jerome's revision of the Latin Bible, pointing out the parallel which exists in every respect between the task accomplished during the fourth century by one of the most illustrious fathers of the Church, and the undertaking now contemplated on this side of the channel. In both cases the amount of opposition to be encountered was extreme, whilst the urgency of the work was evident to all but prejudiced critics. Canon Lightfoot then goes on to shew in detail the necessity for a fresh revision of the authorized version on the following grounds:—*1. False Readings. 2. Artificial distinctions created. 3. Real distinctions obliterated. 4 Faults of Grammar. 5. Faults of Lexicography. 6. Treatment of Proper Names, official titles, etc. 7. Archaisms, defects in the English, errors of the press, etc. *The prospects of the new revision, Canon Lightfoot maintains, are favourable; for the present state of Greek Scholarship in England is a guarantee that the work will be thoroughly done; whilst, on the other hand, the changes contemplated need not alter the character of the old version. The volume is completed by* (1) *an elaborate appendix on the words* ἐπιούσιος *and* περιούσιος, (2) *a table of passages of Scripture quoted, and* (3) *a general index.* "*The book is marked by careful scholarship, familiarity with the subject, sobriety, and circumspection.*"—Athenæum. "*It abounds with evidence of the most extensive learning, and of a masterly familiarity with the best results of modern Greek scholarship.*"—Standard.

Luckock.—THE TABLES OF STONE. A Course of Sermons preached in All Saints' Church, Cambridge, by H. M. LUCKOCK, M.A., Vicar. Fcap. 8vo. 3s. 6d.

Sermons illustrative of the great principles of morality, mostly based on texts from the New Testament Scriptures.

Maclaren.—SERMONS PREACHED at MANCHESTER. By ALEXANDER MACLAREN. Third Edition. Fcap. 8vo. 4s. 6d.

These Sermons, twenty-four in number, are well known for the freshness and vigour of their thought, and the wealth of imagination they display. They represent no special school, but deal with the broad principles of Christian truth, especially in their bearing on practical, every day life. A few of the titles are:—" The Stone of Stumbling," " Love and Forgiveness," " The Living Dead," " Memory in Another World," " Faith in Christ," " Love and Fear," " The Choice of Wisdom," " The Food of the World."

A SECOND SERIES OF SERMONS. Second Edition. Fcap. 8vo. 4s. 6d.

This 2nd Series, consisting of nineteen Sermons, are marked by the same characteristics as the 1st. The Spectator *characterises them as "vigorous in style, full of thought, rich in illustration, and in an unusual degree interesting."*

Maclear.—Works by G. F. MACLEAR, B.D., Head Master of King's College School, and Preacher at the Temple Church :—

THE WITNESS OF THE EUCHARIST ; or, The Institution and Early Celebration of the Lord's Supper, considered as an Evidence of the Historical Truth of the Gospel Narrative and of the Atonement. Crown 8vo. 4s. 6d.

The title of this book, which is the Norrisian Prize Essay for 1863, sufficiently explains its object. The headings of the various Chap-

Maclear (G. F.)—*continued.*

ters will give an idea of the method of treatment :—I. Phenomena of Christian Worship. II. The Religious Revolution thus Attested. III. Alleged Explanations of this Religious Revolution. IV. Examination of the Gospel Narrative. V. The Early Public Ministry. VI. The Later Ministry. VII. The Institution of the Eucharist. VIII. The Eucharist a Sacrificial Feast. IX. The Eucharist a Sacrament of Our Redemption.

A CLASS-BOOK OF OLD TESTAMENT HISTORY.
With Four Maps. Fifth Edition. 18mo. 4*s.* 6*d.*

"The present volume," says the Preface, *"forms a Class-Book of Old Testament History from the Earliest Times to those of Ezra and Nehemiah. In its preparation the most recent authorities have been consulted, and wherever it has appeared useful, Notes have been subjoined illustrative of the Text, and, for the sake of more advanced students, references added to larger works. The Index has been so arranged as to form a concise Dictionary of the Persons and Places mentioned in the course of the Narrative."* The Maps, *prepared by Stanford, materially add to the value and usefulness of the book: they are*—1. *A Map illustrating the Dispersion of Noah's Descendants.* 2. *A Map of Canaan, Egypt, and Sinai, to illustrate the Patriarchal History and the Exodus; with Mt. Sinai enlarged.* 3. *The Holy Land divided among the Twelve Tribes.* 4. *Solomon's Dominions, the Kingdoms of Judah and Israel, and the Lands of the Captivities. In the Appendix are given Tables, I. Of the Patriarchs and their Descendants. II. Of Levi and the Priesthood. III. Of the Kings of Judah and Israel. IV. Of the Prophets. V. Shewing the Connection of Israel with the Surrounding Nations, viz.* (1) *The Later Assyrian Empire,* (2) *Babylonian Empire,* (3) *The Persian Empire and Greece. VI. Tables of Weights, Measures, and Money.* The British Quarterly Review *says of this work:—"It is a careful and elaborate, though brief compendium of all that modern research has done for the illustration of the Old Testament. We know of no work which contains so much important information in so small a compass."*

Maclear (G. F.)—*continued.*

A CLASS-BOOK OF NEW TESTAMENT HISTORY.

Including the Connexion of the Old and New Testament. Third Edition. 18mo. 5s. 6d.

"*The present volume forms a sequel to the Author's Class-Book of Old Testament History, continuing the narrative from the point at which it there ends, and carrying it on to the close of St. Paul's second imprisonment at Rome. In its preparation, as in that of the former volume, the most recent and trustworthy authorities have been consulted, notes subjoined, and references to larger works added. It is thus hoped that it may prove at once a useful Class-Book and a convenient companion to the study of the Greek Testament." The work is divided into three Books—I. The Connection between the Old and New Testaments. II. The Gospel History. III. The Apostolic History. The Index serves a similar purpose to that of the Old Testament History; while in the Appendix are given Chronological Tables, I. Of the Jews under the Empire. II. The Era of the Ptolemies and Seleucidæ. III. Rise of the Herodian Family. IV. The Gospel History. V. The Apostolic History. Appendix VI. is a Table of the Herodian Family. There are five Maps, viz.—1. A Map of the Holy Land to illustrate the Asmonean Period. 2. A Map of the Holy Land to illustrate the New Testament. 3. The Shores of the Sea of Galilee. 4. Jerusalem in the time of our Lord. 5. A Map to illustrate the Apostolic History. "Mr. Maclear," says the* Athenæum, "*has produced in this handy little volume a singularly clear and orderly arrangement of the sacred story. . . . . His work is solidly and completely done." The* Clerical Journal *says, "It is not often that such an amount of useful and interesting matter on biblical subjects, is found in so convenient and small a compass, as in this well-arranged volume.*"

A CLASS-BOOK OF THE CATECHISM OF THE CHURCH OF ENGLAND. Second Edition. 18mo. cloth. 2s. 6d.

The present work is intended as a sequel to the two preceding books. "*Like them, it is furnished with notes and references to larger*

Maclear (G. F.)—*continued.*

works, and it is hoped that it may be found, especially in the higher forms of our Public Schools, to supply a suitable manual of instruction in the chief doctrines of our Church, and a useful help in the preparation of Candidates for Confirmation." The plan *followed by the Author is to go over the Church Catechism clause by clause, and give all needful explanation and illustration, doctrinal, practical, and historical; the Notes make the work especially valuable to the student and clergyman. After a brief Introduction on the Derivation, Division, and History of the Catechism, the book is divided into five Parts:—I. The Christian Covenant. II. The Creed. III. The Ten Commandments. IV. The Lord's Prayer. V. The Sacraments. Appended are a General Index, an Index of Greek and Latin Words, and an Index of the Words explained throughout the book. The* Literary *Churchman says, "It is indeed the work of a scholar and divine, and as such, though extremely simple, it is also extremely instructive. There are few clergy who would not find it useful in preparing candidates for Confirmation; and there are not a few who would find it useful to themselves as well." The* Spectator *says, "A clergyman wanting a manual to use with Confirmation classes, could hardly find a more useful one than this."*

A FIRST CLASS-BOOK OF THE CATECHISM OF THE CHURCH OF ENGLAND, with Scripture Proofs for Junior Classes and Schools. Second Edition. 18mo. 6*d.*

This is an epitome of the larger Class-book, meant for junior students and elementary classes. The Notes, which would have been confusing and unintelligible to young scholars, have been omitted, and the rest of the book has been carefully condensed, so as to contain clearly and fully, the most important part of the contents of the larger book. Like it the present Manual is subdivided into five parts, each part into a number of short chapters, one or more of which might form a suitable lesson, and each chapter is subdivided in a number of sections, each with a prominent title indicative of its contents. It will be found a valuable Manual by parents, Sabbath-school teachers, and others who are concerned with the religious training of children.

Maclear (G. F.)—*continued.*

A SHILLING-BOOK of OLD TESTAMENT HISTORY.
18mo. cloth limp.   1*s.*

This Manual bears the same relation to the larger Old Testament History, that the book just mentioned does to the larger work on the Catechism.   As in it, the small-type notes have been omitted, and a clear and full epitome given of the larger work.   It consists of Ten Books, divided into short chapters, and subdivided into sections, each section treating of a single episode in the history, the title of which is given in bold type.   The Map is clearly printed, and not overcrowded with names.

A SHILLING-BOOK of NEW TESTAMENT HISTORY.
18mo. cloth limp.   1*s.*

This bears the same relation to the larger New Testament History that the work just mentioned has to the large Old Testament History, and is marked by similar characteristics.

THE ORDER OF CONFIRMATION.   A Sequel to the Class-Book of the Church Catechism, with Prayers and Collects. 18mo.   3*d.*

As the title-page indicates, this little Manual forms a suitable sequel to the Class-Book of the Catechism.   *The object of the rite is explained, its appropriateness and beauty set forth, and the different parts of the service expounded in an earnest, simple manner, with suitable exhortations and reflections.   The Order of Confirmation is given in full, after which the Manual is divided into seven brief chapters:—I.   " The Meaning of Confirmation."   II.   " The Origin of Confirmation."   III., IV., V.   " The Order of Confirmation," treating, (1) of " The Interrogation and Answer," (2) " The Laying on of Hands," (3) " The Prayers and Benediction," VI.   " The Holy Communion."   Chapter VII. consists of a few suitable Prayers and Collects intended to be used by the candidate during the days of preparation for Confirmation.   Valuable references, as well as a few explanatory and historical notes are added.   The Manual will be found valuable both by candidates*

Maclear (G. F.)—*continued.*

and by clergymen. The Literary Churchman *calls it "An admirable Manual. Thoroughly sound, clear, and complete in its teaching, with some good, clear, personal advice as to Holy Communion, and a good selection of prayers and collects for those preparing for Confirmation." "Concise and sound," says the* Guardian.

Macmillan.—Works by the Rev. HUGH MACMILLAN. (For other Works by the same Author, see CATALOGUE OF TRAVELS and SCIENTIFIC CATALOGUE).

THE TRUE VINE; or, the Analogies of our Lord's Allegory. Globe 8vo. 6s.

This work is meant to be, not merely an exposition of the fifteenth chapter of St. John's Gospel, but also a general parable of spiritual truth from the world of plants. It describes a few of the points in which the varied realm of vegetable life comes into contact with the higher spiritual realm, and shews how rich a field of promise lies before the analogical mind in this direction. The great majority of the analogies are derived from the grape-vine; but the whole range of the vegetable kingdom is laid under contribution for appropriate illustration. Indeed, Mr. Macmillan has brought into his service many of the results of recent scientific and historic research and biblical criticism; as well as the discoveries of travellers ancient and modern. The work will thus be found not only admirably suited for devotional reading, but also full of valuable and varied instruction. The Nonconformist *says, "It abounds in exquisite bits of description, and in striking facts clearly stated." The* British Quarterly *says, "Readers and preachers who are unscientific will find many of his illustrations as valuable as they are beautiful."*

BIBLE TEACHINGS IN NATURE. Fifth Edition. Globe 8vo. 6s.

In this volume the author has endeavoured to shew that the teaching of nature and the teaching of the Bible are directed to the same

Macmillan (H.)—*continued.*

great end; that the Bible contains the spiritual truths which are necessary to make us wise unto salvation, and the objects and scenes of nature are the pictures by which these truths are illustrated. The lessons of nature in this volume have been gathered at random in different fields of natural science, the object and design of them all being the same. In the first section the objects of nature are described for the sake of their own beauty and wonder, and for the evidences of Divine wisdom, power, and love which they display. In the second section they are viewed entirely. in their typical aspect. The first eight chapters describe, as it were, the exterior appearance of nature's temple—the gorgeous, many-coloured curtain hanging before the shrine. The last seven chapters bring us into the interior—the holy place, where is seen the very core of symbolical ordinances. "He has made the world more beautiful to us, and unsealed our ears.to voices of praise and messages of love that might otherwise have been unheard."—British Quarterly Review. *"Mr. Macmillan has produced a book which may be fitly described as one of the happiest efforts for enlisting physical science in the direct service of religion."*—Guardian.

M'Cosh.—For Works by JAMES McCOSH, LL.D., President of Princeton College, New Jersey, U.S., *see* PHILOSOPHICAL CATALOGUE.

Maurice.—Works by the Rev. F. DENISON MAURICE, M.A., Professor of Moral Philosophy in the University of Cambridge. (For other Works by the same Author, *see* PHILOSOPHICAL and HISTORICAL CATALOGUES).

Mr. Maurice's Sermons and other theological works mark an era, if indeed they have not created a school in modern theology. The deep and wide-spread influence exercised by them as well as by his philosophical writings is acknowledged by all who take heed unto these things. With whatever subject Mr. Maurice deals, he tries to look at it in its bearing on living men and their every-day surroundings, faces unshrinkingly the difficulties which occur to

Maurice (F. D.)—*continued.*

ordinary earnest thinkers in a manner that shews he has intense sympathy with all that concerns our common humanity. By all who wish to understand the varied drifts of thought during the present century, Mr. Maurice's works must be studied ; and they cannot but exercise an ennobling and purifying influence on the hearts and conduct of all who have the faintest aspiration towards a better life.

THE PATRIARCHS AND LAWGIVERS OF THE OLD TESTAMENT. Third and Cheaper Edition. Crown 8vo. 5*s.*

The Nineteen Discourses contained in this volume were preached in the chapel of Lincoln's Inn during the year 1851. The texts are taken from the books of Genesis, Exodus, Numbers, Deuteronomy, Joshua, Judges, and Samuel, and involve some of the most interesting biblical topics discussed in recent times. In his Preface to the First Edition, Mr. Maurice endeavours to explain the mission and justify the position of the Church of England against the attacks of Dissenters and others ; in his Preface to the Second Edition he comments upon some remarks made by Mr. Mansel on the meaning given by Mr. Maurice to the word 'Eternal.' In the latter Preface the writer says,—"My chief object in preaching and writing upon the Old Testament has been to shew that God has created man in His image ; that being so created he is capable of receiving a revelation from God,—of knowing what God is ; that without such a revelation he cannot be truly a man ; that without such knowledge he cannot become what he is always feeling that he ought to become."

THE PROPHETS AND KINGS OF THE OLD TESTAMENT. Third Edition, with new Preface. Crown 8vo. 10*s.* 6*d.*

The previous work brings down Old Testament history to the time of Samuel. The Sermons contained in the present volume—twen'y-

Maurice (F. D.)—*continued.*

seven in number, coming down to the time of Ezekiel—though they commence at that point are distinct in their subject and treatment, and to some extent, even in their purpose. Mr. Maurice, in the spirit which animated the compilers of the Church Lessons, has in these Sermons regarded the Prophets more as preachers of righteousness than as mere predictors—an aspect of their lives which, he thinks, has been greatly overlooked in our day, and than which, there is none we have more need to contemplate. He has found that the Old Testament Prophets, taken in their simple natural sense, clear up many of the difficulties which torment us in the daily work of life; make the past intelligible, the present endurable, and the future real and hopeful. In the Preface to this Third Edition, Mr. Maurice propounds his notions with regard to the connection of Church and State, with special reference to the recent disestablishment of the Irish Church, and the wish in certain quarters to treat the Church of England in the same way.

THE GOSPEL OF THE KINGDOM OF HEAVEN.

A Series of Lectures on the Gospel of St. Luke.   Crown 8vo.   9*s.*

Mr. Maurice, in his Preface to these Twenty-eight Lectures, says,—"In these Lectures I have endeavoured to ascertain what is told us respecting the life of Jesus by one of those Evangelists who proclaim Him to be the Christ, who says that He did come from a Father, that He did baptize with the Holy Spirit, that He did rise from the dead. I have chosen the one who is most directly connected with the later history of the Church, who was not an Apostle, who professedly wrote for the use of a man already instructed in the faith of the Apostles. I have followed the course of the writer's narrative, not changing it under any pretext. I have adhered to his phraseology, striving to avoid the substitution of any other for his." This is necessary on account of the conventional notions which most people are apt to attach to the words of the Gospels; and in the remainder of his Preface, Mr. Maurice points out some of these conventional notions, 1. In relation to Miracles. 2. On the question, Are the Gospels the announcement of a religion? 3. Concerning Eternal Punishment. 4. The Authenticity and Inspiration of the Gospels.

Maurice (F. D.)—*continued.*

THE GOSPEL OF ST. JOHN. A Series of Discourses. Third and Cheaper Edition. Crown 8vo. 6*s.*

These Discourses, twenty-eight in number, are of a nature similar to those on the Gospel of St. Luke. They were preached in Lincoln's Inn during the year 1856, *and will be found to render valuable assistance to any one anxious to understand the Gospel of the beloved disciple, so different in many respects from those of the other three Evangelists. Appended are eleven notes illustrating various points which occur throughout the discourses, such as,* "*Baur's Theory of the Gospels;*" "*On the objections to a Revision of the Scriptures;*" "*On the Resurrection of the Body and the Judgment-day;*" "*On the doctrine of the Atonement—Scotch and English Divinity;*" "*On Corporate Holiness,*" *etc. The* Literary Churchman *thus speaks of this volume:—*"*Thorough honesty, reverence, and deep thought pervade the work, which is every way solid and philosophical, as well as theological, and abounding with suggestions which the patient student may draw out more at length for himself.*"

THE EPISTLES OF ST. JOHN. A Series of Lectures on Christian Ethics. Second and Cheaper Edition. Cr. 8vo. 6*s.*

These Lectures on Christian Ethics were delivered to the students of the Working Men's College, Great Ormond Street, London, on a series of Sunday mornings. There are twenty Lectures in all, founded on various texts taken from the Epistles of St. John, which abound in passages bearing directly on the conduct of life, the duty of men to God and to each other. It will be found that a very complete system of practical morality is developed in this volume, in which the most important points in Ethics are set forth in a clear, interesting, and thoughtful manner. Mr. Maurice believes that the question in which we are most interested, the question which most affects our studies and our daily lives, is the question, whether there is a foundation for human morality, or whether it is dependent upon the opinions and fashions of different ages and countries. This important question will be found amply and fairly discussed in this volume, which the National Review *calls* "*Mr. Maurice's*

Maurice (F. D.)—*continued.*

most effective and instructive work. He is peculiarly fitted by the constitution of his mind, to throw light on St. John's writings." Appended is a note on "Positivism and its Teacher."

EXPOSITORY SERMONS ON THE PRAYER-BOOK. The Prayer-book considered especially in reference to the Romish System. Second Edition. Fcap. 8vo. 5s. 6d.

"There are certain popular notions which," says the Preface, "assume that the Church of England is the result of a compromise; that the Articles embody the opinions of one party to the bargain, the Liturgy those of the other; that every time I put my hand to the former document I proclaim myself in the strictest sense a Protestant, that every time I use the latter I act as a Papist; that in fact, I am neither. . . . In delivering these Sermons [in Lincoln's Inn Chapel in 1848-9], I endeavoured to tell laymen why I could with a clear heart and conscience ask them to take part with me in this Common Prayer. In publishing them I would address myself with equal earnestness and affection to another class, to the younger part of the clergy, and to those who are preparing for Orders." After an Introductory Sermon, Mr. Maurice goes over the various parts of the Church Service, expounds in eighteen Sermons, fully, clearly, and broadly, their intention and significance, points out their beauty, and shews how appropriate they are as expressions of the deepest longings and wants of all classes of men. The last seven Sermons are devoted to the Communion Service.

LECTURES ON THE APOCALYPSE, or Book of the Revelation of St. John the Divine. Crown 8vo. 10s. 6d.

These Twenty-three Lectures on what is generally regarded as the most mysterious Book in the Bible, the Author says are neither controversial nor learned; nor do they demand that extensive knowledge of ancient or modern history which it is necessary to possess to be able to judge of most modern commentaries on Prophecy. The principal historical allusions are to the state of the Roman world during the years preceding the fall of Jerusalem. Mr. Maurice,

Maurice (F. D.)—*continued.*

instead of trying to find far-fetched allusions to great historical events in the distant future, endeavours to discover the plain, literal, obvious meaning of the words of the writer, and shews that as a rule these refer to events contemporaneous with or immediately succeeding the time when the book was written. At the same time he shews the applicability of the contents of the book to the circumstances of the present day and of all times. Here, as in his other expositions of Scripture, Mr. Maurice attempts to shew that the Bible authorises us to believe that the Kingdom of Heaven, instead of being some dull Utopia in the far-distant future, is not "far off from any one of us," is indeed in our very midst. "Never," says the Nonconformist, *"has Mr. Maurice been more reverent, more careful for the letter of the Scripture, more discerning of the purpose of the Spirit, or more sober and practical in his teaching, than in this volume on the Apocalypse."*

WHAT IS REVELATION? A Series of Sermons on the Epiphany; to which are added, Letters to a Theological Student on the Bampton Lectures of Mr. Mansel. Crown 8vo. 10s. 6d.

This volume consists of Seven Sermons preached to the Author's own congregation, and eleven Letters to a Student of Theology. Both Sermons and Letters were called forth by the doctrine maintained by Mr. Mansel in his Bampton Lectures, that Revelation cannot be a Direct Manifestation of the Infinite Nature of God. Mr. Maurice maintains the opposite doctrine, and in his Sermons explains why, in spite of the high authorities on the other side, he must still assert the principle which he discovers in the Services of the Church and throughout the Bible. He has added as a Supplement to these the Letters to a Student of Theology, in which he has followed out all Mr. Mansel's Statements and Arguments step by step. The subjects of the Sermons are:—I. The Magians. II. Christ among the Doctors. III. St. Paul at Athens. IV. The Miracles. V. Casting out the Evil Spirit. VI. Christ's Parables. VII. Practice and Speculation. Among the matters discussed in the Letters are:—Sir William Hamilton; Butler; the Atonement and Incarnation; the Criterion of Truth;

Maurice (F. D.)—*continued.*

Philosophy of Consciousness; the Scotch; Prayer; Knowing and Being; the Trinity; Miracles; Kant; Contents and Evidences of the Bible. The Nonconformist *says, " There will be found ample materials to stimulate Christian faith and earnestness, to quicken and give tenderness to charity, and to vivify conceptions of the ' things not seen which are eternal.'"*

SEQUEL TO THE INQUIRY, "WHAT IS REVELA-
TION?" Letters in Reply to Mr. Mansel's Examination of
"Strictures on the Bampton Lectures." Crown 8vo. 6s.

This, as the title indicates, was called forth by Mr. Mansel's Examination of Mr. Maurice's Strictures on his doctrine of the Infinite, in which Mr. Mansel attacks the latter with considerable acrimony. In a spirit of fairness, and with his usual force, he endeavours to meet Mr. Mansel's attack.

THEOLOGICAL ESSAYS. Third Edition. Crown 8vo.
10s. 6d.

The original reason for publishing this volume was to fulfil the request made by a lady in her will, that Mr. Maurice would write, or procure to be written, some book specially addressed to Unitarians. " The book," says Mr. Maurice, " expresses thoughts which have been working in my mind for years; the method of it has not been adopted carelessly; even the composition has undergone frequent revision." There are seventeen Essays in all, and although meant primarily for Unitarians, to quote the words of the Clerical Journal, *" it leaves untouched scarcely any topic which is in agitation in the religious world; scarcely a moot point between our various sects; scarcely a plot of debateable ground between Christians and Infidels, between Romanists and Protestants, between Socinians and other Christians, between English Churchmen and Dissenters on both sides. Scarce is there a misgiving, a difficulty, an aspiration stirring amongst us now,—now, when men seem in earnest as hardly ever before about religion, and ask and demand satisfaction with a fearlessness which seems almost awful when one thinks what is at stake—which is not recognised and grappled with by Mr. Maurice."*

Maurice (F. D.)—*continued.*

THE DOCTRINE OF SACRIFICE DEDUCED FROM THE SCRIPTURES. Crown 8vo. 7s. 6d.

Throughout the Nineteen Sermons contained in this volume, Mr. Maurice expounds the notions which he has formed of the Doctrine of Sacrifice, as that is set forth in various parts of the Bible. It is well known that he holds peculiar opinions on this matter, opinions, however, which deserve the serious consideration of all thoughtful and earnest Christians. The first five Sermons consider various sacrifices referred to in the Old Testament, while in the remainder the death and resurrection of Christ are looked at from various points of view. He has "tried to speak of Sacrifice under every aspect in which the Bible presents it." In the Dedicatory Letter (occupying fifty pages) to the Members of the Young Men's Christian Association, Mr. Maurice animadverts on an attack made on his opinions and character, by the Rev. Dr. Candlish of Edinburgh, in an address to that Society in Exeter Hall. "The habitual tone," says the Christian Spectator, *"is that of great seriousness and calm,—a seriousness which makes an impression of its own, and a serenity which is only broken by some overpowering feeling forcing itself into expression, and making itself heard in most meaning and stirring words."*

THE RELIGIONS OF THE WORLD, AND THEIR RELATIONS TO CHRISTIANITY. Fourth Edition. Fcap. 8vo. 5s.

These Eight Boyle Lectures were delivered in one of the London Churches at intervals during the years 1845-6. *The title to a considerable extent explains their aim. They are divided into two parts, of four Lectures each. In the first part Mr. Maurice examines the great Religious systems which present themselves in the history of the world, with the purpose of inquiring what is their main characteristic principle. The second four Lectures are occupied with a discussion of the questions, "In what relation does Christianity stand to these different faiths? If there be a faith which is meant for mankind, is this the one, or must we look for another?" In the Preface, the most important authorities on the various subjects discussed in the Lectures are referred to, so that the reader may pursue the subject further.*

Maurice (F. D.)—*continued.*

ON THE LORD'S PRAYER. Fourth Edition. Fcap. 8vo. 2s. 6d.

In these Nine Sermons the successive petitions of the Lord's Prayer are taken up by Mr. Maurice, their real significance fully expounded, and, as usual with him, connected with the every-day lives, feelings, and aspirations of the men of the present time. They were delivered in the momentous year 1848, and frequent allusions are made and lessons drawn from the never-to-be-forgotten events of that year.

ON THE SABBATH DAY; the Character of the Warrior, and on the Interpretation of History. Fcap. 8vo. 2s. 6d.

This volume contains Three Sermons on the Sabbath-day, one of them being in reference to the proposed opening of the Crystal Palace on Sunday—one on the "Character of the Warrior," suggested by the Death of the Duke of Wellington; the fifth being on "The Divine Interpretation of History," delivered during the Great Exhibition of 1851. In this last Mr. Maurice points out a few difficulties which, judging from his own experience, he thinks likely to distress students of history, explaining how the Divine Book has anticipated and resolved them.

THE GROUND AND OBJECT OF HOPE FOR MANKIND. Four Sermons preached before the University of Cambridge. Crown 8vo. 3s. 6d.

In these Four Sermons Mr. Maurice views the subject in four aspects :—I. The Hope of the Missionary. II. The Hope of the Patriot. III. The Hope of the Churchman. IV. The Hope of Man. The Spectator *says, "It is impossible to find anywhere deeper teaching than this;" and the* Nonconformist, *"We thank him for the manly, noble, stirring words in these Sermons—words fitted to quicken thoughts, to awaken high aspiration, to stimulate to lives of goodness."*

Maurice (F. D.)—*continued.*

THE LORD'S PRAYER, THE CREED, AND THE COMMANDMENTS. A Manual for Parents and Schoolmasters. To which is added the Order of the Scriptures. 18mo. cloth limp. 1*s.*

This book is not written for clergymen, as such, but for parents and teachers, who are often either prejudiced against the contents of the Catechism, or regard it peculiarly as the clergyman's book, but, at the same time, have a general notion that a habit of prayer ought to be cultivated, that there are some things which ought to be believed, and some things which ought to be done. Moreover, it will be found to be peculiarly valuable at the present time, when the question of religious education is occupying so much attention. The book consists of four parts:—I. The Lord's Prayer. II. The Belief (Creed). III. The Commandments. IV. The Scriptures. Each part is divided into days, for each day a petition of the Prayer, a clause of the Creed, a Commandment, or a book or connected group of books of the Bible is taken, and a few words of exhortation, explanation, or reflection given on the sentiment suggested.

THE CLAIMS OF THE BIBLE AND OF SCIENCE. A Correspondence on some Questions respecting the Pentateuch. Crown 8vo. 4*s.* 6*d.*

This volume consists of a series of Fifteen Letters, the first and last addressed by a 'Layman' to Mr. Maurice, the intervening thirteen written by Mr. Maurice himself. In the Layman's first letter to Mr. Maurice, immediately called forth by the appearance of Bishop Colenso's attack on the Pentateuch, the writer sets forth some of the difficulties likely to be suggested to an ordinary thinker and believer in Christianity, by recent criticisms on the Bible of the class to which the works of Colenso belong. Three questions especially he propounds, to which, he thinks, a layman may naturally at the present time ask for an answer:—1. Do not our faith in Christ, and our belief in the four Gospels as a real history, rest on grounds independent of the results of any critical inquiry into the authorship of the Pentateuch? 2. May we not continue to read the Pentateuch as the Word of God, speaking of man and to man, without putting

Maurice (F. D.)—*continued.*

a forced construction on the plain meaning of the words, and with-out imposing fetters on the freedom of scientific or critical investiga-tion in any matters which God has given us the power to inquire into ?　3. Is faith in Christ contingent on the proof or disproof of the existence of certain natural phenomena, which seem not to accord with the language of the Bible ?　Mr. Maurice, in his Thirteen Letters, takes up these and the other points suggested by the Layman, and in his own forcible and attractive way endeavours to clear them up and to throw light on the all-important Biblical contro-versy generally.

DIALOGUES ON FAMILY WORSHIP. Crown 8vo. 6s.

"The parties in these Dialogues," says the Preface, "are a Clergy-man who accepts the doctrines of the Church, and a Layman whose faith in them is nearly gone.　The object of the Dialogues is not confutation, but the discovery of a ground on which two English-men and two Fathers may stand, and on which their country and their children may stand when their places know them no more."　In an unconventional and interesting manner some of the most important doctrines of the Church are discussed, the whole series of dialogues tending to shew that men of all shades of belief may look up to and worship God as their common and loving Father.　The key-words of the Dialogues are as follow :—I. A Layman's Perplexities.　II. A Mother's Faith.　III. Male Calvinism.　IV. The Regenerate and the Unregenerate.　V. The Natural and the Supernatural.　VI. The Revelation and the Family of Abraham.　VII. The Father and the Son.　VIII. Repentance and Conversion.　IX. Fathers in God.　X. Heathen and Christ-ian Devotion.　XI. The Method of Prayer.　XII. The Soul and the Spirit.

THE COMMANDMENTS CONSIDERED AS IN-STRUMENTS OF NATIONAL REFORMATION.　Crown 8vo.　4s. 6d.

This is simply a book of practical morality and divinity, and has not the least of a scientific character.　It is to some extent a reply to

Dr. Norman Macleod's Speech on the Sabbath, and his views of the Commandments. The author endeavours to shew that the Commandments are now, and ever have been, the great protectors against Presbyteral and Prelatical assumptions, and that if we do not receive them as Commandments of the Lord God spoken to Israel, and spoken to every people under heaven now, we lose the greatest witnesses we possess for national morality and civil freedom.

Moorhouse.—Works by JAMES MOORHOUSE, M.A., Vicar of Paddington :—

SOME MODERN DIFFICULTIES RESPECTING the FACTS OF NATURE AND REVELATION. Fcap. 8vo. 2*s.* 6*d.*

The first of these Four Discourses is a systematic reply to the Essay of the Rev. Baden Powell on Christian Evidences in "Essays and Reviews." The fourth Sermon, on " The Resurrection," is in some measure complementary to this, and the two together are intended to furnish a tolerably complete view of modern objections to Revelation; so far, at least, as these depend on particular theories as to the connection of matter and spirit. In the second and third Sermons, on the " Temptation" and "Passion," the author has endeavoured " to exhibit the power and wonder of those great facts within the spiritual sphere, which modern theorists have especially sought to discredit." The British Quarterly *says of them,—" The tone of the discussion is able, and throughout conservative of Scriptural truth."*

JACOB. Three Sermons preached before the University of Cambridge in Lent 1870. Extra fcap. 8vo. 3*s.* 6*d.*

In these Three Sermons the author endeavours to indicate the course of that Divine training by which the patriarch Jacob was converted from a deceitful and unscrupulous into a pious and self-denying man. In the first Sermon is considered " The Human Subject," or the nature to be trained ; in the second " The Divine Power," the power by which that training was effected ; and in the third " The Great Change," or the course and form of the training.

Moorhouse (J.)—*continued.*

THE HULSEAN LECTURES FOR 1865. Cr. 8vo. 5*s.*

The following are the subjects of the Four Hulsean Lectures in this volume:—I. "Bearing of Present Controversies on the Doctrine of the Incarnation." II. "How far the Hypothesis of a real Limitation in our Saviour's Human Knowledge is consistent with the Doctrine of His Divinity." III. "The Scriptural Evidence of our Saviour's Sinlessness." IV. "What Kind and Degree of Human Ignorance were left possible to our Lord Jesus Christ by the fact of His Human Sinlessness." The three Sermons which follow are published partly because it seemed to the author that they might be found to elucidate many difficulties which in the Lectures could not be investigated with that degree of care and fulness which was desirable. The subjects are:—I. "The Teaching of the Spirit, —Ordinary and Extraordinary." II. "The Nature of Prophecy, and of Prophetic Inspiration." III. "The Land and the People." "Few more valuable works have come into our hands for many years . . . a most fruitful and welcome volume."—Church Review.

O'Brien.—AN ATTEMPT TO EXPLAIN and ESTAB-
LISH THE DOCTRINE OF JUSTIFICATION by FAITH
ONLY. By JAMES THOMAS O'BRIEN, D.D., Bishop of Ossory.
Third Edition. 8vo. 12*s.*

This work consists of Ten Sermons. The first four treat of the nature and mutual relations of Faith and Justification; the fifth and sixth examine the corruptions of the doctrine of Justification by Faith only, and the objections which have been urged against it. The four concluding sermons deal with the moral effects of Faith. Various Notes are added explanatory of the Author's reasoning.

Palgrave.—HYMNS. By FRANCIS TURNER PALGRAVE.
Third Edition, enlarged. 18mo. 1*s.* 6*d.*

This is a collection of twenty original Hymns, which the Literary Churchman *speaks of as "so choice, so perfect, and so refined,— so tender in feeling, and so scholarly in expression."*

Palmer.—THE BOOK OF PRAISE : From the Best
English Hymn Writers. Selected and arranged by Sir ROUNDELL
PALMER. With Vignette by WOOLNER. 18mo. 4s. 6d.

*The present is an attempt to present, under a convenient arrangement,
a collection of such examples of a copious and interesting branch of
popular literature, as, after several years' study of the subject, have
seemed to the Editor most worthy of being separated from the mass
to which they belong. It has been the Editor's desire and aim to
adhere strictly, in all cases in which it could be ascertained, to the
genuine uncorrupted text of the authors themselves. The names of
the authors and date of composition of the hymns, when known,
are affixed, while notes are added to the volume, giving further
details. The Hymns are arranged according to subjects. "There
is not room for two opinions as to the value of the 'Book of Praise.'"*
—Guardian. *"Approaches as nearly as one can conceive to perfection."*—Nonconformist.

BOOK OF PRAISE HYMNAL. *See* end of this Catalogue.

Prescott.—THE THREEFOLD CORD. Sermons preached
before the University of Cambridge. By J. E. PRESCOTT, B.D.
Fcap. 8vo. 3s. 6d.

*The title of this volume is derived from the subjects of the first three
of these Sermons—Love, Hope, Faith. Their full titles are:—
I. "Christ the Bringer of Peace—Love." II. "Christ the Reno-
vator—Hope." III. "Christ the Light—Faith." The fourth,
an Assize Sermon, is on "The Divinity of Justice." The Sermons
are an attempt to render of practical service certain subjects of no
ordinary weight; to shew that Christian theology is sufficient for
the wants of the present day. There are a considerable number of
Notes throughout the volume, directing the reader to valuable sources
of information. The Churchman says the volume "is evidently
the production of a scholar. Eloquent and striking passages abound
throughout." The Nonconformist styles the Sermons "able,
thoughtful, and earnest."*

Procter.—A HISTORY OF THE BOOK OF COMMON
PRAYER: With a Rationale of its Offices. By FRANCIS
PROCTER, M.A. Ninth Edition, revised and enlarged. Crown
8vo. 10s. 6d.

*The fact that in fifteen years nine editions of this volume have been
called for, shews that such a work was wanted, and that to a large
extent Mr. Procter's book has supplied the want. "In the course
of the last thirty years," the author says, "the whole subject has
been investigated by divines of great learning, and with an accuracy
of research which has given to the present generation of students
the advantage of trustworthy information upon many points of
ritual importance and historical interest; and it was mainly with
a view of epitomizing their extensive publications, and correcting
by their help sundry traditional errors or misconceptions, that the
present volume was put together." The Second Part is occupied
with an account of "The Sources and Rationale of the Offices."
The Athenæum says:—"The origin of every part of the Prayer-
book has been diligently investigated,—and there are few questions
or facts connected with it which are not either sufficiently explained,
or so referred to, that persons interested may work out the truth for
themselves."*

Procter and Maclear.—AN ELEMENTARY INTRO-
DUCTION TO THE BOOK OF COMMON PRAYER.
Fourth Edition, Re-arranged and Supplemented by an Explanation
of the Morning and Evening Prayer and the Litany. By F.
PROCTER, M.A. and G. F. MACLEAR, B.D. 18mo. 2s. 6d.

*This book has the same object and follows the same plan as the
Manuals already noticed under Mr. Maclear's name. The work
is divided into Two Books, and each book subdivided into chapters
and well-marked sections. In Book I. is given a detailed History
of the Book of Common Prayer, from the Service-Books of the Early
Church down to the Attempted Revision in the Reign of William
III. Book II., consisting of four Parts, treats in Part I. of
The Order of Morning Prayer. II. Order of Evening Prayer.
III. The Litany. IV. Occasional Prayers and Thanksgivings.
Valuable Notes, etymological, historical, and critical, are given*

throughout the book, while the Appendix contains several articles of much interest and importance. Appended is a General Index and an Index of Words explained in the Notes. The Literary Churchman *characterizes it as "by far the completest and most satisfactory book of its kind we know. We wish it were in the hands of every schoolboy and every schoolmaster in the kingdom."*

Psalms of David CHRONOLOGICALLY ARRANGED.

An Amended Version, with Historical Introductions and Explanatory Notes. By FOUR FRIENDS. Second and Cheaper Edition, much enlarged. Crown 8vo. 8s. 6d.

One of the chief designs of the Editors, in preparing this volume, was to restore the Psalter as far as possible to the order in which the Psalms were written. They give the division of each Psalm into strophes, and of each strophe into the lines which composed it, and amend the errors of translation. In accomplishing this work they have mainly followed the guidance of Professor Henry Ewald. A Supplement contains the chief specimens of Hebrew Lyric poetry not included in the Book of Psalms. The Spectator *calls it "One of the most instructive and valuable books that have been published for many years."*

THE GOLDEN TREASURY PSALTER; a Student's Edition of the above, with Briefer Notes. 18mo. 3s. 6d.

Ramsay.—THE CATECHISER'S MANUAL; or, the

Church Catechism Illustrated and Explained, for the Use of Clergymen, Schoolmasters, and Teachers. By ARTHUR RAMSAY, M.A. Second Edition. 18mo. 1s. 6d.

This Manual, which is in the form of question and answer, is intended to afford full assistance both to learners and teachers, to candidates for Confirmation as well as to clergymen, in the understanding of the Church Catechism, and of all the matters referred to therein. It is divided into seven chapters:—I. "The Church Catechism," in which the meaning and object of the Catechism is explained, as well as the significance and object of

4

Confirmation. II. The various parts of the Catechism are analysed and explained. III. The Creeds—the Apostles', the Nicene, and the Athanasian. IV. The Apostles' Creed. V. The Commandments. VI. The Lord's Prayer. VII. The Sacraments. The English Journal of Education *says,—"This is by far the best Manual on the Catechism we have met with, adapted not only for the use of the national schoolmaster, but also for the clergyman and the tutor . . . There is much original observation in it, hints for the application of the Catechism to the questions of the present day, and an extensive range of inquiry on collateral points of interest."*

Rays of Sunlight for Dark Days. A Book of Selections for the Suffering. With a Preface by C. J. VAUGHAN, D.D. 18mo. New Edition. 3s. 6d. Also in morocco, old style.

Dr. Vaughan says in the Preface, after speaking of the general run of Books of Comfort for Mourners, "It is because I think that the little volume now offered to the Christian sufferer is one of greater wisdom and of deeper experience, that I have readily consented to the request that I would introduce it by a few words of Preface." The book consists of a series of very brief extracts from a great variety of authors, in prose and poetry, suited to the many moods of a mourning or suffering mind. "Amongst the many books of Comfort," says the Nonconformist, *"for the sorrowful and afflicted that have at different times come to our hands, scarcely has there been one that has the fitness to its end that we find in this little volume." "Mostly gems of the first water."*—Clerical Journal.

Reynolds.—NOTES OF THE CHRISTIAN LIFE. A Selection of Sermons by HENRY ROBERT REYNOLDS, B.A., President of Cheshunt College, and Fellow of University College, London. Crown 8vo. 7s. 6d.

This work may be taken as representative of the mode of thought and feeling which is most popular amongst the freer and more cultivated Nonconformists. "The reader throughout," says the Patriot, *"feels himself in the grasp of an earnest and careful thinker." "It is long," says the* Nonconformist, *"since we have met with*

*any published sermons better calculated than these to stimulate
devout thought, and to bring home to the soul the reality of a
spiritual life."*

Roberts.—DISCUSSIONS ON THE GOSPELS. By the
Rev. ALEXANDER ROBERTS, D.D. Second Edition, revised and
enlarged. 8vo. 16s.

> *This volume is divided into two parts. Part I. "On the Language
> employed by our Lord and His Disciples," in which the author
> endeavours to prove that Greek was widely diffused and commonly
> employed for all public purposes in Palestine, during the period
> of Christ and His Apostles ; and especially that it was the
> language usually employed by Christ Himself, in opposition to the
> common belief that Our Lord spoke Aramæan. The Second Part
> is occupied with a discussion "On the Original Language of St.
> Matthew's Gospel," and on "The Origin and Authenticity of the
> Gospels." In the Second Part, as well as in the First, the author
> propounds some novel views on the points discussed, the result of
> long and deep study and research. The volume abounds in valu-
> able and learned Notes, and in the Second Part is a chapter bearing
> chiefly on the proper authenticity of the Gospels as recently challenged
> by M. Renan. "The author brings the valuable qualifications of
> learning, temper, and an independent judgment. . . . It is but bare
> justice to affirm that his arguments render it [his proposition]
> extremely probable."—*Daily News.* "This volume is of intense
> interest to every Biblical student. It enters a field of inquiry
> hitherto untrodden."—*British Standard.*

Robertson.—PASTORAL COUNSELS. Being Chapters
on Practical and Devotional Subjects. By the late JOHN ROBERT-
SON, D.D. Third Edition, with a Preface by the Author of
"The Recreations of a Country Parson." Extra fcap. 8vo. 6s.

> *These Sermons are the free utterances of a strong and independent
> thinker. He does not depart from the essential doctrines of his
> Church, but he expounds them in a spirit of the widest charity, and
> always having most prominently in view the requirements of prac-
> tical life. "The sermons are admirable specimens of a practical,
> earnest, and instructive style of pulpit teaching."*—Nonconformist.

Rowsell.—MAN'S LABOUR AND GOD'S HARVEST.
Sermons preached before the University of Cambridge in Lent,
1861. Fcap. 8vo. 3s.

*This volume contains Five Sermons, the general drift of which is
indicated by the title. "We strongly recommend this little volume
to young men, and especially to those who are contemplating working for Christ in Holy Orders."*—Literary Churchman. *"Mr.
Rowsell's Sermons must, we feel sure, have touched the heart of
many a Cambridge Undergraduate, and are deserving of a wide
general circulation. It is seldom we meet with so much zeal, combined with so much sobriety."*—The Ecclesiastic.

Sergeant.—SERMONS. By the Rev. E. W. SERGEANT,
M.A., Balliol College, Oxford; Assistant Master at Westminster
College. Fcap. 8vo. 2s. 6d.

*This volume contains Nine Sermons on a variety of topics, preached
by the author at various times and to various classes of heqrers.
The First Sermon is on Free Inquiry.*

Smith.—PROPHECY A PREPARATION FOR CHRIST.
Eight Lectures preached before the University of Oxford, being the
Bampton Lectures for 1869. By R. PAYNE SMITH, D.D., Dean
of Canterbury. Second and Cheaper Edition. Crown 8vo. 6s.

*The author's object in these Lectures is to shew that there exists in the
Old Testament an element, which no criticism on naturalistic
principles can either account for or explain away: that element is
Prophecy. The author endeavours to prove that its force does not
consist merely in its predictions. Prophecy means more than this.
The Bible describes man's first estate of innocency, his fall, and the
promise given by God of his restoration. The author asserts that
throughout the Old Testament there is an express and manifest
working of the Deity for the accomplishment of this promise.
Virtually the promise meant that God would give man a true
religion; and the author asserts that Christianity is the sole religion
on earth that fulfils the conditions necessary to constitute a true
religion. God has pledged His own attributes in its behalf; this*

pledge He has given in miracle and prophecy. The author en-
deavours to shew the reality of that portion of the proof founded on
prophecy. "These Lectures overflow with solid learning."—Record.

Smith.—CHRISTIAN FAITH. Sermons preached before
the University of Cambridge. By W. SAUMAREZ SMITH, M.A.,
Principal of St. Aidan's College, Birkenhead. Fcap. 8vo. 3*s.* 6*d.*

The first two sermons in this volume have special reference to the
Person of Christ; the next two are concerned with the inner life
of Christians; and the last speaks of the outward development of
Christian faith. "Appropriate and earnest sermons, suited to the
practical exhortation of an educated congregation."—Guardian.

Stanley.—THE ATHANASIAN CREED, with a Preface
on the General Recommendations of the RITUAL COMMISSION.
By A. P. STANLEY, D.D., Dean of Westminster. Cr. 8vo. 2*s.*

The present volume is a reprint of two articles which appeared in the
Contemporary Review *of August and November* 1870. *Its object*
is not so much to urge the omission or change of the Athanasian
Creed, as to shew that such a relaxation ought to give offence to no
reasonable or religious mind. With this view, the Dean of West-
minster discusses in succession—(1) *the Authorship of the Creed,*
(2) *its Internal Characteristics,* (3) *the Peculiarities of its Use in*
the Church of England, (4) *its Advantages and Disadvantages,*
(5) *its various Interpretations, and* (6) *the Judgment passed upon*
it by the Ritual Commission. In conclusion, after quoting two
recent cases which bear out his theory, Dr. Stanley maintains that
the use of the Athanasian Creed should no longer be made com-
pulsory. "Dr. Stanley puts with admirable force the objections
which may be made to the Creed; equally admirable, we think, in
his statement of its advantages."—Spectator.

Sunday Library. See end of this Catalogue.

Swainson.—Works by C. A. SWAINSON, D.D., Canon of Chichester :—

THE CREEDS OF THE CHURCH IN THEIR RE-LATIONS TO HOLY SCRIPTURE and the CONSCIENCE OF THE CHRISTIAN. 8vo. cloth. 9s.

*The Lectures which compose this volume discuss, amongst others, the following subjects: "Faith in God," "Exercise of our Reason," "Origin and Authority of Creeds," and "Private Judgment, its use and exercise." "Treating of abstruse points of Scripture, he applies them so forcibly to Christian duty and practice as to prove eminently serviceable to the Church."—*John Bull.

THE AUTHORITY OF THE NEW TESTAMENT, and other LECTURES, delivered before the University of Cambridge. 8vo. cloth. 12s.

*The first series of Lectures in this work is on "The Words spoken by the Apostles of Jesus," "The Inspiration of God's Servants," "The Human Character of the Inspired Writers," and "The Divine Character of the Word written." The second embraces Lectures on "Sin as Imperfection," "Sin as Self-will," "Whatsoever is not of Faith is Sin," "Christ the Saviour," and "The Blood of the New Covenant." The third is on "Christians One Body in Christ," "The One Body the Spouse of Christ," "Christ's Prayer for Unity," "Our Reconciliation should be manifested in common Worship," and "Ambassadors for Christ." "All the grave and awful questions associated with human sinfulness and the Divine plan of redemption are discussed with minute and painstaking care, and in the Appendix all the passages of Scripture referring to them are marshalled and critically reviewed."—*Wesleyan Times.

Taylor.—THE RESTORATION OF BELIEF. New and Revised Edition. By ISAAC TAYLOR, Esq. Crown 8vo. 8s. 6d.

The earlier chapters are occupied with an examination of the primitive history of the Christian Religion, and its relation to the Roman government; and here, as well as in the remainder of the work, the author shews the bearing of that history on some of the difficult and interesting questions which have recently been claiming the attention of all earnest men. The book will be found to contain a clear and full statement of the case as it at present stands in behalf of Christianity. The last chapter of this New Edition treats of " The Present Position of the Argument concerning Christianity," with special reference to M. Renan's Vie de Jésus. *The* Journal of Sacred Literature *says,—" The current of thought which runs through this book is calm and clear, its tone is earnest, its manner courteous. The author has carefully studied the successive problems which he so ably handles."*

Temple.—SERMONS PREACHED IN THE CHAPEL of RUGBY SCHOOL. By F. Temple, D.D., Bishop of Exeter. New and Cheaper Edition. Extra fcap. 8vo. 4*s.* 6*d.*

This volume contains Thirty-five Sermons on topics more or less intimately connected with every-day life. The following are a few of the subjects discoursed upon :—"Love and Duty;" "Coming to Christ;" "Great Men ;" "Faith;" " Doubts ;" " Scruples;" "Original Sin ;" "Friendship;" "Helping Others;" " The Discipline of Temptation;" "Strength a Duty;" "Worldliness;" "Ill Temper;" " The Burial of the Past." The Critic *speaks of them thus :—"We trust that the tender affectionate spirit of practical Christianity which runs through every page of the volume will have its due effect. . . . desiring to rouse the youthful hearers to a sense of duty, and to arm them against the perils and dangers of the world against which they are so soon to battle."*

A SECOND SERIES OF SERMONS, preached in the Chapel of Rugby School. Extra fcap. 8vo. 6*s.*

This Second Series of Forty-two brief, pointed, practical Sermons, on topics intimately connected with the every-day life of young and old, will be acceptable to all who are acquainted with the First Series. The following are a few of the subjects treated of :—"Disobedience," "Almsgiving," " The Unknown Guidance of God," "Apathy one of our Trials," "High Aims in Leaders," "Doing our Best," " The Use of Knowledge," "Use of Observances," "Martha and

Mary," "*John the Baptist*," "*Severity before Mercy*," "*Even Mistakes Punished*," "*Morality and Religion*," "*Children*," "*Action the Test of Spiritual Life*," "*Self-Respect*," "*Too Late*," "*The Tercentenary.*"

Thring.—SERMONS DELIVERED AT UPPINGHAM SCHOOL. By the Rev. E. THRING, M.A. Crown 8vo. 5*s*.

> *In this volume are contained Forty-seven brief Sermons, all on subjects more or less intimately connected with Public-school life. "These Sermons," the author says, "are sent into the world as parts of a system, and as exponents, in some degree, of the experience of working men, that it is possible to have a free and manly school-life, complete in all its parts, neither lost in a crowd, nor shut up in a prison, nor reared in a hot-bed."—"We desire very highly to commend these capital Sermons which treat of a boy's life and trials in a thoroughly practical way and with great simplicity and impressiveness. They deserve to be classed with the best of their kind."*—Literary Churchman.

Tracts for Priests and People. By VARIOUS WRITERS.

THE FIRST SERIES. Crown 8vo. 8*s*.

THE SECOND SERIES. Crown 8vo. 8*s*.

The whole Series of Fifteen Tracts may he had separately, price One Shilling each.

> *A series of papers written after the excitement aroused by the publication of "Essays and Reviews" had somewhat abated, and designed, by the exposition of positive truth, to meet the religious difficulties of honest inquirers. Amongst the writers are Mr. Thomas Hughes, Professor Maurice, the Rev. J. Llewellyn Davies, and Mr. J. M. Ludlow.*

Trench.—Works by R. CHENEVIX TRENCH, D.D., Archbishop of Dublin. (For other Works by the same author, *see* BIOGRAPHICAL, BELLES LETTRES, and LINGUISTIC CATALOGUES).

> *Archbishop Trench is well known as a writer who has the happy faculty of being able to take with discrimination the results of the*

Trench—*continued.*

highest criticism and scholarship, and present them in such a shape as will be not only valuable to scholars, but interesting, intelligible, and of the greatest use even to the ordinary reader. It is generally acknowledged that few men have been more successful in bringing out the less obvious meanings of the New Testament, or done more for the popular yet scholarly exposition of the Bible generally.

NOTES ON THE PARABLES OF OUR LORD.
Eleventh Edition. 8vo. 12s.

This work has taken its place as a standard exposition and interpretation of Christ's Parables. The book is prefaced by an Introductory Essay in four chapters :—I. On the definition of the Parable, a point on which there has been much difference of opinion. II. On Teaching by Parables. III. On the Interpretation of the Parables. IV. On other Parables besides those in the Scriptures. The author then proceeds to take up the Parables one by one, and by the aid of philology, history, antiquities, and the researches of travellers, shew forth the significance, beauty, and applicability of each, concluding with what he deems its true moral interpretation. In the numerous Notes are many valuable references, illustrative quotations, critical and philological annotations, etc., and appended to the volume is a classified list of fifty-six works on the Parables.

NOTES ON THE MIRACLES OF OUR LORD.
Ninth Edition. 8vo. 12s.

In the 'Preliminary Essay' to this work, all the momentous and interesting questions that have been raised in connection with Miracles, are discussed with considerable fulness, and the author's usual candour and learning. The Essay consists of six chapters : —I. On the Names of Miracles, i. e. the Greek words by which they are designated in the New Testament. II. The Miracles and Nature—What is the difference between a Miracle and any event in the ordinary course of Nature? III. The Authority of Miracles—Is the Miracle to command absolute obedience? IV. The Evangelical, compared with the other cycles of

Trench—*continued.*

*Miracles. V. The Assaults on the Miracles—*1. *The Jewish.* 2. *The Heathen (Celsus etc.).* 3. *The Pantheistic (Spinosa etc.).* 4. *The Sceptical (Hume).* 5. *The Miracles only relatively miraculous (Schleiermacher).* 6. *The Rationalistic (Paulus).* 7. *The Historico-Critical (Woolston, Strauss). VI. The Apologetic Worth of the Miracles. The author then treats the separate Miracles as he does the Parables.*

SYNONYMS OF THE NEW TESTAMENT. New Edition, enlarged. 8vo. cloth. 12s.

The study of synonyms in any language is valuable as a discipline for training the mind to close and accurate habits of thought; more especially is this the case in Greek—"a language spoken by a people of the finest and subtlest intellect; who saw distinctions where others saw none; who divided out to different words what others often were content to huddle confusedly under a common term. . . . Where is it so desirable that we should miss nothing, that we should lose no finer intention of the writer, as in those words which are the vehicles of the very mind of God Himself?" This work is recognised as a valuable companion to every student of the New Testament in the original. This, the Seventh Edition, has been carefully revised, and a considerable number of new synonyms added. Appended is an Index to the Synonyms, and an Index to many other words alluded to or explained throughout the work. "He is," the Athenæum *says, "a guide in this department of knowledge to whom his readers may intrust themselves with confidence. His sober judgment and sound sense are barriers against the misleading influence of arbitrary hypotheses."*

ON THE AUTHORIZED VERSION OF THE NEW TESTAMENT. Second Edition. 8vo. 7s.

Archbishop Trench's familiarity with and many-sided study of the New Testament makes him peculiarly fitted to estimate the value of the present translation, and to give directions as to how a new one should be proceeded with. After some Introductory Remarks, in which the propriety of a revision is briefly discussed, the whole

Trench—*continued.*

question of the merits of the present version is gone into in detail, in eleven chapters. A few of the titles of the chapters are:—III. On the English of the Authorized Version. IV. On some Questions of Translation. IX. On some Questionable Renderings of Words. X. On some Incorrect Renderings. XI. On the Best Means of carrying out a Revision. Appended is a chronological list of works bearing on the subject, an Index of the principal Texts considered, an Index of Greek Words, and an Index of other Words referred to throughout the book.

STUDIES IN THE GOSPELS. Second Edition. 8vo. 10s. 6d.

This book is published under the conviction that the assertion often made is untrue,—viz. that Gospels are in the main plain and easy, and that all the chief difficulties of the New Testament are to be found in the Epistles. In the Epistles, the difficulties are often mere difficulties of form, whereas in the Gospels it is the thought itself, the Divine fact or statement, which itself constitutes the difficulty. These "Studies," sixteen in number, are the fruit of a much larger scheme, and each Study deals with some important episode mentioned in the Gospels, in a critical, philosophical, and practical manner. Many learned references and quotations are added to the Notes. Among the subjects treated are:—The Temptation; Christ and the Samaritan Woman; The Three Aspirants; The Transfiguration; Zacchæus; The True Vine; The Penitent Malefactor; Christ and the Two Disciples on the way to Emmaus.

COMMENTARY ON THE EPISTLES to the SEVEN CHURCHES IN ASIA. Third Edition, revised. 8vo. 8s. 6d.

Bengel was wont above all things to recommend the study of these Epistles to youthful ministers of Christ's Word and Sacraments; and, as the author says in his Preface, the number of aspects in which they present themselves to us as full of interest, is extraordinary. They are full of interest to the student of ecclesiastical history; possess a strong attraction for those who occupy themselves with questions of pure exegesis, from the fact of their con-

Trench—*continued.*

taining so many unsolved problems of interpretation; their purely
theological interest is great; their practical interest in their
bearing on the whole pastoral and ministerial work is extreme;
and finally, there is about these Epistles a striking originality,
an entire unlikeness, in some points at least, to anything else in
Scripture.   The present work consists of an Introduction, being
a commentary on Rev. i. 4—20, a detailed examination of each of
the Seven Epistles, in all its bearings, and an Excursus on the
Historico-Prophetical Interpretation of the Epistles.

THE SERMON ON THE MOUNT.   An Exposition
drawn from the writings of St. Augustine, with an Essay on his
merits as an Interpreter of Holy Scripture.   Third Edition, enlarged. 8vo. 10s. 6d.

*This volume is not a mere translation of St. Augustine's Commentary
on the Sermon on the Mount, but an attempt to draw from the
whole circle of his writings (that one of course included) what of
most important he has contributed for the elucidation, or for the
turning to practical uses, of this portion of Holy Scripture.   The
first half of the present work consists of a dissertation in eight
chapters on "Augustine as an Interpreter of Scripture," the titles
of the several chapters being as follow:—I. Augustine's General
Views of Scripture and its Interpretation.   II. The External
Helps for the Interpretation of Scripture possessed by Augustine.
III. Augustine's Principles and Canons of Interpretation.   IV.
Augustine's Allegorical Interpretation of Scripture.   V. Illustrations of Augustine's Skill as an Interpreter of Scripture.   VI.
Augustine on John the Baptist and on St. Stephen.   VII. Augustine on the Epistle to the Romans.   VIII. Miscellaneous Examples of Augustine's Interpretation of Scripture.   The latter half
of the work consists of Augustine's Exposition of the Sermon on
the Mount, not however a mere series of quotations from Augustine,
but a connected account of his sentiments on the various passages of
that Sermon, interspersed with criticisms by Archbishop Trench.
The Notes consist mostly of quotations from Augustine in the
original Latin.*

Trench—*continued.*

SERMONS PREACHED in WESTMINSTER ABBEY.
Second Edition. 8vo. 10s. 6d.

> *This volume consists of Thirty-three Sermons preached by the author in the Abbey, when Dean of Westminster. They embrace a wide variety of topics, and are thoroughly practical, earnest, and evangelical, and simple in style. The following are a few of the subjects:—"Tercentenary Celebration of Queen Elizabeth's Accession;" "Conviction and Conversion;" "The Incredulity of Thomas;" "The Angels' Hymn;" "Counting the Cost;" "The Holy Trinity in Relation to our Prayers;" "On the Death of General Havelock;" "Christ Weeping over Jerusalem;" "Walking with Christ in White."*

SHIPWRECKS OF FAITH. Three Sermons preached before the University of Cambridge in May, 1867. Fcap. 8vo. 2s. 6d.

> *These Sermons are especially addressed to young men. The subjects are "Balaam," "Saul," and "Judas Iscariot," three of the mournfullest lives recorded in Scripture, "for the greatness of their vocation, and their disastrous falling short of the same, for the utter defeat of their lives, for the shipwreck of everything which they made." These lives are set forth as beacon-lights, "to warn us off from perilous reefs and quicksands, which have been the destruction of many, and which might only too easily be ours." "The Archbishop of Dublin's Sermons," says the* John Bull, *"before the University of Cambridge are, like all he writes, affectionate and earnest discourses."*

Tudor.—The DECALOGUE VIEWED as the CHRISTIAN'S LAW. With Special Reference to the Questions and Wants of the Times. By the Rev. RICH. TUDOR, B.A. Crown 8vo. 10s. 6d.

> *In complying with the request to publish these Lectures, and in preparing them for the press, the author has expanded them into a consecutive treatise on the Ten Commandments. His aim is to*

bring out the Christian sense of the Decalogue in its application to existing needs and questions. Many questions of the highest importance have been treated in an earnest and reverent manner, and the work will be found to occupy ground which no other single work has hitherto filled. It is divided into Two Parts, the First Part consisting of three lectures on "Duty," and the Second Part of twelve lectures on the Ten Commandments. The Guardian *says of it, "As a series· of practical sermons, and as a whole, his volume throughout is an outspoken and sound exposition of Christian morality, based deeply upon true foundations, set forth systematically, and forcibly and plainly expressed—as good a specimen of what pulpit lectures ought to be as is often to be found." The* Westminster Review *says, · " There is an earnestness in his purpose and evidently a sincere endeavour to apply the words of Scripture to present needs."*

Tulloch.—THE CHRIST OF THE GOSPELS AND THE CHRIST OF MODERN CRITICISM. Lectures on M. RENAN'S "Vie de Jésus." By JOHN TULLOCH, D.D., Principal of the College of St. Mary, in the University of St. Andrew's. Extra fcap. 8vo. 4s. 6d.

These Lectures were written originally during the heat of the commotion caused by the publication of M. Renan's Vie de Jésus. *While Dr. Tulloch does not hesitate to grapple boldly with the statements and theories of Renan, he does so in a spirit of perfect fairness and courtesy, eschewing all personalities and sinister insinuations as to motives and sincerity. The work will be found to be a fair and full statement, in Dr. Tulloch's eloquent style, of the case as it stands against Renan's theory. "Amongst direct answers," says the* Reader, *"to M. Renan, this volume will not be easily surpassed... The style is animated, pointed, and scholarly; the tone fair and appreciative; the philosophy intelligent and cautious; the Christianity liberal, reverent, and hearty."*

Vaughan.—Works by CHARLES J. VAUGHAN, D.D., Master of the Temple :—

Few men of the present day have won so much of the respect and love of their fellow-men of all creeds as the Rev. Dr. Vaughan.

His genuine sympathy with the difficulties, sorrows and struggles of all classes of his fellow-men, his thorough disinterestedness, and his high views of life have been acknowledged by critics of all creeds. No sermons can be more applicable to the ever-recurring ills, bodily, mental, and spiritual, that flesh is heir to; they are eloquent because they glow with love and enthusiasm for the highest good of men. His commentaries and expository lectures are those of a faithful evangelical, but at the same time liberal-minded interpreter of what he believes to be the Word of God.

CHRIST SATISFYING THE INSTINCTS OF HU-MANITY. Eight Lectures delivered in the Temple Church. Extra fcp. 8vo. 3*s.* 6*d.*

The object of these Sermons is to exhibit the spiritual wants of human nature, and to prove that all of them receive full satisfaction in Christ. The various instincts which He is shewn to meet are those of Truth, Reverence, Perfection, Liberty, Courage, Sympathy, Sacrifice, and Unity. "We are convinced that there are congregations, in number unmistakeably increasing, to whom such Essays as these, full of thought and learning, are infinitely more beneficial, for they are more acceptable, than the recognised type of sermons." —John Bull.

MEMORIALS OF HARROW SUNDAYS. A Selection of Sermons preached in Harrow School Chapel. With a View of the Chapel. Fourth Edition. Crown 8vo. 10*s.* 6*d.*

These Sermons were preached in the Chapel of Harrow School, and while they deal with subjects that in a peculiar way concern the young, and in a manner that cannot fail to attract their attention and influence their conduct, they are in every respect applicable to people of all ages. "Discussing," says the John Bull, *"those forms of evil and impediments to duty which peculiarly beset the young, Dr. Vaughan has, with singular tact, blended deep thought and analytical investigation of principles with interesting earnestness and eloquent simplicity."* . *The* Morning Chronicle *says, "The number of view-points from which he regards his subject, the various motives he appeals to, and the range of duties and*

Vaughan (Dr. C. J.)—*continued.*

situations to which he demonstrates its applicability, his copiousness of illustration and breadth of view in practical teaching, are conspicuous in almost every sermon."   The Nonconformist *says "the volume is a precious one for family reading, and for the hand of the thoughtful boy or young man entering life."*

THE BOOK AND THE LIFE, and other Sermons, preached before the University of Cambridge. New Edition. Fcap. 8vo. 4s. 6d.

These Sermons are all of a thoroughly practical nature, and some of them are especially adapted to those who are in a state of anxious doubt.   " They meet," the Freeman *says, "in what appears to us to be the one true method, the scepticism and indifference to religious truth which are almost sure to trouble young men who read and think.   In short, we know no book more likely to do the young and inquiring good, or to help them to gain that tone of mind wanting which they may doubt and ask for ever, because always doubting and asking in vain."*

TWELVE DISCOURSES on SUBJECTS CONNECTED WITH THE LITURGY and WORSHIP of the CHURCH OF ENGLAND. Fcap. 8vo. 6s.

Four of these discourses were published in 1860, *in a work entitled* Revision of the Liturgy; *four others have appeared in the form of separate sermons, delivered on various occasions, and published at the time by request ; and four are new.   All will be found to fall strictly under the present title, reviewing the chief matters suggested by the Church Liturgy.   The Appendix contains two articles,—one on "Subscription and Scruples," the other on the "Rubric and the Burial Service."   The* Press *characterises the volume as "eminently wise and temperate."*

LESSONS OF LIFE AND GODLINESS.   A Selection of Sermons preached in the Parish Church of Doncaster.   Fourth and Cheaper Edition.   Fcap. 8vo.   3s. 6d.

This volume consists of Nineteen Sermons, mostly on subjects connected with the every-day walk and conversation of Christians.

Vaughan (Dr. C. J.)—*continued.*

They bear such titles as "The Talebearer," "Features of Charity," "The Danger of Relapse," "The Secret Life and the Outward," "Family Prayer," "Zeal without Consistency," "The Gospel an Incentive to Industry in Business," "Use and Abuse of the World." "A more useful book," says the Press, *"or one more fitted to be under almost every possible circumstance the guide and support of all earnest young people, could not well be conceived." The* Spectator *styles them "earnest and human. They are adapted to every class and order in the social system, and will be read with wakeful interest by all who seek to amend whatever may be amiss in their natural disposition or in their acquired habits."*

WORDS FROM THE GOSPELS. A Second Selection of Sermons preached in the Parish Church of Doncaster. Second Edition. Fcap. 8vo. 4s. 6d.

In this volume are Twenty-two Sermons on subjects taken from one or other of the four Gospels. The Nonconformist *characterises these Sermons as "of practical earnestness, of a thoughtfulness that penetrates the common conditions and experiences of life, and brings the truths and examples of Scripture to bear on them with singular force, and of a style that owes its real elegance to the simplicity and directness which have fine culture for their roots. . . . A book than which few could give more holy pleasantness and solemn purpose to their Sabbath evenings at home."*

LESSONS OF THE CROSS AND PASSION. Six Lectures delivered in Hereford Cathedral during the Week before Easter, 1869. Fcap. 8vo. 2s. 6d.

This volume contains Six Sermons on subjects mainly connected with the death and passion of Christ. The titles of the Sermons are:— I. "Too Late" (Matt. xxvi. 45). II. "The Divine Sacrifice and the Human Priesthood." III. "Love not the World." IV. "The Moral Glory of Christ." V. "Christ made perfect through Suffering." VI. "Death the Remedy of Christ's Loneliness." "This little volume," the Nonconformist *says, "exhibits all his*

5

Vaughan (Dr. C. J.)—*continued.*

best characteristics. Elevated, calm, and clear, the Sermons owe much to their force, and yet they seem literally to owe nothing to it. They are studied, but their grace is the grace of perfect simplicity."

LIFE'S WORK AND GOD'S DISCIPLINE.   Three Sermons.   Fcap. 8vo. cloth.   2s. 6d.

The Three Sermons contained in this volume have a oneness of aim indicated by the title, and are on the following subjects:—I. "The Work burned and the Workmen saved." II. "The Individual Hiring." III. "The Remedial Discipline of Disease and Death."

THE WHOLESOME WORDS OF JESUS CHRIST. Four Sermons preached before the University of Cambridge in November 1866.   Second Edition.   Fcap. 8vo. cloth.   3s. 6d.

Dr. Vaughan uses the word "Wholesome" here in its literal and original sense, the sense in which St. Paul uses it, as meaning healthy, sound, conducing to right living; *and in the Four Sermons contained in this volume he points out and illustrates several of the "wholesome" characteristics of the Gospel,—the Words of Christ. The subjects of these Sermons are as follow:— I. "Naturalness and Spirituality of Revelation—Grandeur and Self-Control—Truthfulness and Tenderness." II. "Universality and Individuality of Christ's Gospel." III. "Oblivions and Ambitions of the Life of Grace." IV. "Regrets and Preparations of Human Life." The* John Bull *says this volume is "replete with all the author's well-known vigour of thought and richness of expression."*

FOES OF FAITH.   Sermons preached before the University of Cambridge in November 1868.   Fcap. 8vo.   3s. 6d.

The "Foes of Faith" preached against in these Four Sermons are:— I. "Unreality." II. "Indolence." III. "Irreverence." IV. "Inconsistency,"—"Foes," says the author, "which must be manfully fought against by all who would be finally admitted into that holy communion and fellowship which is, for time and eternity,

Vaughan (Dr. C. J.)—*continued.*

the blessed company of all faithful people." "*They are written,*" *the* London Review *says,* "*with culture and elegance, and exhibit the thoughtful earnestness, piety, and good sense of their author.*" "*They are thoroughly excellent,*" *says the* Literary Churchman.

LECTURES ON THE EPISTLE to the PHILIPPIANS.
Second Edition. Crown 8vo. 7s. 6d.

This series of Lectures, twenty-one in number, was delivered by Dr. Vaughan to his own congregation. Each Lecture is prefaced by a literal translation from the Greek of the paragraph which forms its subject, contains first a minute explanation of the passage on which it is based, and then a practical application of the verse or clause selected as its text. The Press *speaks of these Lectures thus:—"Replete with good sense and practical religious advice... The language of the Apostle assumes a practical significance, which it seldom wears in the eyes of any ordinary reader, and Dr. Vaughan's listeners would feel themselves placed in the position of men receiving inspired instruction on the ordinary business of life. We can scarcely praise this plan too highly.*"

LECTURES ON THE REVELATION OF ST. JOHN.
Third and Cheaper Edition. Two Vols. Extra fcap. 8vo. 9s.

In this the Third Edition of these Lectures, the literal translations of the passages expounded will be found interwoven in the body of the Lectures themselves. The whole has been carefully revised, but without any material change. In attempting to expound this most-hard-to-understand Book, Dr. Vaughan, while taking from others what assistance he required, has not adhered to any particular school of interpretation, but has endeavoured to shew forth the significance of this Revelation by the help of his strong common sense, critical acumen, scholarship, and reverent spirit. "Dr. Vaughan's Sermons," the Spectator *says, "are the most practical discourses on the Apocalypse with which we are acquainted." Prefixed is a Synopsis of the Book of Revelation, and appended is an Index of passages illustrating the language of the Book. There are in all Thirty-eight Lectures.*

Vaughan (Dr. C. J.)—*continued.*

EPIPHANY, LENT, AND EASTER. A Selection of
Expository Sermons. Third Edition. Crown 8vo. 10*s*. 6*d*.

> *The first eighteen of these Sermons were preached during the seasons
> of* 1860, *indicated in the title, and are practical expositions of passages taken from the lessons of the days on which they were delivered.
> The last eight Sermons were added to the Second Edition, and were
> preached in the following July. The Third Edition has been carefully revised, and one or two important alterations made in the
> interpretation of the text. As in the case of the Lectures on
> Philippians, each Lecture is prefaced with a careful and literal
> rendering of the original of the passage of which the Lecture is an
> exposition. The* Nonconformist *says that "in simplicity, dignity,
> close adherence to the words of Scripture, insight into 'the mind
> of the Spirit,' and practical thoughtfulness, they are models of that
> species of pulpit instruction to which they belong."*

THE EPISTLES OF ST. PAUL. For English Readers.
PART I., containing the FIRST EPISTLE TO THE THESSALONIANS.
Second Edition. 8vo. 1*s*. 6*d*. Each Epistle will be published
separately in its chronological order.

> *It is the object of this work to enable English readers, unacquainted
> with Greek, to enter with intelligence into the meaning, connection,
> and phraseology of the writings of the great Apostle.* (1) *Each
> Epistle will be prefaced by an Introduction containing information
> as to the circumstances, design, and order of its composition.* (2)
> *The Authorized English Version occupies the foremost place in
> each page.* (3) *Beside it, in smaller type, is a literal English
> Version, made from the original Greek.* (4) *A free paraphrase
> stands below, in which it is attempted to express the sense and
> connection of the Epistle.* . (5) *The Notes include both doctrinal
> explanation and verbal illustration; occasionally a brief word of
> application has been introduced.*

ST. PAUL'S EPISTLE TO THE ROMANS. The Greek
Text, with English Notes. Third Edition, greatly enlarged.
Crown 8vo. 7*s*. 6*d*.

Vaughan (Dr. C. J.)—*continued.*

This volume contains the Greek Text of the Epistle to the Romans as settled by the Rev. B. F. Westcott, D.D., for his complete recension of the Text of the New Testament; his name is a sufficient guarantee for its accuracy. Appended to the text are copious critical and exegetical Notes, the result, when first published, of almost eighteen years' study on the part of the author. This the Third Edition has for the most part been entirely re-written; the main features of the work are, however, unchanged. The author has sought more and more to render the work serviceable to students of the Greek Testament generally, and of St. Paul's Epistle in particular. The "Index of Words illustrated or explained in the Notes" will be found, in some considerable degree, an Index to the Epistles as a whole. "I have desired," the author says, "to catch and to represent the meaning of each passage and of the whole, without deriving it from any secondary source. Each single note is the result of some honest labour. One of my principal endeavours has been, to trace through the New Testament the uses of the more remarkable words or phrases which occur in the Epistle, arranging them, where the case required it, under their various modifications of sense." Prefixed to the volume is a discourse on "St. Paul's Conversion and Doctrine," suggested by some recent publications on St. Paul's theological standing. In the Preface to the Third Edition, among other things, is a Synopsis of the contents of the Epistle. The Guardian *says of the work,—"For educated young men his commentary seems to fill a gap hitherto unfilled... As a whole, Dr. Vaughan appears to us to have given to the world a valuable book of original and careful and earnest thought bestowed on the accomplishment of a work which will be of much service and which is much needed."*

THE CHURCH OF THE FIRST DAYS.

Series I.   The Church of Jerusalem.   Second Edition.
   "   II.   The Church of the Gentiles.   Second Edition.
   " III.   The Church of the World.   Second Edition.
Fcap. 8vo. cloth.   4s. 6d. each.

These Lectures on the Acts *of the* Apostles *were delivered by the author during* 1862-64, *in the Parish Church of Doncaster, in*

Vaughan (Dr. C. J.)—*continued.*

the ordinary course of parochial ministration. The work is in three volumes:—I. "The Church of Jerusalem," extending from the 1st to the 8th chapter (inclusive) of the Acts. II. "The Church of the Gentiles," from the 9th to the 16th chapter. III. "The Church of the World," from the 17th to the 28th chapter. The titles are of necessity only approximately appropriate. Where necessary, the Authorized Version has been departed from, and a new literal translation taken as the basis of exposition. All possible topographical and historical light has been brought to bear on the subject; and while thoroughly practical in their aim, these Lectures will be found to afford a fair notion of the history and condition of the Primitive Church. The British Quarterly says,— "These Sermons are worthy of all praise, and are models of pulpit teaching." In reference to this work, the Patriot says,—"We are indebted to Dr. Vaughan for shewing how interesting and effective expository preaching may be made."

COUNSELS for YOUNG STUDENTS. Three Sermons preached before the University of Cambridge at the Opening of the Academical Year 1870-71. Fcap. 8vo. 2s. 6d.

The titles of the Three Sermons contained in this volume are:—I. "The Great Decision." II. "The House and the Builder." III. "The Prayer and the Counter-Prayer." They all bear pointedly, earnestly, and sympathisingly upon the conduct and pursuits of young students and young men generally, to counsel whom, Dr. Vaughan's qualifications and aptitude are well known.

NOTES FOR LECTURES ON CONFIRMATION, with suitable Prayers. Seventh Edition. Fcap. 8vo. 1s. 6d.

In preparation for the Confirmation held in Harrow School Chapel, Dr. Vaughan was in the habit of printing week by week, and distributing among the Candidates, somewhat full notes of the Lecture he purposed to deliver to them, together with a form of Prayer adapted to the particular subject. He has collected these weekly Notes and Prayers into this little volume, in the hope that it may assist the labours of those who are engaged in preparing Candidates for Confirmation, and who find it difficult to lay their hand upon any one book of suitable instruction, at once sufficiently full to furnish a synopsis of the subject, and sufficiently elastic to give free scope to the individual judgment in the use of it. The Press says the work *"commends itself at once by its simplicity and by its logical arrangement. . . . While points of doctrine, as they arise, are not lost sight of, the principal stress is laid on the preparation of the heart rather than the head. . . . This little Manual will prove, as it is well calculated to be, extensively useful."*

Vaughan.—Works by DAVID J. VAUGHAN, M.A., Vicar of St. Martin's, Leicester :—

SERMONS PREACHED IN ST. JOHN'S CHURCH, LEICESTER, during the Years 1855 and 1856. Crown 8vo. 5s. 6d.

This volume contains Twenty-five Sermons preached in St. John's Church, Leicester, in the ordinary course of the author's ministration. They embrace a great variety of topics, all of the highest interest, are thoroughly practical in their nature, and calculated to give a hopeful view of life as seen in the light shed upon it by Christianity.

SERMONS on the RESURRECTION. With a Preface. Fcap. 8vo. 3s.

In the Preface to this work, the author expounds and endeavours to justify his view of the Atonement, shewing it to be more reasonable and scriptural than the ordinary doctrine. There are Seven Sermons in all, bearing the following titles:—I. "The Fellowship of Christ's Sufferings." II. "Christ the Resurrection and the Life." III. "Christ our Passover." IV. "Christ the Shepherd." V. "The True Light which lighteth every man." VI. "The City of God, and the Light thereof." VII. "Christ going to the Father, and the Way to the Father."

CHRISTIAN EVIDENCES AND THE BIBLE. New Edition, revised and enlarged. Fcap. 8vo. cloth. 5s. 6d.

The main object of this series of Twelve Sermons is to shew, that,

Vaughan (D. J.)—*continued.*

quite irrespective of any theory as to the nature of the Bible and the special inspiration of its authors, there is good and sufficient reason for believing that Jesus Christ is the Son of God, who reveals and reconciles men to the Father. The author thinks it impossible to build our Christian faith upon the assumed infallibility of the Bible as its foundation; and that the true and solid rock, upon which the Church really stands and ought consciously to stand, is simply the confession that "Jesus is the Christ, the Son of the living God." The Preface to this, the Second Edition, consists of a somewhat lengthened "Analysis of the Nature of Scientific Truth," —the nature of the evidence which is universally held to be sound and conclusive. In the Sermons themselves the Internal and External Evidences of Christianity and cognate subjects are discussed, and throughout the volume are several long notes on points occurring in the text. Appended is a short Essay on " The Nature and Sphere of Law."—" This little volume," the Spectator *says, "is a model of that honest and reverent criticism of the Bible which is not only right, but the duty of English clergymen in such times as these to put forth from the pulpit."*

Venn.—ON SOME OF THE CHARACTERISTICS OF BELIEF, Scientific and Religious. Being the Hulsean Lectures for 1869. By the Rev. J. VENN, M.A. 8vo. 6s. 6d.

These discourses are intended to illustrate, explain, and work out into some of their consequences, certain characteristics by which the attainment of religious belief is prominently distinguished from the attainment of belief upon most other subjects. The first Lecture is an attempt to explain what is the nature of the logical foothold for differences of opinion among men is; to shew what there is in the constitution of the evidence which makes it possible for these differences to commence and persist. The second meets the question, What is the criterion of truth? How are we to decide which of the varying but honest judgment on the same subject is right and which wrong? The third and fourth Lectures are devoted to working out into several of their consequences the characteristics of evidence on religious subjects which were explained and illustrated in the first.

Warington.—THE WEEK OF CREATION; OR, THE COSMOGONY OF GENESIS CONSIDERED IN ITS RELATION TO MODERN SCIENCE. By GEORGE WARINGTON, Author of "The Historic Character of the Pentateuch Vindicated." Crown 8vo. 4s. 6d.

The greater part of this work is taken up with the teaching of the Cosmogony. Its purpose is also investigated, and a chapter is devoted to the consideration of the passage in which the difficulties occur. "A very able vindication of the Mosaic Cosmogony by a writer who unites the advantages of a critical knowledge of the Hebrew text and of distinguished scientific attainments."—Spectator.

Westcott.—Works by BROOKE FOSS WESTCOTT, D.D., Regius Professor of Divinity in the University of Cambridge; Canon of Peterborough :—

The London Quarterly, speaking of Mr. Westcott, says,—" To a learning and accuracy which command respect and confidence, he unites what are not always to be found in union with these qualities, the no less valuable faculties of lucid arrangement and graceful and facile expression."

AN INTRODUCTION TO THE STUDY OF THE GOSPELS. Third Edition. Crown 8vo. 10s. 6d.

The author's chief object in this work has been to shew that there is a true mean between the idea of a formal harmonization of the Gospels and the abandonment of their absolute truth. After an Introduction on the General Effects of the course of Modern Philosophy on the popular views of Christianity, and Holy Scripture specially, as regards its Inspiration, Completeness, and Interpretation, he proceeds to determine in what way the principles therein indicated may be applied to the study of the Gospels, to determine how far their origin and contents fall in with the general order of Providence, and suggest the presence of that deep and hidden wisdom in which he believes the characteristic of Inspiration to lie. The treatise is divided into seven Chapters :—I. The Preparation for the Gospel. II. The Jewish Doctrine of the Messiah. III. The

Westcott (Dr. B. F.)—*continued.*

Origin of the Gospels.   IV. The Characteristics of the Gospels. V. The Gospel of St. John.   VI. and VII. The Differences in detail and of arrangement in the Synoptic Evangelists.   VIII. The Difficulties of the Gospels.   The Appendices contain much valuable subsidiary matter.

A GENERAL SURVEY OF THE HISTORY OF THE CANON OF THE NEW TESTAMENT DURING THE FIRST FOUR CENTURIES. Third Edition, revised. Crown 8vo. 10s. 6d.

The object of this treatise is to deal with the New Testament as a whole, and that on purely historical grounds.   The separate books of which it is composed are considered not individually, but as claiming to be parts of the apostolic heritage of Christians.   The Author has thus endeavoured to connect the history of the New Testament Canon with the growth and consolidation of the Catholic Church, and to point out the relation existing between the amount of evidence for the authenticity of its component parts and the whole mass of Christian literature.   "The treatise," says the British Quarterly, *"is a scholarly performance, learned, dispassionate, discriminating, worthy of his subject and of the present state of Christian literature in relation to it."*

THE BIBLE IN THE CHURCH.   A Popular Account of the Collection and Reception of the Holy Scriptures in the Christian Churches.   Third Edition. 18mo. 4s. 6d.

The present work is an attempt to answer a request frequently made to the author, to place in a simple form, for the use of general readers, the substance of his large work on the Canon of the New Testament.   *The present volume has been written under the impression that a History of the whole Bible, and not of the New Testament only, would be required, if those unfamiliar with the subject were to be enabled to learn in what manner and with what consent the collection of Holy Scriptures was first made and then enlarged and finally closed by the Church.   Though the work is intended to be simple and popular in its method, the*

Westcott (Dr. B. F.)—*continued.*

author, for this very reason, has aimed at the strictest accuracy. The author has endeavoured to make the work complete in itself: every technical term is explained when it first occurs; and the addition of slight historical characteristics of men or ages will enable the reader to appreciate fairly the relative importance of the evidence which they contribute. The History of the Bible is brought down to the 16th century, and the Appendix contains two articles,—I. "On the History of the Canon of the Old Testament before the Christian Era." II. "On the Contents of the most ancient MSS. of the Christian Bible." Appended is a copious Index. "We would recommend," the Literary Churchman *says, "every one who loves and studies the Bible to read and ponder this exquisite little book. . . . Mr. Westcott's account of the 'Canon' is* true history *in the very highest sense."*

A GENERAL VIEW OF THE HISTORY OF THE ENGLISH BIBLE. Crown 8vo. 10s. 6d.

Previous writers in this department have in the main confined themselves to outward facts, without tracing the facts back to their ultimate sources, or noticing the variety of elements which go to form the final result. In the present work Mr. Westcott endeavours to solve this problem as far as possible. In the Introduction the author notices briefly the earliest vernacular versions of the Bible, especially those in Anglo-Saxon. Chapter I. is occupied with an account of the Manuscript English Bible from the 14th century downwards; and in Chapter II. is narrated, with many interesting personal and other details, the External History of the Printed Bible. In Chapter III. is set forth the Internal History of the English Bible, shewing to what extent the various English Translations were independent, and to what extent the translators were indebted to earlier English and foreign versions. In the Appendices, among other interesting and valuable matter, will be found "Specimens of the Earlier and Later Wycliffite Versions;" "Chronological List of Bibles;" "An Examination of Mr. Froude's History of the English Bible." The Pall Mall Gazette *calls the work "A brief, scholarly, and, to a great extent, an original contribution to theological literature."*

Westcott (Dr. B. F.)—*continued.*

THE CHRISTIAN LIFE, MANIFOLD AND ONE.
Six Sermons preached in Peterborough Cathedral. Crown 8vo.
2*s.* 6*d.*

*The Six Sermons contained in this volume are the first preached by
the author as a Canon of Peterborough Cathedral. The subjects
are:—I. "Life consecrated by the Ascension." II. "Many Gifts,
One Spirit." III. "The Gospel of the Resurrection." IV.
"Sufficiency of God." V. "Action the Test of Faith." VI.
"Progress from the Confession of God." The* Nonconformist
calls them "Beautiful discourses, singularly devout and tender."

THE GOSPEL OF THE RESURRECTION. Thoughts
on its Relation to Reason and History. New Edition. Fcap.
8vo. 4*s.* 6*d.*

*The present Essay is an endeavour to consider some of the elementary
truths of Christianity as a miraculous Revelation from the side of
History and Reason. The author endeavours to shew that the
Resurrection, with all that it includes, is the key to the history of
man, and the complement of reason; that a devout belief in the
Life of Christ is quite compatible with a broad view of the course
of human progress and a frank trust in the laws of our own minds.
After a "Statement of the Question," and an Introduction on
"Ideas of God, Nature, Miracles," Chapter I. treats of "The
Resurrection and History;" Chapter II. "The Resurrection and
Man;" Chapter III. "The Resurrection and the Church."—
"We owe," the* Patriot *says, "Mr. Westcott a very great debt of
gratitude for his very able little treatise, so faithful to the great
truths which are so precious to us, so catholic and spiritual in its
conceptions of these truths, and, moreover, so philosophical in
analysis, organism, and presentation."*

Wilkins.—THE LIGHT OF THE WORLD. An Essay,
by A. S. WILKINS, M.A., Professor of Latin in Owens College,
Manchester. Second Edition. Crown 8vo. 3*s.* 6*d.*

*The present Essay obtained the Hulsean Prize in the University of
Cambridge for the year* 1869. *The subject proposed by the Trustees
was, "The Distinctive Features of Christian as compared with
Pagan Ethics." This the author treats in six chapters:—I.
"The Object and Scope of the Discussion." II. "Pagan Ethics—
—their Historical Development." III. "Pagan Ethics—their
Greatest Perfection." IV. "Christian Ethics—their Method."
V. "Christian Ethics—their Perfection." VI. "Christian Ethics
—their Power." The author has tried in this Essay to give his
reasons for believing that the Christian ethics so far transcend the
ethics of any or all of the Pagan systems in method, in purity and
in power, as to compel us to assume for them an origin, differing in
kind from the origin of any purely human system. "It would be
difficult to praise too highly the spirit, the burden, the conclusions, or
the scholarly finish of this beautiful Essay."*—British Quarterly
Review.

Wilson.—RELIGIO CHEMICI. With a Vignette beautifully engraved after a Design by Sir NOEL PATON. By GEORGE
WILSON, M.D. Crown 8vo. 8s. 6d.

*"George Wilson," says the Preface to this volume, "had it in his
heart for many years to write a book corresponding to the* Religio
Medici *of Sir Thomas Browne, with the title* Religio Chemici.
*Several of the Essays in this volume were intended to form chapters
of it, but the health and leisure necessary to carry out his plans
were never attainable, and thus fragments only of the designed
work exist. These fragments, however, being in most cases like
finished gems waiting to be set, some of them are now given in
a collected form to his friends and the public." The Contents
of the volume are:—"Chemistry and Natural Theology." "The
Chemistry of the Stars; an Argument touching the Stars and
their Inhabitants." "Chemical Final Causes; as illustrated by
the presence of Phosphorus, Nitrogen, and Iron in the Higher
Sentient Organisms." "Robert Boyle." "Wollaston." "Life
and Discoveries of Dalton." "Thoughts on the Resurrection; an
Address to Medical Students."—"A more fascinating volume,"
the* Spectator *says, "has seldom fallen into our hands."*

Wilson.—THE BIBLE STUDENT'S GUIDE TO THE MORE CORRECT UNDERSTANDING of the ENGLISH TRANSLATION OF THE OLD TESTAMENT, BY REFERENCE TO THE ORIGINAL HEBREW. By WILLIAM WILSON, D.D., Canon of Winchester. Second Edition, carefully revised. 4to. 25*s*.

> "*The work now presented to the public*," says the Preface, "*has been the result of almost incredible labour bestowed on it during many years. It was commenced for the purpose of illustrating the precise meaning of Hebrew words ; to be a kind of manual of consultation when longer time could not be spared for further investigation. The author believes that the present work is the nearest approach to a complete Concordance of every word in the original that has yet been made: and as a Concordance, it may be found of great use to the Bible student, while at the same time it serves the important object of furnishing the means of comparing synonymous words, and of eliciting their precise and distinctive meaning. The knowledge of the Hebrew language is not absolutely necessary to the profitable use of the work ; and it is believed that many devout and accurate students of the Bible, entirely unacquainted with it, will derive great advantage from frequent reference to these pages.*" *Introductory to the body of the work, the author gives a sketch of the Construction of Hebrew. The plan of the work is simple: every word occurring in the English Version is arranged alphabetically, and under it is given the Hebrew word or words, with a full explanation of their meaning, of which it is meant to be a translation, and a complete list of the passages where it occurs. Following the general work is a complete Hebrew and English Index, which is, in effect, a Hebrew-English Dictionary. Appended are copious examples of the Figure* Paronomasia, *which occurs so frequently in the Bible.*

Worship (The) of God and Fellowship among Men. Sermons on Public Worship. By Professor MAURICE, and others. Fcap. 8vo. 3*s*. 6*d*.

> *This volume consists of Six Sermons preached by various clergymen, and although not addressed specially to any class, were suggested by*

recent efforts to bring the members of the Working Class to our Churches. As the title-page indicates, the subjects are all connected with public worship. The preachers were—Professor Maurice, I. "Preaching, a Call to Worship." II. "The Bible, a Revelation of the Beginning and End of Worship." Rev. T. J. Rowsell, "Common Prayer, the Method of Worship." Rev. J. Ll. Davies, I. "Baptism, an Admission to the Privilege of Worship." II. "The Sabbath Day, the Refreshment of Worship." Rev. D. J. Vaughan, "The Lord's Supper, the most Sacred Bond of Worship." "They are very suggestive to those who may have to prepare sermons, and well calculated to be lent amongst the more thoughtful parishioners."—Literary Churchman.

Yonge (Charlotte M.)—SCRIPTURE READINGS for SCHOOLS AND FAMILIES. By CHARLOTTE M. YONGE, Author of "The Heir of Redclyffe." Globe 8vo. 1*s.* 6*d.* With Comments. 3*s.* 6*d.*

Actual need has led the author to endeavour to prepare a reading book convenient for study with children, containing the very words of the Bible, with only a few expedient omissions, and arranged in Lessons of such length as by experience she has found to suit with children's ordinary power of accurate attentive interest. The verse form has been retained because of its convenience for children reading in class, and as more resembling their Bibles; but the poetical portions have been given in their lines. When Psalms or portions from the Prophets illustrate or fall in with the narrative, they are given in their chronological sequence. The Scripture portion, with a very few notes explanatory of mere words, is bound up apart to be used by children, while the same is also supplied with a brief comment, the purpose of which is either to assist the teacher in explaining the lesson, or to be used by more advanced young people to whom it may not be possible to give access to the authorities whence it has been taken.

In crown 8vo. cloth extra, Illustrated, price 4*s.* 6*d.* each Volume ; also
kept in morocco and calf bindings at moderate prices, and in
Ornamental Boxes containing Four Vols., 21*s.* each.

MACMILLAN'S SUNDAY LIBRARY.

A Series of Original Works by Eminent Authors.

The projectors of the Sunday Library *feel that there is a want of
books of a kind that will be welcome in many Households for reading
on Sundays, and will be in accordance with earnest convictions as to
the nature of the "Sabbath Day."*

*Sunday should contain the theory, the collective view, of our work-day
lives; and these work-days should be the Sunday in action. Our
Sunday Books, therefore, ought to do more than afford abstract subjects of meditation; they should exercise a living power, by bringing
us into direct contact with all that is true and noble in human nature
and human life, and by shewing us the life of Christ as the central
truth of humanity.*

*For Sunday reading, therefore, we need not only history, but history in
its relation to Christianity; not only biography, but the lives of men
who have consciously promoted the Christian religion—Christian
heroes in art, in science, in divinity, and in social action. The
history of Christianity, permanent and progressive, is also the history
of civilization, and from the growth of the latter we may be strengthened
in the faith that the former will ultimately prevail throughout the
whole world.*

*The Publishers have secured the co-operation of very eminent writers,
a list of whom, with the works they undertake, is herewith given.*

THE FOLLOWING VOLUMES ARE NOW READY:—

The Pupils of St. John the Divine.—By Charlotte M. Yonge, Author of "The Heir of Redclyffe."

*St. John's personal influence and share in organising the Church were
greater than those of any of the other Apostles, except perhaps St.
Paul. The author first gives a full sketch of the life and work of the
Apostle himself, drawing the material from all the most authoritative
sources, sacred and profane; then follow the lives of his immediate
disciples, Ignatius, Quadratus, Polycarp, and others; which are suc-*

ceeded by the lives of many of their pupils. The author then proceeds to sketch from their foundation the history of the many churches planted or superintended by St. John and his pupils, both in the East and West. In the last chapter is given an account of the present aspect of the Churches of St. John,—the Seven Churches of Asia mentioned in Revelations ; *also those of Athens, of Nîmes, of Lyons, and others in the West. Throughout the volume, much of early Church History is necessarily introduced, and details are given of the many persecutions to which Christianity was subjected during its struggling infancy. "Young and old will be equally refreshed and taught by these pages, in which nothing is dull, and nothing is far-fetched."*—Churchman.

The Hermits.—By CANON KINGSLEY.

In the Introduction to this volume, Mr. Kingsley shews that early hermit-life was a natural outcome of the corrupt condition of Roman society. Christianity, he shews, in its first crude form, working upon the minds of earnest men aspiring after the better life, impelled many of them to "commit a new and grand form of suicide," by taking refuge in desert places, and thus cutting themselves off from a world "which was no place for honest men,"—"where but to think was to be full of sorrow and leaden-eyed despair." The hermits "were a school of philosophers who altered the whole current of human thought ; their influence is being felt around us in many a puzzle—educational, social, and political ;" these lives afford a "key to many a lock, which just now refuses to be tampered with or burst open." The volume contains the lives of some of the most remarkable early Egyptian, Syrian, Persian, and Western hermits. The lives are mostly translations from the original biographies ; "the reader will thus be able to see the men as wholes, to judge of their merits and defects. The very style of their biographers will teach him, if he be wise, somewhat of the temper and habits of the age in which they lived."—"It is from first to last a production full of interest, written with a liberal appreciation of what is memorable for good in the lives of the Hermits, and with a wise forbearance towards legends which may be due to the ignorance, and, no doubt, also to the strong faith of the early chroniclers."—London Review.

Seekers after God.—By the Rev. F. W. FARRAR, M.A., F.R.S., Head Master of Marlborough College.

In this volume the author seeks to record the lives, and gives copious samples of the almost Christ-like utterances of three of the most clear-sighted ancient moralists, and, with perhaps the exception of Socrates, "the best and holiest characters presented to us in the records of antiquity." They are Seneca, Epictetus, and Marcus Aurelius, most appropriately called "Seekers after God," seeing that "amid infinite difficulties and surrounded by a corrupt society, they devoted themselves to the earnest search after those truths which might best make their lives 'beautiful before God.'" Besides being stimulated by the lofty example of these men, and taught wisdom by their almost Divine sayings, the reader will find in this volume much information concerning the moral and political condition of the Roman world, and learn in what kind of atmosphere the influences of Christianity were forced to work. Many details are also given which afford an insight into Roman life and manners, the kind of education bestowed on Roman youth, and the characteristics of the chief systems of ancient philosophy. The volume contains portraits of Aurelius, Seneca, and Antoninus Pius. "We can heartily recommend it as healthy in tone, instructive, interesting, mentally and spiritually stimulating and nutritious. Mr. Farrar writes as a scholar, a thinker, an earnest Christian, a wise teacher, and a genuine artist."—Nonconformist.

England's Antiphon.—By GEORGE MACDONALD.

"Antiphon means the responsive song of the parted choir," and is used in the title to indicate that this volume deals chiefly with the lyric or song-form of English religious poetry, other kinds, however, being not infrequently introduced. The author has sought to trace the course of our religious poetry from the 13th to the 19th centuries, from before Chaucer to Tennyson. He endeavours to accomplish his object by selecting the men who have produced the finest religious poetry, setting forth the circumstances in which they were placed, characterising the men themselves, critically estimating their productions, and giving ample specimens of their best religious lyrics, and quotations from larger poems, illustrating the religious feeling

of the poets or their times. Thus the volume, besides providing a concert of the sweetest and purest music, will be found to exhibit the beliefs held and aspirations cherished by many of the noblest, purest, and most richly endowed minds during the last 600 years. "This," as Mr. Macdonald says, "could hardly be done without reference to some of the principal phases of religious history of the nation."—"Dr. Macdonald has very successfully endeavoured to bring together in his little book a whole series of the sweet singers of England, and makes them raise, one after the other, their voices in praise of God."—Guardian.

Great Christians of France : St. Louis and Calvin. By M. Guizot.

The author in his Preface says :—"From the brightest epochs of Catholicism and Protestantism, I have endeavoured to select some of their most earnest and noble representatives,—men whom no intelligent and well-informed man of the present day can refuse to recognise as Christians." From among French Catholics, M. Guizot has, in this volume, selected Louis, King of France in the 13th century, and among Protestants, Calvin the Reformer in the 16th century, "as two earnest and illustrious representatives of the Christian faith and life, as well as of the loftiest thought and purest morality of their country and generation." In setting forth with considerable fulness the lives of these prominent and representative Christian men, M. Guizot necessarily introduces much of the political and religious history of the periods during which they lived. "A very interesting book," says the Guardian.

Christian Singers of Germany. — By Catherine Winkworth.

"The hymns of Germany are so steadily becoming naturalized in England that English readers may be glad to know something of the men who wrote them, and the times in which they had their origin." In this volume the authoress gives an account of the principal hymn-writers of Germany from the 9th to the 19th century, introducing ample (altogether about 120 translations) specimens from their best productions. In the translations, while the English is perfectly idiomatic and harmonious, the characteristic

differences of the poems have been carefully imitated, and the general style and metre retained. The book is divided into chapters, the writers noticed and the hymns quoted in each chapter, being representative of an epoch in the religious life of Germany. In thus tracing the course of German hymnology, the authoress is necessarily led to notice to some extent the religious history of the country, is "brought into contact with those great movements which have stirred the life of the people."—"Miss Winkworth's volume of this series is, according to our view, the choicest production of her pen."
—British Quarterly Review.

Apostles of Mediæval Europe.—By the Rev. G. F. MACLEAR, B.D., Head Master of King's College School, London.

In two Introductory Chapters the author notices some of the chief characteristics of the mediæval period itself; gives a graphic sketch of the devastated state of Europe at the beginning of that period, and an interesting account of the religions of the three great groups of vigorous barbarians—the Celts, the Teutons, and the Sclaves—who had, wave after wave, overflowed its surface. He then proceeds to sketch the lives and work of the chief of the courageous men who devoted themselves to the stupendous task of their conversion and civilization, during a period extending from the 5th to the 13th century; such as St. Patrick, St. Columba, St. Columbanus, St. Augustine of Canterbury, St. Boniface, St. Olaf, St. Cyril, Raymond Sull, and others. In narrating the lives of these men, many glimpses are given into the political, social, and religious life of Europe during the Middle Ages, and many interesting and instructive incidents are introduced. "Mr. Maclear will have done a great work if his admirable little volume shall help to break up the dense ignorance which is still prevailing among people at large."—Literary Churchman.

Alfred the Great.—By THOMAS HUGHES, M.P., Author of "Tom Brown's School Days."

"The events of the last few years, particularly of the last few months, have forced on those who think on such subjects at all, the practical need of examining once more the principles upon which society, and

the life of nations, rest. . . . The time is come when we English can no longer stand by as interested spectators only, but in which every one of our institutions will be sifted with rigour, and will have to shew cause for its existence. . . . As a help in this search, this life of the typical English King is here offered." After two Introductory Chapters, one on Kings and Kingship, and another depicting the condition of Wessex industrially, socially, politically, and ecclesiastically, when Alfred became its ruler, the author proceeds to set forth the life and work of this great prince, shewing how he conducted himself as a man, a Christian, a husband, a father, a friend, a student, a financier, a warrior, a king. In the last chapter the author shews the bearing which Christianity has on the kingship and government of the nations and people of the world in which we live. Besides other illustrations in the volume, a Map of England is prefixed, shewing its divisions about 1000 A.D., *as well as at the present time. "Mr. Hughes has indeed written a good book, bright and readable we need hardly say, and of a very considerable historical value."*—Spectator.

Nations Around.—By Miss A. KEARY.

This volume contains many details concerning the social and political life, the religion, the superstitions, the literature, the architecture, the commerce, the industry, of the Nations around Palestine, an acquaintance with which is necessary in order to a clear and full understanding of the history of the Hebrew people. Among the nations concerning which much valuable information is brought together in this volume, are Chaldea, Egypt, the Kingdoms of Canaan, and Assyria with its great city Babylon, the influence of all which can be traced to a greater or less extent in the history, manners, and customs of the Jews. The authoress has brought to her aid all the most recent investigations into the early history of these nations, referring frequently to the fruitful excavations which have brought to light the ruins of many of their buried cities, and making considerable use of the writings and hieroglyphics found upon the walls of their palaces, as these have been interpreted by the most accomplished Eastern scholars. "Miss Keary has skilfully availed herself of the opportunity to write a pleasing and instructive book."—Guardian. *"A valuable and interesting volume."*—Illustrated Times.

St. Anselm.—By the Very Rev. R. W. CHURCH, M.A., Dean of St. Paul's.

> *In this biography of the great and good Archbishop of Canterbury during the end of the 11th and beginning of the 12th century, while the story of his life as a man, a Christian, a clergyman, and a politician, is told impartially and fully, much light is shed on the ecclesiastical and political history of the time during which he lived. Throughout the volume many interesting details are given concerning the internal economy of the monastic establishments of the period. Of the worthiness of St. Anselm to have his life recorded, Mr. Church says, " It would not be easy to find one who so joined the largeness and daring of a powerful and inquiring intellect, with the graces and sweetness and unselfishness of the most loveable of friends, and with the fortitude, clear-sightedness, and dauntless firmness of a hero, forced into a hero's career in spite of himself." The author has drawn his materials from contemporary biographers and chroniclers, while at the same time he has consulted the best recent authors who have treated of the man and his time. " It is a sketch by the hand of a master, with every line marked by taste, learning, and real apprehension of the subject." — Pall Mall Gazette.*

Francis of Assisi.—By Mrs. OLIPHANT.

> *The life of this saint, the founder of the Franciscan order, and one of the most remarkable men of his time, illustrates some of the chief characteristics of the religious life of the Middle Ages. Mrs. Oliphant, in an Introduction, gives a slight sketch of the political and religious condition of Europe in the 13th century, in order to shew that the kind of life adopted by St. Francis was a natural result of the influences by which he was surrounded. In the subsequent biography much information is given concerning the missionary labours of the saint and his companions, as well as concerning the religious and monastic life of the time. Many graphic details are introduced from the saint's contemporary biographers, which shew forth the prevalent beliefs of the period ; and abundant samples are given of St. Francis's own sayings, as well as a few specimens of his simple tender hymns. The main authorities for*

the biography are two lives by contemporaries, and one by the distinguished and eloquent Bonaventura, who had the fullest access to all documents on the subjects. "We are grateful to Mrs. Oliphant for a book of much interest and pathetic beauty, a book which none can read without being the better for it."—John Bull.

Pioneers and Founders; or, Recent Workers in the Mission Field. By CHARLOTTE M. YONGE, Author of "The Heir of Redclyffe." With Frontispiece, and Vignette Portrait of BISHOP HEBER.

The author has endeavoured in these narratives to bring together such of the more distinguished Missionaries of the English and American Nations as might best illustrate the character and growth of Mission-work in the last two centuries. The object has been to throw together such biographies as are most complete, most illustrative, and have been found most inciting to stir up others— representative lives, as far as possible—from the time when the destitution of the Red Indians first stirred the heart of John Eliot, till the misery of the hunted negro brought Charles Mackenzie to the banks of the fever-haunted Zambesi. The missionaries whose biographies are here given, are—John Eliot, the Apostle of the Red Indians; David Brainerd, the Enthusiast; Christian F. Schwartz, the Councillor of Tanjore; Henry Martyn, the Scholar-Missionary; William Carey and Joshua Marshman, the Serampore Missionaries; the Judson Family; the Bishops of Calcutta,—Thomas Middleton, Reginald Heber, Daniel Wilson; Samuel Marsden, the Australian Chaplain and Friend of the Maori; John Williams, the Martyr of Erromango; Allen Gardener, the Sailor Martyr; Charles Frederick Mackenzie, the Martyr of Zambesi. "Likely to be one of the most popular of the 'Sunday Library' volumes."—Literary Churchman.

THE "BOOK OF PRAISE" HYMNAL

COMPILED AND ARRANGED BY

SIR ROUNDELL PALMER,

In the following four forms :—

A. Beautifully printed in Royal 32mo., limp cloth, price 6d
B.   „   „   Small 18mo., larger type, cloth limp
C. Same edition on fine paper, cloth, 1s. 6d.
Also an edition with Music, selected, harmonized, and compc
    by **JOHN HULLAH**, in square 18mo., cloth, 3s. 6d.

The large acceptance which has been given to " The Book of Pra
by all classes of Christian people encourages the Publishers in entertain
the hope that this Hymnal, which is mainly selected from it, may be
tensively used in Congregations, and in some degree at least meet
desires of those who seek uniformity in common worship as a m
towards that unity which pious souls yearn after, and which our i
prayed for in behalf of his Church. " The office of a hymn is n
teach controversial Theology, but to give the voice of song to prac
religion. No doubt, to do this, it must embody sound doctrine ; b
ought to do so, not after the manner of the schools, but with the brea
freedom, and simplicity of the Fountain-head." On this principle
Sir R. Palmer proceeded in the preparation of this book.

The arrangement adopted is the following :—

PART I. *consists of Hymns arranged according to the subjects of*
Creed—"God the Creator," "Christ Incarnate," "Christ Crucifi
"Christ Risen," "Christ Ascended," "Christ's Kingdom and Ju
ment," etc.

PART II. *comprises Hymns arranged according to the subjects of*
Lord's Prayer.

PART III. *Hymns for natural and sacred seasons.*

There are 320 Hymns in all.

CAMBRIDGE :—PRINTED BY J. PALMER.

www.ingramcontent.com/pod-product-compliance
Lightning Source LLC
Chambersburg PA
CBHW020811060726

47498CB00017B/1666